# MÉXICO PROFUNDO:
## Reclaiming a Civilization

**Translations from Latin America Series**

# MÉXICO PROFUNDO:
# Reclaiming a Civilization

## by
## Guillermo Bonfil Batalla

Translated by Philip A. Dennis

 **University of Texas Press, Austin**
**Institute of Latin American Studies**

First Edition, 1996

Requests for permission to reproduce material from this work should be sent to Permissions, University of Texas Press, P.O. Box 7819, Austin, Texas 78713-7819

⊛ The paper used in this publication meets the minimum requirements of American National Standard for Information Sciences—Permanence of Paper for Printed Library Materials, ANSI Z39.48–1984.

**Library of Congress Cataloging-in-Publication Data**

Bonfil Batalla, Guillermo
  [México profundo. English]
  México profundo : reclaiming a civilization / by Guillermo Bonfil Batalla ; translated by Philip A. Dennis.
       p.   cm. — (Translations from Latin America Series)
    ISBN 0-292-70844-0 (cloth : alk. paper). — ISBN 0-292-70843-2 (pbk. : alk. paper)
      1. Mexico—Civilization—Indian influences. 2. Indians of Mexico—Ethnic identity. 3. Indians of Mexico—Government relations—History. 4. Government, Resistance to—Mexico—History.   I. Dennis, Philip Adams, 1945– . II. Title. III. Series.
F1210.B6613 1996
972'.00497—dc20                                                        95-43407
                                                                          CIP

# Contents

Translator's Foreword                                         vii

Preface to the Second Edition                                 xi

Introduction                                                  xv

Part I. A Civilization Denied

  1. A Land of Millenarian Civilization               3

  2. The Indian Recognized                             19

  3. De-Indianizing That Which Is Indian               41

Part II. How We Came to Be Where We Are

  4. The Problem of National Culture                   61

  5. The Colonial Order                                70

  6. Forging a Nation                                  94

  7. Our (Revolutionized) Modern Times                 108

  8. The Paths of Indian Survival                      129

Part III. The National Program and the Civilizational Project

  9. The Nation We Have Today                          153

  10. Civilization and Alternatives                    163

References Cited                                              177

Bibliographic Appendix                                       181

Index                                                        185

# Translator's Foreword

Guillermo Bonfil Batalla's book *México profundo: una civilización negada* seems prophetic in retrospect. He predicted the collapse of what he called the imaginary Mexico and hoped that the strengths of the "México profundo" would serve as the basis for building a new Mexico. According to Bonfil Batalla, Mexico is not a mestizo country. Rather, it is a country whose majority population continues to be rooted in Mesoamerican civilization and whose way of life reflects cultural patterns and values with thousands of years of history. The peoples embodying this Mesoamerican civilization include the remaining communities that speak an Indian language and identify themselves as Indian, the "de-Indianized" rural communities, and large sectors of the urban poor, many of them recent immigrants to the cities. These people constitute, for Bonfil Batalla, the *México profundo*. Their way of life has endured, he argues, as they have resisted outside forces, appropriated and adopted as their own useful items from outside, and in turn created new and original elements of Mesoamerican civilization. The bearers of this civilization have been in continual confrontation with peoples of European background, who arrived convinced that the existing civilization had to be uprooted and something different imposed in its place. However, the struggle to survive and maintain their own cultural patterns has given the people of the *México profundo* an incredible willpower and strength to survive. Bonfil Batalla saw these qualities as providing the basis for building a new Mexico, based on the country that really exists, instead of on imitations of European or U.S. models.

The *México profundo* erupted into national consciousness on January 1, 1994, when the Zapatista National Liberation Army (Ejército Zapatista de la Liberación Nacional—EZLN) took over four towns in the southeastern state of Chiapas. Their struggle provoked a still-unresolved confrontation with the Mexican government. Most of the EZLN fighters are Maya Indians from a poor state whose population includes more than a million Maya people. Their rebellion responds to years of injustice and oppression. In recent years in Chiapas, large cattle ranchers have continued to usurp Indian land, with the support of paid gunmen and the judicial police. Land and wealth and political power in Chiapas are highly concentrated in the hands of a local elite, while the Indian and peasant majority live in extreme poverty. The EZLN rebellion erupted when President Salinas de Gortari repealed Article 27 of the Constitution, ending federal protection for the ejido lands held by local communities, and signed the NAFTA agreement with the United States, which threatened to impoverish the communities even further. The rebellion provoked enormous popular support in Mexico. In interviews, EZLN members stated that it was better to die fighting for what they still had, rather than face daily violence, poverty, malnutrition, political corruption, and economic exploitation. Bonfil Batalla's description of the relationship between the *México profundo* and the national system was brought to life for millions of television viewers in Mexico and throughout the world, as they watched the crisis in Chiapas unfold.

For me, the concept of a *México profundo* put into perspective many of my own fieldwork experiences in Zapotec Oaxaca during the 1970s and 1980s. In translating Bonfil Batalla's book, I wanted to make this major work in Mexican anthropology accessible to English-language readers. Although anthropology has played an important role in twentieth-century Mexico, very few of the classic works by Mexican anthropologists have been translated into English. Works by U.S. anthropologists, on the other hand, are widely available in Spanish. In the 1970s, the National Indian Institute (Instituto Nacional Indigenista, or INI) translated dozens of ethnographies of Mexican communities, written by foreign scholars, into Spanish. My own work was among them. However, the reverse process has not taken place, reflecting a continuing gulf in communications between the English- and Spanish-speaking scholarly worlds. With this translation, I hope to help bridge this gulf. *México profundo* is a book with far-reaching implications about Mexico's identity and its future. The original Spanish version of the book was published in 1987 and has been widely read, making the phrase "México profundo" common parlance in the Mexican intellectual world. The book's thesis will be thought-provoking to all students and general readers who want to understand our "distant neighbors" to the south.

I made a number of attempts to adequately translate Bonfil Batalla's concept of the *México profundo* into English, but none of them did justice to the powerful idea compressed in his simple phrase. Therefore, throughout the text I have simply used the term *México profundo.* After a diligent search, I have also added references to most of the works Bonfil quotes in the text. Readers will find them listed in the References Cited at the end of the book, along with Bonfil Batalla's own Bibliographic

Appendix. I would like to thank Salomón Nahmad for helping find some of the references. In the translation, I have tried to preserve the eloquence and flavor of Bonfil's prose as well as the content of his ideas. I am grateful to the Institute of Latin American Studies at the University of Texas, which provided a small grant to allow me to work on the manuscript in the Benson Collection. At ILAS, I would especially like to thank Virginia Hagerty and Carolyn Palaima for their helpfulness and encouragement in working with me on the manuscript, and for their enthusiasm about completing this translation project.

Guillermo Bonfil Batalla had a distinguished career in Mexican anthropology, cut tragically short by his death in an automobile accident in July 1991. As director of the National Institute of Anthropology and History (Instituto Nacional de Antropología e Historia—INAH), he founded the regional centers that today coordinate research in different areas of the country, thus decentralizing the Institute's work. He founded and directed the National Museum of Popular Culture and directed the Center for Research and Advanced Study in Social Anthropology (Centro de Investigaciones y Estudios Superiores en Antropología Social—CIESAS). His other books include *Cholula, la ciudad sagrada en la era industrial* (1973), *Utopía y revolución* (1981), and *Pensar nuestra cultura* (1991), a collection of essays about cultural pluralism, which appeared shortly before his death. Bonfil Batalla began his career as one of the early critics of *indigenismo,* a continent-wide movement concerned with Indian welfare, but directed by non-Indians. He and other Mexican anthropologists of the early 1970s concluded that the paternalistic stance of *indigenismo* obscured the truly multicultural nature of Mexico, and they supported, instead, Indian efforts at self-determination. In 1975, for example, Bonfil helped organize Mexico's first National Congress of Indian Peoples, attended by twenty-five hundred Indian delegates from the all over the country. Along with Salomón Nahmad and other colleagues, he argued that Indian peoples should manage development efforts on their own behalf, thus escaping the control of government bureaucracies. His belief that Indian peoples have the right to control their own destiny follows directly from the ideas and concerns developed in this book. *México profundo* stands as a summary of and monument to his life as a scholar and an advocate of justice for the Indian peoples of Mexico.

—Philip A. Dennis
July 1995

# Preface to the Second Edition

It is always tempting to make changes in the text when the decision is made to bring out a second edition. This time I resisted the temptation, not because I think this book is perfect, lacking nothing and with nothing that could be eliminated. I realized from the beginning that it should be an open text, full of questions, lacunae, and preliminary ideas sketched many times that would require better documentation and broader development. Nevertheless, I think that in order to overcome those limitations it would be necessary to write a different book. As it is, I think that this version of *México Profundo* fulfills the major intention for which it was written. Perhaps it would lose its value for intellectual and political stimulus if I now tried to fill out arguments and amplify options with my own opinions. It might close the spectrum of alternatives that I have tried to contribute in rethinking our history, the present, and the future we should try to build. It has also been said many times that a book leads its own life and takes its own path. Even the author, after placing the final period, has no right to interfere by modifying it. Thus, I decided to leave it as is.

I take the opportunity of adding this brief preface to mention recent events and to try to see them from the general perspective of this book. In the little more than a year since the first edition was published, the country has lived through unusual moments, particularly related to the elections of July 6, 1988. "The country changed" and "Mexico is different" are phrases that became commonplace in the months that followed. Broad sectors of society were surprised and excited. Some were enthusiastic, others, fearful, but all realized that it was necessary to revise the visions and convictions on which the image of the country was based. What happened on July 6 demonstrated, in effect, a different Mexico, at least from the viewpoint of those who do not see beyond the limits of the imaginary Mexico. The question remains: What really were the motivations capable of mobilizing hundreds of thousands of Mexicans, from the most varied living conditions, to simultaneously express their protest and their renewed hopes in a heretofore unthinkable opposition? Let us ask it in this fashion: To what degree, in fact, did the *México profundo* awaken? What happened in the hamlets, the villages, the barrios, which have remained at the margin of imaginary political activity, an exercise imposed by that other, unreal, dominant Mexico, but that has no roots or flesh and blood?

From what I can see, little notice has been taken of something that seems basic to me. The Cardenist program, beyond its lack of precision and its poorly drawn and in many ways contradictory outline, was perceived by many as hope for a step backward. Perhaps it was not clear how far back, but in any case, back to a previous place. It was an invitation to begin again, to retrace the steps that had already been traveled. It was a reactionary program, some might say.

But it was not really reactionary, if you look at things from the other side, from the point of view of those who have been attacked, who have nothing but who are nevertheless denied. From this other point of view, going backward is necessary, indispensable in order to advance along the true path, one that leads somewhere besides disaster. I would interpret what happened in the 1988 elections, following the basic ideas I advance in this book, as the political expression—at least that expression manifested in the electoral exercise—of what large sectors live and feel. It was a reaction to the complete failure of the development model that the imaginary Mexico has tried to impose. The turn backward would signify the recovery of a true, deeply rooted nationalism. It was no coincidence that people, including youth, sang the national anthem with moving conviction, beyond the obligatory requirements of empty ritual.

The other side of the coin is that the vote in important indigenous areas confirmed the tradition of absolute dominance of the PRI [Partido Revolucionario Institucional]. Are the Indians the pillars of the system, content with the benefits they receive? I agree with the interpretation offered by Arturo Warman, that the Indians voted with short-term results in mind; their considerations have nothing to do with political programs that plant alternative models of society for the future. Voting in these communities is more of a resource for the here and now, exercised with the hope of getting a road finished, constructing a school, obtaining potable water, making progress in acquiring land titles, and other minor support in resolving the everyday, ancestral problems that overwhelm all else in life. Everything else is a matter of "the others," the superimposed world forged by the imaginary Mexico. The political parties will have to dig deep to reach the level where the motivations capable of mobilizing the *México profundo* exist. Some progress was made in 1988, but it would be a myopic error to suppose that since then the whole country, not just the part with an audible voice and a visible face, is really different.

I do not mean to deny the importance of recent social and political events. I do mean to put them into relative perspective, to complement a vision that is centralist, urban, and somewhat elitist and according to which what occurs around me is also occurring elsewhere. As in the Mexican Revolution, in the elections of 1988 very diverse motivations were involved, producing convergence and joint action that are not necessarily compatible in the short run. Nevertheless, the events were important. What I will call a conscience of inconsistency was born in large sectors. That is to say, deeply rooted convictions that seemed unshakable were questioned. There is an intellectual opening that seems to allow revising the explanations of the country's nature, completing our amputated vision of its reality, and rethinking a possible future. Fortunately, dogmatism is at a low point. There is an intellectual space favorable to pluralism. Will we be capable of taking advantage of this moment by taking firm steps toward putting our country back on its feet, instead of, as has been the case, on its head?

These changes, although largely confined to the imaginary Mexico, would still require putting into practice some of the ideas that are simply noted in the third part of this book. Most certainly, it would be necessary to add others not even mentioned. Various readers and some reviewers have indicated the shortcomings of the last two chapters. I readily admit them. I intend to work more on the topic, although with the clear realization that reflection on our future is a matter for all. Individual contributions, although necessary, are simply that. The debate should be opened, giving it the space and amplitude it deserves. It is not just a matter of debating my ideas. I say frankly in the text that in many cases these are others' ideas, which I have used without any pangs of conscience to construct a broader argument. Such ideas exist only because of our effort to understand reality. It is that reality and its problems that are important to analyze and discuss. There is a challenge to the imagination, which we can confront only by beginning with an authentic recognition of our reality. And we will learn, after unmasking our prejudices, after liberating our colonial thinking, after deciding that it is we ourselves who must understand who we are, that the central protagonist of our history and the indispensable component of our future is the *México profundo*.

—Guillermo Bonfil Batalla
Mexico City, April 1989

# Introduction

This book has two purposes. On the one hand, it attempts to present a panoramic vision of the constant and multiform presence of that which is Indian in Mexico. "The Indian" refers to the persistence of Mesoamerican civilization today among specific indigenous peoples. It is also expressed in diverse ways in larger sectors of the national society that form, together with the Indian communities, what I have called the *México profundo*. Based on the recognition of this *México profundo*, the second purpose of the book is to present arguments for broader analysis, which all Mexicans should take into account. What does the coexistence of two civilizations, Mesoamerican and Western, mean in our history, our present, and, above all, our future?

It might seem that reflecting on the problem of civilization is inopportune at a time when the country is going through difficult circumstances and faces economic, political, and social problems that demand immediate solutions. What sense does it make to think about civilization? I think that it makes a profound kind of sense. I suggest that the immediate problems that besiege us with their simultaneous and growing presence will be only partially and incompletely understood, and only partially and incompletely solved in the best of cases, if they are not placed in the context of the unresolved dilemma of the presence of two civilizations. Two civilizations mean two civilizational programs, two ideal models for the society sought after, two different possible futures. Whatever decision is made about reorienting the country, whatever path is chosen to escape from the current crisis, implies a choice for one of those civilizational projects and against the other.

The recent history of Mexico, that of the last five hundred years, is the story of permanent confrontation between those attempting to direct the country toward the path of Western civilization and those, rooted in Mesoamerican ways of life, who resist. The first plan arrived with the European invaders but was not abandoned with independence. The new groups in power, first the creoles and later the mestizos, never renounced

the westernization plan. They still have not renounced it. Their differences and the struggles that divide them express only disagreement over
the best way of carrying out the same program. The adoption of that
model has meant the creation within Mexican society of a minority
country organized according to the norms, aspirations, and goals of
Western civilization. They are not shared, or are shared from a different
perspective, by the rest of the national population. To the sector that
represents and gives impetus to our country's dominant civilizational
program, I have given the name "the imaginary Mexico."

The relations between the *México profundo* and the imaginary Mexico
have been conflictive during the five centuries of their confrontation.
Imaginary Mexico's westernization plan has been exclusionary and has
denied the validity of Mesoamerican civilization. No room has been
allowed for a convergence of civilizations through a slow fusion that
gives rise to a new civilizational plan, different from the two original
ones but arising from them. On the contrary, the groups embodying the
two civilizations have permanently confronted each other, sometimes
violently. They constantly confront each other in the activities of daily
life, which put into practice the deeper principles of their respective
cultural matrices.

This confrontation does not happen between cultural elements but
between the social groups that bear them, use them, and develop them.
It is those social groups that participate in two different civilizations that
over the period of half a millennium have maintained a constant
opposition. The colonial origin of Mexican society has meant that the
dominant groups and classes are also those who foment the project of
westernization, the creators of the imaginary Mexico. At the base of the
social pyramid are the peoples resisting, those who embody Mesoamerican
civilization, who sustain the *México profundo*. Power and Western
civilization coincide, on one pole, and subjugation and Mesoamerican
civilization coincide on the other.

This is not a fortuitous coincidence, but, rather, the necessary result
of a colonial history that until now has not been superseded inside
Mexican society. A basic characteristic of every colonial society is that
the invading group, with a different culture from the dominated, ideologically affirms its immanent superiority in all areas of life and denies
and excludes the culture of those colonized. The decolonization of
Mexico was incomplete. Independence from Spain was achieved, but the
internal colonial structure was not eliminated. The groups that have
held power since 1821 have never abandoned the civilizational project of
the West and have never overcome the distorted view of the country that
is the essence of the colonizers' viewpoint. Thus, the diverse national
visions used to organize Mexican society during different periods since

independence have all been created within a Western framework. In none of them has the reality of the *México profundo* had a place. Instead, it has been viewed only as a symbol of backwardness and an obstacle to be overcome.

The *México profundo*, meanwhile, keeps resisting, appealing to diverse strategies, depending on the scheme of domination to which it is subjected. It is not a passive, static world, but, rather, one that lives in permanent tension. The peoples of the *México profundo* continually create and re-create their culture, adjust it to changing pressures, and reinforce their own, private sphere of control. They take foreign cultural elements and put them at their service; they cyclically perform the collective acts that are a way of expressing and renewing their own identity. They remain silent or they rebel, according to strategies refined by centuries of resistance.

At present, when the plans of the imaginary Mexico are falling apart, we must rethink our country and its trajectory. It would be irresponsible and suicidal to pretend to find solutions to the crisis without taking into account what we really are and what resources we really have to move ahead. We cannot continue to close our eyes to the *México profundo*. We cannot continue to ignore and deny the potential represented by the living presence of Mesoamerican civilization. We should not continue wasting energy and resources in an effort to substitute another reality for that which the majority of the population experiences. Instead, we should create conditions in which the existing reality can be transformed using its own potential. Its creative force has been unable to extend itself in other areas because colonial domination has denied it and forced it to take refuge in resistance in order to survive.

When we discuss the dilemma of civilization in Mexico, we are really considering the necessity of formulating a new vision or plan for the country in which all the patrimony that we Mexicans have inherited can be incorporated as active capital. This includes not only natural resources, but also various ways of understanding and making use of them through knowledge and technology that are inherited from the diverse peoples composing the nation. We mean not only the work force composed of millions of countrymen, but also the ways of organizing production and consumption that persist in the *México profundo* and that have made its survival possible. We refer not only to the Western knowledge that with so much effort has been accumulated (more than developed) in Mexico, but also to the rich gamut of knowledge that is the product of millenarian experience. Thus, what is needed is to find the ways in which the enormous cultural potential that has been negated in Mexico can flourish. It is with that civilization, and not in opposition to it, that we can construct our own, authentic plans for the country and displace forever the imaginary Mexico, the proof of whose invalidity is now being shown.

This book is divided into three parts. In the first part, I try to present a general picture of Mesoamerican civilization in modern Mexico. Its presence is undeniable in the countryside and in the names and the faces of the people throughout the length and breadth of the country. In order to give that presence its true historical depth, I briefly trace the origin and development of Mesoamerican civilization up to the moment of the European invasion. Much of what we have, and that will be indispensable in building the future, has behind it thousands of years of history.

Next, our attention will be centered on a brief and synthetic description of Mesoamerican civilization as it is lived in Indian communities today. My design is to draw a single picture, in spite of the particularities that express the individual character of each cultural group. I try to show the internal coherence of the cultures of Mesoamerican origin, a coherence explained by the worldview they conserve. Implicit in this worldview are the deepest values of Mesoamerican civilization, values that form the matrix that gives meaning to all its acts.

In the first part I also explore the presence of Mesoamerican civilization in other groups within Mexican society that do not recognize themselves as Indian. Here we find evidence of de-Indianization, that is, the loss of these groups' original collective identity as a result of the process of colonial domination. Nevertheless, the change of identity does not necessarily imply the loss of Indian culture. This is indicated by the cultural reality of the traditional rural communities that identify themselves as mestizo. Even in the cities, old bastions of colonial power, it is possible to find the presence of Indian culture manifested in various forms. Some, such as Indian barrios, result from historical processes, and others result from more recent social processes, such as emigration from the countryside to the city.

The first part concludes with a rapid look at what happens in other sectors of Mexican society, those that embody the imaginary Mexico, the proponent of the Western civilizational program. Here I can represent only a few cultural traits of those groups, particularly those that reveal a contradictory relationship with the *México profundo*. My emphasis is really on exposing the hidden face of the great mass of the population whose lives are organized around a Mesoamerican cultural matrix.

The image of Mexico that is derived from this schematic x-ray view is of a plural and heterogeneous country with a variety of cultures that do not form a continuous sequence. That is, we do not have societies with different levels of development on a common scale. Far from it. What is clearly profiled is a division into cultural forms belonging to two different civilizations that have never fused, although they interpenetrate. The ties between these two cultural universes are those that correspond to a situation of colonial domination in which the imaginary Mexico tries to subordinate the rest of the population to its plans. This is the dilemma of Mexican culture that introduces Part II.

In the second part we try to understand how our current situation came about. We look at important parts of the historical process that have led Mexican society to deny its substance and repeatedly to undertake a program of substitution instead of development. I do not attempt a detailed summary of the history of the last five centuries. I try only to highlight general tendencies and key moments that help explain the persistence of an external, colonial program brought up to the present without substantial change since the Spanish creoles began imagining independence. This selective account also allows us to understand the diverse ways in which the peoples of Mesoamerican origin and their culture have been attacked in an age-old effort to deny them and subject them to the cultural order proposed by successive dominant groups.

In concluding Part II, I briefly summarize the *México profundo*'s response to colonial domination. The forms of resistance have varied, from armed defense and rebellion to the apparently conservative attachment to traditional practices. I attempt to demonstrate that all these forms of resistance are really facets of the same permanent, tenacious struggle. Each community and all of them in conjunction have fought to continue being themselves, not to give up being the protagonists of their own history.

Part III, based on the previous chapters, reflects on the current and future situation of Mexico. My intent is to present the country we have inherited on two planes. One is the collapse of the development model that has been promulgated, with its disastrous consequences and the dangers implied in trying to promote it once again. The other is the resources we actually have, and with which we should construct our own authentic future. Based on these considerations I suggest possible options for constructing a new national program, which should be framed in a civilizational project that makes explicit our reality instead of hiding it. I consider these ideas as notes for an inescapable and urgent debate in which the question of democracy must take first place. This is not the formal, docile, and awkwardly traced democracy of the West, but a real democracy derived from our history and responding to the rich and varied composition of Mexican society. This too is a civilizational problem.

I wrote this book between May 1985 and April 1987, and its preparation was my principal task during that period as an investigator in the

Center for Research and Advanced Study in Social Anthropology (CIESAS). During the first year my time was devoted to building an analytical model that would allow me to approach the main theme with clarity and that would serve as a unifying guide for a work that touches so many and such varied aspects of the historical and present reality of Mexico. The analytical model was formulated in an essay, "La teoría del control cultural en el estudio de procesos étnicos," whose first draft served as a framework for the seminar I directed in the doctoral program of CIESAS between January and October 1986. The contributions and criticisms of the participants were taken into account in producing the final version of that essay.

The reader will encounter references to a theory of cultural control in various sections of the book. I included only such references as were necessary to clarify the meaning of important terms employed. Such terms include our own culture and foreign culture, cultural control, resistance processes, appropriation, innovation, imposition, alienation, and suppression, as well as the meanings I give to ethnic group and ethnic identity. Apart from those clarifying paragraphs, I opted not to expound the theory of cultural control, although it is implicit in the general focus of the book. I made that decision while thinking of the general reader of the book, for whom a theoretical and methodological discussion might be confusing. Neither would its exposition contribute anything substantial to my purpose in writing the book.

For the same reason I eliminated from the text the footnotes and exact bibliographic references that we tend to assume demonstrate seriousness and rigor in an academic work. [Trans. note: Wherever possible, references have been added for the English-language edition.] I decided to write freely, less constrained by the daily habits of research in the social sciences, with the aim of reaching, in a simple, clear, and direct way, a larger reading public than that accustomed to reading academic books. The reader interested in pursuing in depth any of the themes discussed here will encounter in the Bibliographic Appendix some suggestions for further reading. The Appendix also gives credit to the principal sources from which I have taken the data upon which this vision of Mexico is based. I list only the principal sources and perhaps those most recently consulted, because a work like this represents, in the final analysis, an attempt to synthesize many things learned from many sources over the years. It would have been inappropriate and even useless to try to specify in detail the source of the data for making this or that statement or generalization. Specialists will easily be able to find specific ways in which my global analysis is inexact. I hope, however, that the broad lines of argument will not be seen as invalid because of an inexactness that would have been difficult to avoid.

In another area, that of ideas, I realize that this book is not an individual effort, although I appear as the author. In two senses it is a collective work. First, there are a number of us who, for many years, have felt the need to explore the *México profundo* from an academic and political perspective. We have been certain that in it exist the keys and indispensable answers for finding the path to a better future. I have used with no pangs of conscience the reflections, data, and intuitions of many colleagues and friends who have thought in similar ways. This book is also theirs, although without any responsibility for the limitations and errors it may contain. The second sense, even richer and more solid, resides in the millions of Mexicans who experience the *México profundo* in their daily lives. In their thought and their hopes, they constantly renew the fundamentals that make possible the conviction that they are the bearers of a civilizational project that might also be ours. I have wanted to learn from them. This stammering attempt to translate what I have learned can only be dedicated to them, the indigenous people of Mexico.

—Guillermo Bonfil Batalla
Avándaro and Mexico City, 1985–1987

# MÉXICO PROFUNDO:
## Reclaiming a Civilization

# PART I.

## A Civilization Denied

The *México profundo* is formed by a great diversity of peoples, communities, and social sectors that constitute the majority of the population of the country. What unifies them and distinguishes them from the rest of Mexican society is that they are bearers of ways of understanding the world and of organizing human life that have their origins in Mesoamerican civilization and that have been forged here in Mexico through a long and complicated historical process. The contemporary expressions of that civilization are quite diverse: from those indigenous peoples who have been able to conserve an internally cohesive culture of their own, to a multitude of isolated traits distributed in different ways in urban populations. The civilization of Mesoamerica has been denied but it is essential to recognize its continuing presence.

# 1.

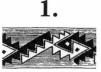

# A Land of Millenarian Civilization

Let us start from a basic fact: one of the few original civilizations that humanity has created throughout all its history arose and developed in what today is Mexico. This is Mesoamerican civilization, from which derives all that is "Indian" in Mexico. Mesoamerican civilization is the starting point and indeed the most profound aspect of our country.

Every schoolchild knows something about the precolonial world. The great archaeological monuments stand as national symbols. There is a circumstantial pride in a past that is somehow assumed to be glorious, but that is experienced as something dead, a matter for specialists and an irresistible attraction for tourists. Above all, it is assumed to be something apart from ourselves, something that happened long ago in the same place where we, the Mexicans, live today. The only connection is based on the fact of *them* and *us* occupying the same territory, but in different time periods.

We do not recognize a historical connection or a continuity with the past. Some believe that Mesoamerican civilization was destroyed by the European invasion; others seem to regard that event as a sort of redemption. What remains of Mesoamerican civilization is regarded as ruins, some of stone but others still living. We accept and utilize the precolonial past as the history of the national territory, but not as our own past. *They* are simply the Indians, the Indian part of Mexico.

In this way of regarding the matter one notes a rupture, accentuated by a revealing and disquieting tone of superiority. That renunciation, that denial of the past—does it really correspond to a total and irreme-diable historical break? Did Mesoamerican civilization really die, and are the remaining Indian populations simply fossils, condemned five hundred years ago to disappear because they have no place in the present or in the future? Upon the answers to these fundamental questions depend many other urgent questions and responses about the Mexico of today and about the Mexico that we want to build for the future.

## The Forging of a Civilization

In Mexico, as in most countries of the world, the last several thousand years have seen the origin, the disappearance, and the passing through of a great number of different societies and peoples. Here, however, unlike what occurred in many areas, there exists a cultural continuity that made possible the origin and development of a specific kind of civilization.

According to the information available, human beings have been living in Mexico for at least thirty thousand years. The earliest groups lived by hunting and gathering wild products. Some groups seem to have specialized in hunting large mammal species such as mammoths and mastodons, camels, and horses, which later disappeared. Others, depending on local conditions, hunted smaller species of game and depended more on gathering plant foods. The large game animals disappeared in Mexico approximately seven thousand years ago, perhaps because they could not survive changing climatic conditions. Of those early bands we have recovered fossil remains, stone tools, and weapons directly associated with the skeletons of the great animals they hunted. They were nomadic groups who required very large territories to survive. They lived in caves and temporary structures that were abandoned after short periods of occupation.

The reduction in available game animals and the greater dependence on gathering wild products certainly influenced a basic process: the domestication and later cultivation of plants. Mesoamerican civilization arises directly from the invention of agriculture. This was a long process, not an instantaneous transformation. Agriculture began in the semiarid watersheds and valleys of Central Mexico between about five thousand and seventy-five hundred years ago. In that period people began to domesticate beans, squashes, *huautli* [*Amaranthus paniculathus*, also called *alegría*], chiles, *miltomate* [*Physalix ixocarpa*, or tomatillo], gourds, avocados, and, of course, corn or maize. The cultivation of corn was a momentous achievement and remains linked in an inseparable way to Mesoamerican civilization. Its domestication produced the greatest morphological changes in any domesticated plant. Adaptation over time also permitted its cultivation in a wider range of climates and altitudes than any other domesticated plant of importance. One must remember that corn can grow only with human intervention, since the corn cob has no mechanism to disperse its seeds without human help. It is, in effect, a human creation, a child of Mesoamerican parents. Its parents, in turn, are children of corn, as poetically related in the *Pop Wuj*, "The Book of Events," of the Quiché Maya:

Thus they found food and it was what they employed to make the bodies of the people who were made, who were formed; the blood was liquid, the blood of the people; corn was used by Created and by Male Created . . . Later they thought about how to make our first mother and father. Of yellow corn and white corn they made the bodies, of food were made the arms and legs of the people, of our first parents. Four people were created, of pure foodstuffs were their bodies. [Chávez 1979: 65a]

Corn and agriculture in general did not immediately acquire the importance they would have later. Agriculture's inventors continued practicing gathering and hunting as primary subsistence activities and used the products of agriculture in a complementary fashion, although they constantly increased in importance. About three thousand years before Christ, the inhabitants of the small villages that have been discovered near Tehuacán obtained only about 20 percent of their food from cultivated plants; 50 percent came from gathering and the rest from hunting. Nevertheless, they already had a sedentary life; they had increased the variety of plants cultivated, and they were already raising dogs as a food source. Between 2,000 and 1,500 BC the process of sedentarization was completed and, of the products consumed, half were cultivated. This change has been explained by the fact that 440 to 550 pounds [200 to 250 kilograms] of corn can be harvested per hectare, which made it more productive as a food source than gathered products.

The first permanent villages were formed, and pottery, which had been invented about 2300 BC, was produced in them. It can be said that at this point, about 1500 BC, Mesoamerican civilization began. At this time the Olmecs, considered the bearers of Mesoamerican civilization's mother culture, were found in the hot country of southern Veracruz.

This is not the place to present a panorama, even a schematic one, of the development of this civilization from its beginnings to the sixteenth century. It was a complicated and diverse process that is understood better as archaeological and historical research proceeds. Suffice it to say that the experts have established certain chronological periods that, in their general outlines, coincide in the different Mesoamerican regions. Thus, a Preclassic or Formative period is known, which extends from about 2000 BC until approximately AD 200. Between 800 and 200 BC is the climax of Olmec culture, in which the first inscriptions on stone are found, the calendar (to be perfected by later peoples) is invented, and monumental sculptures in stone are carved whose technical quality and plastic harmony surprise us even today.

The influence of the mother culture is evident in various places. In northern Veracruz the culture called Remojadas develops, a tradition that the Totonacs will continue later. In Oaxaca, Zapotec culture begins. In the Yucatan peninsula, apparently through Olmec influences, the basis of Maya culture is established, a culture whose unmistakable profile will appear at the end of the Preclassic. During this time in the central valleys, an intensive agriculture develops in certain places that makes use of artificial terraces, canals, reservoirs, and *chinampas* [raised garden plots built in shallow lakes]. All are made possible by the development of a form of social organization that the archaeologists have called "theocratic chiefdoms." By the end of the Preclassic the bases of Mesoamerican civilization have been established, and its various component cultures begin to crystallize.

At the beginning of the Classic period, about AD 200, Teotihuacán culture begins. It expands greatly in the following five centuries and its later influence lasts until the arrival of the Spaniards. Teotihuacán, at the moment of its greatest splendor, was perhaps the largest city in the world. Its power and influence depended on the intensive agriculture practiced in the central valleys and the tribute it received from the peoples who submitted to its hegemony. At this time the central valleys acquired importance as the political and economic axis of a vast region, a role they have maintained to the present. In some periods the region was larger than the modern boundaries of Mexico.

The power of the central valleys was originally based on optimum use of the natural environment, using Mesoamerican agricultural technology and the development of forms of social organization that permitted the control of a large and dispersed population. Without metal tools, without plows or the wheel, without draft animals, an intensive high-yield agriculture was practiced with relatively limited labor. The lakes in the Valley of Mexico were used to construct *chinampas*, which are highly productive. Great dams were constructed to prevent the passage of saltwater into the freshwater reservoirs. The lakes themselves served to transport people and merchandise between many areas in the valley. On the slopes of the mountains that encircle the valley, terraces were constructed to cultivate the land and canals were built to use the water sources. Their geographical position allowed the central valleys to become the point of convergence of products from many different climatic zones, not necessarily far distant. Different ecological niches were regularly articulated by commercial interchanges, at times imposed by military force and its corresponding political power. This relationship made possible one of the key features of Mesoamerican civilization: Central Mexico would be constantly nourished by very diverse influences, including those from beyond the northern limits of

Mesoamerica. There was continual contact with groups of hunters and gatherers from the arid lands to the north, contact that was sometimes peaceful and sometimes warlike.

But is was not only Central Mexico that developed culturally, based on its intense contacts with other regions. In fact, all the cultures of the area maintained direct or indirect contact with each other. The Toltec diaspora at the end of the tenth century AD influenced places very distant from the great cities of Tula, Teotihuacán, and Cholula. For example, it produced important changes in the Maya area from Chiapas to Honduras and Yucatan. The local cultures of the peoples located on the peripheries of the centers of greater development presented characteristics that can be related to specific cultural traits of one or the other of their larger neighbors. This happened, for example, with the Itzás, who occupied Chichén about AD 918. They were Chontales from the coast of Tabasco in whose original culture both Maya and Toltec influences can be seen.

The slow cultural advance of the first thousands of years accelerates from the moment in which agriculture becomes the principal economic base. It gives rise to collective forms of social life that, within the diversity of their particular cultural traits, maintain common elements of civilization. Intense and prolonged contact occurred between cultures with their own historically developed profiles, and between the peoples who created those cultures. Thus, different and once autonomous peoples created a unified Mesoamerican civilization. This common origin is recognized in the myths and traditions of different peoples. A fragment of the *Pop Wuj* will serve to illustrate:

> What happened to our own language? What has happened to us? We are lost. Where can they have deceived us? Our language was one when we came from Tulan, one was our manner of subsistence, our origin. What has happened to us is not good, said the tribes beneath the trees, beneath the foliage. [Chávez 1979: 72a]

The definition of Mesoamerica as a cultural region with precise boundaries and characteristics was originally proposed by Paul Kirchhoff [1967]. He based the definition on the distribution of a hundred or more kinds of cultural traits, about half of which were found exclusively in Mesoamerica. Mesoamerica's remaining cultural traits were shared with other regions of the continent. The physical boundaries of this area were approximately from the Pánuco River to the Sinaloa River, passing along the Lerma River in the north; and from the mouth of the Motagua River to the Gulf of Nicoya, passing through Lake Nicaragua in the south. Kirchhoff's seminal study referred to the situation at the moment of the European invasion, and the author himself advised that later research would show variation in the Mesoamerican frontiers during different historical periods, especially in the north.

Of course, the simple presence or absence of cultural traits of such different significance as "cultivation of corn," "use of rabbit fur to decorate textiles," "specialized markets," "hieroglyphic writing," "chinampas," and "thirteen as a ritual number" is clearly insufficient to characterize a civilization. Kirchhoff indicates as much himself. He provides other facts and reflections among which stands out an important conclusion based on linguistic information. The distribution of Mesoamerican languages indicates, on the one hand, an ancient presence in the region, and, on the other, constant contact between the peoples who spoke those different languages. "This all indicates," according to Kirchhoff, "the reality of Mesoamerica as a region whose inhabitants, both the ancient immigrants and those recently arrived, were united by a common history, and in terms of which they confronted other tribes of the continent" [1967: 4].

In effect, there is a continuity between the invention of corn cultivation by the hunting and collecting bands of the Tehuacán caves seven thousand years ago and the florescence of Teotihuacán at the beginning of the seventh century AD. In the same way there is an undeniable relationship between Teotihuacán culture and the development of the various Mesoamerican cultures up to the European invasion, independent of the fact that the different groups spoke distinct languages and identified themselves by different names. Mesoamerican civilization is not the product of the intrusion of foreign elements, unknown in the region, but, rather, of cumulative development based on local experiences. This suggests a theme that will occur throughout this book: Indian cultures have adapted to the physical conditions in which they are found, a fact that explains their diversity. At the same time, the unity that they manifest is explained by their belonging to the same level or horizon of civilization.

Another fact that stands out is that practically the entire habitable area was in fact occupied at some point in the precolonial period. This means that Mesoamerican civilization was nourished by confronting an extreme variety of different situations. There was a great variety of ecological niches in which local cultural development took place, and a variety in the cultural characteristics of the peoples who successively occupied those niches. It is only after the European invasion and the installation of the colonial regime that the country becomes "unknown territory" whose contours and secrets need to be "discovered." The viewpoint of the colonizer ignored the profound ancestral perspective of the Indian who saw and understood this land, in the same way that it ignored the Indian's experience and memory.

Historical contacts included those with the peoples who inhabited the areas north of Mesoamerica, in so-called Arid America. It was an unstable and fluctuating frontier. Its inhabitants were not of Mesoamerican origin, but they had constant relations with the civilization to the south, and these relations were not always violent. Some Mesoamerican peoples originated as northern hunters and gatherers who migrated to and assimilated the agricultural, urban civilization of the south. Huitzilopochtli, the major god of the Aztecs, presents characteristics that distinguish him in the Mesoamerican pantheon. This is understandable, since he came from that small, nomadic group that, after long wandering, established itself finally in Tenochtitlán and became "the People of the Sun."

The distinction between Mesoamerica and the groups to the north is real and useful for understanding the general history of precolonial Mexico. However, the boundary should not be understood as a barrier that separated two radically different worlds, but, rather, as a variable limit between climatic regions. To the south these conditions, especially annual rainfall, permitted an agricultural life based on the available technology. There were differences in many aspects of life between south and north, but there was not isolation or lack of contact. The experience of the hunters and gatherers of the north is not alien to Mesoamerican civilization.

In the current geographic conformation of Mexico one notes the contrast between north and south and the central plateau and the coasts, and the preeminence of the central valleys. Although that conformation is based on geographic facts, the important features of the country are also the result of thousands of years of history, whose marks have not been erased by the last five hundred years. This is not to deny the importance of changes since the European invasion, but to point out that geographic transformations did not take place on an empty landscape. Rather, the changes Europeans introduced affected groups of people with a cultural heritage elaborated over many centuries in the same places, where local adaptations allowed different sorts of responses.

It is important to underline that thousands of years of human presence in the present-day Mexican territory produced a civilization. This fact has profound implications. For one thing, the diverse cultures that existed in the precolonial past and that, transformed, exist today as a continuation of them all have a common origin. They are the results of a unique civilizational process that gives them a unity apart from their differences and particularities. In addition, when we speak of "civilization," we are making reference to a certain level of cultural development, in the broadest and most inclusive sense of the term. This level is complex enough to serve as a common base and principle of orientation for the historical development of all the peoples who share that civilization. It does not consist of a simple aggregate of isolated cultural traits, however complicated such an aggregate might be. Rather, it refers to a general plan for human life, which gives meaning and transcendence to human actions and which locates people in a certain manner within the natural world and the universe. It gives coherence to human plans and values. It also allows constant change in responding to the fortunes of history without denying the civilization's profound underlying meaning; rather, it applies that meaning to the circumstances at hand. Mesoamerican civilization is a large framework—stable and permanent but by no means immutable—within which various cultures are encompassed and by which various histories are made comprehensible. Nothing less than this was bequeathed to us: a civilization, created by hundreds of successive generations who, during thousands of years, worked, thought, and dreamed in this land.

The legacy of this civilizational process surrounds us on all sides. We constantly have in front of us a material vestige, a way of feeling and of doing certain things, a name, a food, a face. All of these things reiterate the dynamic continuity of what has been created here over many centuries. These objects and beings are not mute, although we stubbornly persist in not listening to them.

## A Humanized Nature

There are hardly any virgin landscapes in Mexico. One always finds evidence of human presence, of the ancient passing of others over these lands. Thousands of abandoned habitation sites may be found, from the imposing ruins of the great cities to the barely visible vestiges of small villages beneath mounds that appear natural. Many contemporary Mexican towns have been continuously occupied since centuries before the European invasion. There are ancient canals, no longer in use. There are *chinampas*, some still productive and others converted into tourist attractions. In the mountainous zones of the central and southern part of the country, at sunrise or in late afternoon one can still see the outlines of terraces that permitted cultivation of very steep hillsides. Without too much effort one can still traverse long stretches of road over which the Maya walked a thousand years ago. There are waterworks of surprising magnitude, such as those of Tezcutzingo, near Texcoco. Hundreds of caves and springs preserve evidence of ancestral rites, some of which are still practiced regularly. Potsherds, obsidian knives, fragments of stone or pottery figurines are dispersed over every corner of the country, testifying to the human relationship with the natural world since remote times. Incessant human activity has changed our landscape, sometimes in spectacular fashion, but more commonly in a subtle, slow, and constant manner.

The transformation of the natural world includes the creation of spaces adapted for the development of human life. In many cultivated area the original vegetation was eliminated more than a thousand years ago. Patiently, generation after generation, cultivators have contributed to smoothing the profile of the land to facilitate the tasks of farming. The lithe stalks of corn peacefully invaded the countryside from the coasts to altitudes of more than 9,950 feet [3,000 meters] above sea level. And this is a plant invented by humans living on this land. For many centuries corn has been a controlling force in a large part of Mexico [Museo Nacional de Culturas Populares 1982]. Even the least alert observation will verify the reciprocal adaptation of corn to humans and humans to corn in any peasant village of Mesoamerican ancestry. Houses in small villages, for example, may be located on adjacent properties along straight streets, or along curved, winding paths. In other places one finds dispersed households scattered among the fields. These differences in human settlement may be a function of the local require-ments for corn cultivation, depending on the conformation and slope of the land, the climate, and different ways of using the available water. The use of space within households also reveals the importance of corn. For instance, there is always a place to store the ears of corn. The storehouse's form and manner of construction vary from region to region, according to the materials available, the climatic conditions, and the kinds of noxious pests to be dealt with. There is also a space for shelling the corn, which is a daily task in which all members of the family participate and which is an occasion for intensifying domestic relations. Occupying a prominent place in the home is a hearth and *metate* [grinding stone] for making tortillas, the basic and indispensable foodstuff. Here the women spend many hours, beginning long before sunrise, and here the family gathers to eat, talk, and discuss work and daily events. Space itself, from the boundaries that mark different kinds of occupation in different regions of the country to the interior details of living quarters, ultimately has a relation to corn cultivation forged over centuries and millennia.

Along with corn, Mesoamerican civilization domesticated and culti-vated many other useful plants. Beans, squash, chiles, and other products that form part of the daily diet continue to be sown together with corn in the fields called *milpas*. The maguey [agave plant] is characteristic of the landscape in high areas, where it functions to mark boundaries and to arrest soil erosion. It has, in addition, so many other useful qualities that Father Acosta commented, "It is a tree of miracles, innumerable are the uses of this plant." The prickly pear cactus [*nopal*] frequently accompanies it, accentuating the harshness of the landscape.

The cultivation of plants with several thousand years' antiquity in the service of humankind continues in every part of the country. The list is impressive and includes some products now for general use or consumption in many parts of the world, such as tomatoes, chocolate, tobacco, avocados, and cotton. It also includes plants, such as the *alegría*, that were once of great importance but whose cultivation and use have declined, and that today are harbored only in small corners of the country.

Whether one goes to humid tropical lands, the valleys of the high plateau, the semiarid north, or the flat limestone peninsula of Yucatan, one will find a vegetation largely transformed by human hands and intelligence. It is to some degree an invented landscape. Even in the depths of the forest, the distribution and relative density of certain species is due to human intention. Here, without being cultivated, the usefulness of some species has been known for centuries, which has resulted in their protection.

The fauna has also suffered changes in adapting to human presence. Turkeys and several species of dogs were domesticated from the animal kingdom, and their survival now depends on human company. Many other animals arrived with the Europeans and were easily incorporated into rural life, since Mesoamerican civilization had the cultural space available to make those animals its own. There are also methods of hunting wild animals, of attracting them, and of driving them away that have been practiced constantly over centuries and that have affected the natural distribution of animals and altered the size of their populations.

The use of certain mineral products, such as salt, clay, building stone, and sand, is also an ancient practice that has contributed to humanizing the Mexican landscape, transforming it and making it more adequate for human life. Many settlements and roads that are still in use had their beginnings in the necessity of obtaining salt for consumption in regions where it was not found. Several decades ago, Miguel Othón de Mendizábal [1929] called attention to the great importance of the salt trade in precolonial times.

A millennial interrelationship of man with nature can be seen in all the diverse ways in which the peoples of Mexico relate to the natural world, use it, and transform it daily. We see the depth of relationship in the natural contours of Mexico, in the landscapes that we all hold in our memories as an inescapable part of our lives, in the vegetation that is so familiar it goes unperceived, and in the slopes and the forms of human occupation. In this interrelationship there have been changes, which seem to have accelerated in modern times. But there is also a profound continuity that makes us part of the civilizational process that took place here, in these lands, in this natural setting. It is not simply that we occupy today the same territory in which the original civilization flourished in ancient times. Today the relationship with the natural world and all that it implies presents a pressing problem on whose satisfactory solution the future of Mexico depends to a large degree. The multiple ways in which we Mexicans turn to elements from Meso-american civilization to establish a harmonious and beneficial relation-ship with the natural world that surrounds us reveal something much richer and more complex than appears at first sight. It is not that isolated, backward technologies survive and are the cause of our backwardness. Rather, the persistence of those technologies is related to a body of knowledge that represents the accumulated, systematized experience of centuries. This knowledge and experience are consistent with particular ways of understanding the natural world, and with profoundly rooted systems of values, forms of social organization, and ways of organizing daily life. This is to say, they are part of a living culture.

## To Name Is to Create

We Mexicans who do not speak an indigenous language have lost the possibility of understanding much of the meaning of our countryside. We memorize the names of mountains and rivers, of towns and trees, of caves and geographical configurations, but we do not capture the mes-sage in those names. Here, everything geographical has a name. To a large extent, geographical names in Indian languages have been adopted as official designations. This has occurred in spite of the insistence of the Spanish crown and republican Mexico that new names be introduced. The new names signify the eternal remembrance of the symbols of the moment: saints and virgins, lands across the ocean, exalted personages of diverse background. Many indigenous names were grotesquely de-formed in the first European attempts to pronounce aboriginal lan-guages: Churubusco for Huitzilopochco, Cuernavaca for Cuauhnáhuac. The original names of many localities became the last names of saints through the policy of evangelization. Republican Mexico, more radical although less extensive in efforts at changing nomenclature, renamed some localities completely. Eminent republican figures, unlike the saints, already had last names! In spite of all the efforts of five centuries at changing the place names in our geography, many of the old names remain. They are a stubborn reserve of knowledge and testimony that will be within reach of the majority of Mexicans only when our relationship with indigenous languages changes substantially.

At the bottom of this question is the fact that to name is to understand, to create. What has a name has a meaning. If you prefer, that which has a meaning necessarily has a name. In the case of place names, their richness demonstrates the knowledge that exists of local geography. Many describe exactly the site to which they apply, and others refer to an abundance of whatever natural elements characterize the locale. But our geography is also history, and place names report this as well, telling us what happened here in terms of human affairs. Frequently, house plots, gardens, and fields have names of their own that signify some peculiar characteristic of the land, its use, or to whom it belongs. In some parts of the country there are multiple place names in two or more indigenous languages, indicating successive occupation by different peoples, or the domination of one group by another, as is frequent in areas of Nahua expansion. In these situations, nevertheless, when the local population preserves its original language, it also preserves its own system of place names and not the others that have been imposed, whatever their origin.

In the popular speech of Mexicans, even those who speak only Spanish, there are a great number of words of indigenous origin. Many of these words are in general use and have been adopted into other languages besides Spanish, because they refer to products that originally came from Mexico. But the phenomenon is most interesting in local regions of Mexico, where indigenous terms are used to refer to items that also have common names in Spanish.

This vast terminology gives name and meaning to the natural world that surrounds us and makes it comprehensible in the semantic context of dozens of aboriginal languages. It is conclusive proof of the ancestral appropriation of nature on the part of the peoples who created and maintained the underlying Mexican civilization. In-depth study of these vocabularies, hardly begun until the present, will provide information of singular importance about the diverse principles and codes that Mesoamerican peoples have employed to classify and understand the natural world in which they live and of which they form a part. From the research already published it is possible to infer the richness of information behind those names. A comparison of the terms designating the different parts of the corn plant, its variations and stages of development, has shown that the indigenous languages are richer than Spanish. This denotes a more detailed classification, which in turn is based on more precise knowledge of the botanical characteristics of corn. In addition, the botanical terminologies that have been studied allow a first approximation to the principles on which the classifications are made. These principles, along with what is being learned little by little about the human body and its illnesses, the animal kingdom, the soils, and the celestial vault of the heavens, will tell us about the way in which the universe is understood in Mesoamerican terms. This in turn will permit a more specific understanding of the relation between human beings and nature.

It is important to underline the fact that we are not referring to dead nomenclatures whose vestiges have lost coherence and meaning. On the contrary, to the extent that they belong to living languages, they conserve their full significance in the semantic context in which they originated. Consequently, they continue as linguistic systems that express and condense the knowledge base of Mesoamerican civilization. The secular continuity of common names, then, is a way of channeling the inevitable transformations in speech, which are a response to ever-changing reality. Names are like solid points of reference that prevent linguistic change from erasing the basic structures of thought through which it has been possible to understand the world and one's place in it.

## Disavowing the Indian Face of Mexico

If nature, its transformation, and its names testify at every point to the unavoidable presence of Mesoamerican civilization, what can we say about the faces of our people? One principle must be clarified. Genetic continuity and the fact that the immense majority of us have somatic traits that loudly proclaim our Indian heritage does not in itself prove the continuity of Mesoamerican civilization. Culture is not inherited like the color of the skin or the shape of the nose. Social and biological processes are quite different matters; however, they are not unconnected phenomena. If one objectively observes certain somatic traits among the Mexican population, for example, skin color, one notes that it is not distributed in a homogeneous manner. Lighter skin is encountered more frequently in certain social groups than in the rest of the population. The processes of biological reproduction that have given rise to this peculiar distribution of traits ultimately have social and cultural determinants that form part of our history right up to the present. It is worth exploring these factors further.

It is common to say that Mexico is a mestizo country both biologically and culturally. In terms of physical features, the mixture can be seen in large sectors of the population, although the intensity varies and Indian traits predominate in many groups. This can be attributed in the first place to the size of the original Indian population, which was much larger than the European, African, and other groups that participated in the racial fusion. It is well to remember that the indigenous population of Mexico has been estimated at twenty-five million at the time of the European invasion. This figure suffered a brutal decline during the first decades of the colonial period, so that only in the present century has the country again grown to twenty-five million inhabitants.

It is evident that the Indian genetic contribution was the fundamental one in the physical makeup of the Mexican population. This is an undeniable reality. However, the predominance of Indian traits in the majority sectors of the population and their much lower frequency in the dominant classes indicates that racial fusion did not occur in a uniform fashion and that we are far from being the racial democracy that is often proclaimed. The racial differences are a basic historical fact that indicates the most profound aspect of our reality during the last five centuries. A colonial society was established whose nature made it necessary to distinguish subject populations from those who were dominant. This distinction was indispensable and included racial differences. The colonial order was based ideologically on affirmation of the superiority of the dominant society over those colonized, in all terms of comparison, including racial ones.

Racial mixture occurs, to a greater or lesser degree, in all colonial societies. It must be denied socially or, when admitted, the mestizo must be assigned an inferior position in the social hierarchy. In slave societies the child of a female slave was always a slave, whatever his or her color might be, or whatever other evidence of racial mixture he or she might exhibit. In some contemporary situations there has been an effort to quantify an individual's percentage of Indian blood to determine legally aboriginal status, as has occurred in the United States. In New Spain the colonial regime formally imposed caste distinctions based on relative amounts of Indian, African, and Spanish blood. It assigned a different rank to each caste, with corresponding rights, obligations, and prohibitions. Whatever its form or extent, racial mixture did not imply at any moment that colonial society had renounced its ideological affirmation of racial superiority. These somatic differences emphatically distinguished the dominant classes from the variegated collection of dominated peoples. This separation of colonial society, in both biological and cultural terms, continued to be a burning problem throughout the sixteenth century, and even persists today, as we will see in more detail shortly.

What is important to emphasize here are the implications of the unequal racial mixture presented by different strata of the population: the absolute dominance of Indian traits in many groups and their absence or very weak presence in others. The Indian faces of the great majority indicate the existence, throughout five centuries, of forms of social organization that made it possible for those traits to predominate biologically. These forms of social organization also permitted cultural continuity. This was the result of colonial segregation, which established defined social spaces in which the biological reproduction of the Indian population took place. Inevitably, it also allowed the corresponding maintenance of culture, within certain limits. This continuity has occurred within the framework of colonial domination, with all the attendant consequences. Biological mixture was frequently the product of violence, and cultural persistence had to confront or elude the most varied forms of oppression, imposition, and rejection.

From this perspective, the mestizo nature of Mexico allows less simple and evasive interpretations than those suggested in the "racial democracy" argument. A first question has to do with the mestizo. Here I will suggest only a few ideas to be developed in later sections. Much of the mestizo Mexican population, which today forms the largest part of the rural and urban non-Indian population, is very hard to distinguish in physical appearance from the members of any community that is recognized without question as indigenous. From a genetic point of view, both are the products of mixture in which Mesoamerican traits predominate. The social differences between "Indians" and "mestizos" do not follow, then, a radically different history of racial mixture. The problem can be better understood in different terms: the mestizos are the contingent of "de-Indianized" Indians. "De-Indianization" is a different process from the biological one of racial mixture. To use the term *mestizaje* in different sorts of situations—for example, "cultural *mestizaje*"—carries the risk of introducing an incorrect view. It is an inappropriate way to understand nonbiological processes, such as those that occur in the cultures of different groups in contact, within the context of colonial domination.

De-Indianization is a historical process through which populations that originally possessed a particular and distinctive identity, based upon their own culture, are forced to renounce that identity, with all the consequent changes in their social organization and culture. De-Indianization is not the result of biological mixture, but of the pressure of an ethnocide that ultimately blocks the historical continuity of a people as a culturally differentiated group. Many cultural traits may continue to be present in a de-Indianized collectivity. In fact, if one looks in detail at the cultural repertoire, the way of life, of a traditional agricultural mestizo community and compares it with what happens in an Indian community, it is easy to see that the similarities are greater than the differences. Similarities are obvious in housing, foodways, *milpa* agriculture, medical practices, and many other aspects of social life. Even in language one can find the mark of the Indian past, since the local Spanish of a "mestizo" community frequently includes a great number of words from the original Mesoamerican language.

What is the difference then? On what basis can we say that some are

Indians and others are not? Before giving a detailed answer, let me mention a major achievement of the process of de-Indianization, begun almost five centuries ago. Working largely through mechanisms of compulsion, it has succeeded in convincing large parts of the Mesoamerican population to renounce their identification as members of a specific Indian collectivity. An Indian community considers itself the sole heir of a defined cultural patrimony and assumes the exclusive right to make decisions related to all its components—natural resources, forms of social organization, knowledge, symbolic systems, motivations, and so on. Separation from its cultural patrimony is the culmination of the de-Indianization process. As I have noted, it does not necessarily imply a break with cultural tradition, but it does restrict the scope in which cultural continuity is possible and makes any ongoing cultural development more difficult.

It remains to mention the problem of the correlation between physical features of European derivation and the socially and economically privileged groups. It is obvious that any explanation that involves notions of "natural" superiority or inferiority of groups with different racial characteristics must be discounted. History has undertaken the task of discounting such ideas, sometimes in a bloody and painful fashion. History itself helps us find the thread running through the tangle. Again, it was the colonial experience that organized society on the basis of hierarchical divisions. Physical features were used as social principles for ordering groups and individuals. The old structures of domination with their supporting ideologies continue in effect in many parts of our contemporary society. The privileges of the groups that inherited and continue to hold wealth and power tend to be justified as the necessary result of a natural superiority visible in physical differences. Faced with the new metropolis, which proclaims its Western, Christian, and white affiliations, neocolonialism and dependence reinforce the racist ideology of the old elites, in spite of rhetoric that disguises it. The ideals of physical beauty, discriminatory language, and the daily conduct of those elites demonstrate an underlying, unmasked racism.

This racism consists of much more than a preference for certain physical traits or skin color. Discrimination against that which is Indian, its denial as a major part of what we ourselves are, has much more to do with the rejection of Indian culture than with rejection of bronzed skin. There is an attempt to hide and ignore the Indian face of Mexico because no real connection with Mesoamerican civilization is admitted. The clear and undeniable evidence of our Indian ancestry is a mirror in which we do not wish to see our own reflection.

# 2.

# The Indian Recognized

One of the ways of avoiding the problem of Mexico's Indian identity has been to ideologically convert one sector of the national population into the repository of the remnants that, in spite of everything, admittedly remain from that foreign past. "The Indians," generically labeled, thus resolve the absurdity of a civilization declared defunct by decree. What remains of all that was? Only this: the Indians.

And, in fact, they are here. In the Indian regions of the country they are recognized through external evidence: the clothes they wear, the "dialect" they speak, the appearance of their huts, their fiestas and customs. Nevertheless, we Mexicans in general know little about "our Indians." How many are there? How many different peoples compose that diverse ethnic mosaic that the colonizers lumped under the single term "Indian," that is, those who were defeated and colonized? How many indigenous languages are spoken?

These cold facts are difficult to specify precisely, a situation that in itself is symptomatic of the problem. But the real problem lies in the fact that rejection of that which is Indian makes it impossible to understand different and alternative ways of life. Very few people care to understand what it means to be Indian, to share the life and the culture of an Indian community, suffer its troubles and delight in its pleasures. The Indian is viewed through the lens of an easy prejudice: the lazy Indian, primitive, ignorant, perhaps picturesque, but always the dead weight that keeps us from being the country we should have been.

### What It Means to Be Indian

It is not possible to give a precise figure for the number of Mexicans who consider themselves members of an indigenous group—that is, those who assume a particular ethnic identity and consider themselves collectively members of an "us" who are different from "the others." In Mexico there is no legal definition of what it means to be Indian. Such a definition would at least provide a formal way of estimating numbers. Instead, we are all equal here—although there are also Indians.

The census data record only one piece of information, which is pertinent but by no means sufficient: the population five years old and above who speak an indigenous language. The census of 1980 recorded a total of 5,181,038 such individuals, of whom 3,699,653 also speak Spanish. These data and those from previous censuses have been criticized frequently and thrown into doubt. A "statistical ethnocide," that is, a substantial reduction in the real figures caused by insufficient and defective data collection, has even been suggested. It is well known that many people who speak an indigenous language as their maternal tongue hide and deny that fact.

These problems carry us back to the colonial situation, to prohibited identities and proscribed languages, to the final accomplishment of colonization, when the colonized finally accepted internally the inferiority that the colonizers attributed to them, renounced their own identity, and assumed another and different one. Add to this, in many cases, the attitude of "progressive" local authorities, anxious to prove at any price that here, in this village, there are no more Indians, or at least there are fewer. We have become "cultured people" [*gente de razón*].

Nevertheless, apart from purifying the census figures, the problem consists in the fact that speaking an indigenous language, although an important fact, does not mean that all the speakers and only the speakers of indigenous languages constitute the total Indian population. The problem is not of a linguistic nature, although certainly language plays a role of great importance. Rather, it is social and cultural elements that determine membership in a specific cultural group. It is useful, then, to try to characterize Indian groups or peoples and, on this basis, to try to estimate how many Indians there are in Mexico.

Indian peoples, like all others at any time or place in history, have their own particular history. Throughout that often ancient history, each generation transmits a heritage—its culture—to the next. Culture includes many diverse elements: objects and material goods considered as property, a territory and the natural resources it contains, habitations, public spaces and buildings, productive and ceremonial installations, sacred sites, the place where our dead ancestors are buried, instruments of work and of daily life—in sum, all the material repertoire that has been invented or adopted through time and that we consider ours, as belonging to the Maya or the Tarahumara or the Mixe.

Also transmitted as a part of the cultural heritage are the forms of social organization: what rights and responsibilities individuals have as members of families, communities, and cultural groups as a whole; how to solicit the collaboration of others and to repay it; to whom to turn for orientation, decision making, or help. All this leads to another area, inherited knowledge.

We learn how to do things, to do the kind of work that is done here, to interpret the natural world and its expressions, to find ways of confronting problems, to name things. Along with this we also receive values: what is right and wrong, what is desirable and what is not, what is permitted and what is forbidden, what should be—the relative value of all acts and things. One generation transmits to those that follow the codes that allow communication and mutual understanding. It transmits a particular language that expresses the vision of the world and the ideas created by the group throughout its history. Also transmitted are particular gestures, tones of voice, ways of looking, and attitudes that have meaning for us, and often for us alone. At a deeper level a spectrum of sentiments are also transmitted. Because they are shared, they allow us to participate, to accept, and to believe. Without them personal relations and collective effort would be impossible. All this is culture, and each new generation receives it enriched by the efforts and the imagination of those who went before. As each generation is shaped within a culture, it in turn helps enrich that culture.

Our own culture belongs to us; it is the one to which we have exclusive access. History has defined who "we" are by specifying who belongs and who does not and when one stops belonging to the social universe that is the heir, depository, and legitimate owner of our own culture. Each group establishes the limits and the norms. There are ways to join and ways to be accepted. There are also ways of losing one's membership. This is what is expressed in cultural identity. To know and look upon oneself as a member of a group, and to be recognized as such by other members and outsiders, means to form part of a society that has as its exclusive patrimony its own culture. The individual benefits from his or her culture and has decision-making rights, according to the norms, rights, and privileges one's culture establishes (and that change over time), all of which are recognized as group membership, or membership in a unique, different, specific group.

From this perspective we can better understand what it means to belong to an ethnic group. We all necessarily belong to a defined society, large or small, but one that always has boundaries, membership rules, and a store of culture that is considered exclusive and its own. The Indian does not define himself in terms of a series of external cultural traits— dress, language, customs, and so on—that make him different in the eyes of outsiders. Rather, he defines himself as belonging to an organized collectivity, a group, a society, a village that possesses a cultural heritage formed and transmitted through history by successive generations. In relation to one's own culture, one knows and feels oneself to be Maya, Purépecha, Seri, or Huastec.

In the specific case of the Indian peoples of Mexico, there is another historical condition that is necessary for understanding their basic characteristics and current situation: for five hundred years these people have been the colonized. Colonial domination has had profound effects in every area of indigenous life. It has constrained cultural development, imposed foreign traits, dispossessed people of resources and cultural elements that form part of their historical patrimony. Colonial domination provoked various forms of resistance but always tried by any means to ensure the subjugation of those colonized. It was most effective when it was able to convince the colonized of their own inferiority. Throughout these pages there will be continual reference to the process of colonial domination. I do not wish to repeat myself unnecessarily, but, rather, to constantly and necessarily place Indian peoples in the social context within which their history has taken place from five centuries ago until the present.

The preceding reflections should make it easier to understand the difficulties of taking any census of the indigenous population and the inadequacy of the available figures. To make sense, it would be necessary to employ criteria of social group membership and not simply sum up individual characteristics.

An estimate of the Indian population of Mexico as being between eight and ten million seems reasonable. This would represent 10 to 12.5 percent of the total population. Remember that we are speaking of individuals who maintain their membership in a local group; the group identifies itself as different from others because it has a common and exclusive cultural patrimony. Not counted in this figure are other individuals and groups who have lost their sense of ethnic identity, although they conserve a way of life that is basically Mesoamerican.

How many Indian cultures exist in Mexico currently? This question cannot be answered precisely either, for reasons that are quickly noted here but that will be explained later. First, the identification of cultures in terms of the languages they speak is not sufficient. In general, it is estimated that there are fifty-six surviving Indian languages, but some scholars claim there are many more and argue in some cases that different dialects are in reality different languages. Besides, although speaking a common language is one of the principal requirements for constituting an ethnic group, it is not necessarily true that all the speakers of a language form a single ethnic unit. This means that detailed information on the number of languages spoken does not in itself resolve the problem of how many cultures exist. The basic problem is not linguistic. Colonial domination, as we will see in some detail, tried to systematically destroy the broader levels of existing social organization, which included vast populations occupying broad territories. It insisted on reducing indigenous life exclusively to the local community level.

This atomization of the original Indian peoples has affected the course of Mesoamerican civilization. It has reinforced local identity to the detriment of the broader social identities characteristic of Indian social organization before the European invasion. Thus, current identities should be understood as the result of the colonization process and not simply as diverse local communities, each of which constitutes a distinct people or culture. I will return to this point.

In spite of the foregoing comments, it is possible to identify contrasting situations that indicate the different demographic conditions characteristic of Mexico's Indian peoples. For example, it is estimated that the Maya of the Yucatan peninsula have a population of more than 700,000. They occupy a continuous territory, speak the same language (the local dialects never prevent mutual communication in Yucatec Maya), and to a large degree share the same culture and cultural matrix. Thus we can speak of the Maya people and Maya culture. The problem is different with the more than 300,000 Zapotecs. They occupy different territories (the mountains of Oaxaca, the central valleys, and the Isthmus of Tehuantepec), speak dialects of the language whose most distant representatives are mutually unintelligible and present very striking cultural differences. Here we must speak of a historical people and culture whose internal diversity has been accentuated by colonial domination.

But one must understand that many Indian peoples are of nowhere near the demographic magnitude of the Maya, the Nahua, the Zapotecs, the Purépecha, or the Mixtecs. About twenty ethnic groups have fewer than ten thousand members, and half of those have fewer than one thousand. These are the dramatic cases of cultures at risk of extinction, besieged by the unceasing action of ethnocidal forces.

It is easy to understand that this diversity of situations is reflected also in the characteristics that each culture has been able to maintain and elaborate. In spite of their differences, it is possible to present an outline of Indian cultures that brings to light their essential characteristics, over and above their individual differences.

### A Profile of Indigenous Culture

Each of the Indian cultures of Mexico has a distinctive cultural profile that is the result of a particular history whose beginnings date to remote times. At first glance, faced with this mosaic of different peoples, it seems difficult to make valid generalizations. Nevertheless, a careful comparison of different Indian cultures discovers similarities and correspondences beyond their particular traits. This should not be surprising if one keeps in mind two basic facts. First is the existence of a common civilization in which all Mesoamerican peoples participated and which also influenced the nomadic groups to the north. This civilization is the background, the common cultural heritage, of each people. Second, the common experience of colonial domination produced similar effects, even though in some cases the definitive subjugation may have occurred centuries apart. In fact, some peoples were subjugated or "pacified" only in the first decade of this century.

The territorial distribution of the Indian population shows a greater concentration in areas that had achieved notable cultural development before the European invasion. It is not a perfect correspondence, because diverse factors have influenced the original distribution since the beginning of the colonial period. The devastating decline in population during the sixteenth century, caused by previously unknown diseases, wars, and the hard conditions of forced labor, led to the disappearance of entire peoples and the depopulation of formerly inhabited sites. The seizure of their lands and their stubborn desire to remain free drove many groups to inhospitable regions quite different from their original homelands, the sorts of areas that Gonzalo Aguirre Beltrán [1967] has quite accurately called "refuge regions." Greed for land and the demand for forced labor were perennial forces, and their effects were felt with renewed intensity in the nineteenth century, altering once more the distribution of the Indian population in much of the country.

In many regions the Indian population effectively disappeared. In some cases it was expelled, in others, exterminated, as was the case with the Great Chichimeca of the arid north. Most frequently it was subjected to conditions that made continuity as a culturally different people impossible. This last process, de-Indianization, has been called "mixture" [*mestizaje*], but it really was, and is, ethnocide. We will return to it later.

Today, the population recognized as Indian is distributed unequally in the national territory. The central, southern, and southeastern regions are home to the largest groups and contain vast regions in which the Indians are the majority, particularly in comparison with the rest of the rural population. Indian communities are situated in diverse ecological zones, from the humid tropical forests to the semiarid plateaus more than 6,600 feet [2,000 meters] above sea level. Areas of steep mountain slopes, where making a living is difficult, are frequently isolated refuge regions whose only occupants are Indians. Few Indian communities are on the coasts. Mesoamerican civilization is more at home along the rivers and lakes, in the mountains and fertile valleys, although it has sometimes adapted to semiarid conditions.

The colonial occupation of the territory, the gradual and variable growth of what was the "useful Mexico" to the colonizers, has in most regions interrupted the original contiguity of the indigenous territories. Physical space has been fragmented as a consequence of the expropriation of Indian lands, policies of dividing the land for administrative purposes, the establishment of non-Indian cities and enterprises, networks of roads, and the construction of large public projects. Nevertheless, in certain zones, for example, among the Maya of Yucatan, territorial continuity survives. Other groups, however, have become enclaves within their own territories, which are now occupied by non-Indian Mexico. The initial impression one gains from a rapid tour through any Indian region is of a rural, peasant world composed of communities that seem similar to one another. The people are different from those in the cities, although not absent in them.

The basic productive activity of the Indian communities is agriculture. There are many systems of cultivation, depending on soil types, topographic relief, the yearly rainfall, average temperatures, and, of course, the cultural traditions represented. These systems always seek the optimum utilization of the local resources and the best adaptation to the local conditions, starting from the system of knowledge, technology, social organization of work, and the preferences and values of the group. The popular image of Indian agriculture portrays it as "primitive" and of low productivity. Quite to the contrary, however, we can observe a situation that offers a varied and rich panorama.

The first general characteristic of Indian agriculture is that several different products are raised simultaneously on the same plot. The best known example is the classic *milpa*, in which corn, beans, squash, and chiles are grown together. Actually, the number of crops grown together is usually larger. In some cases, as among the Huastec of northern Veracruz, the list of things grown in the *milpa* includes root crops, tubers, cereal grains, agaves, vegetables, and fruits. In many areas of the humid tropics a system of shade-producing zones is utilized, which depends on the height of each cultivated species to best utilize the available solar energy and increase the variety of crops grown. In other areas, the diversification of cultivated crops is achieved by complementing the basic products of the *milpa* with many others, grown in small quantities on a piece of land next to the living quarters. In this case, it is usually the women who cultivate the family garden while the men work in the *milpa*.

It is important to note that the diversification of agricultural products, which implies different harvests at different seasons, plays an important role in the diet available in indigenous communities. To evaluate the Mesoamerican diet one cannot simply quantify the calories or protein consumed in any particular day or week. Rather, one must take into account the annual cycle, in which the absence of certain nutrients in a given period is compensated by their abundance in others. The dietary cycle also includes meals during fiestas, some of which occur on obligatory, established days, and others of which occur irregularly, on the occasion of baptisms, weddings, and house construction celebrations. Finally, one must not lose sight of the fact that the indigenous diet also includes a great variety of insects and animals, available in different seasons, which provide nutrients in the annual cycle.

An agricultural system that continues in use in the lake regions of the Valley of Mexico is the cultivation of *chinampas*. The *chinampas* utilize shallow lake waters, and along their banks parcels of farmland are constructed. These parcels, the *chinampas* themselves, remain constantly damp and are systems that are highly productive for horticulture.

The tools used in Indian agriculture are usually simple and frequently manufactured in the communities themselves. For planting on steep or rocky lands, either an *espeque*, a stick with a fire-hardened point, or an *azada*, a large curved hoe, is used. On flatlands a wooden plow is used. Along with these basic instruments the machete, the sickle, a knife for husking the ears of corn, and little else are used. There are more complex Indian agricultural systems in which water is controlled by dams and canals. There are also ways of cultivating hillsides and avoiding soil erosion through the construction of rock terraces or maguey hedges.

Altogether, agricultural technology is far from "primitive," in spite of the elementary tools used. It implies putting into practice a complex variety of knowledge that is the accumulation of long-term experience. This knowledge includes knowing the characteristics of the soils, selecting compatible varieties of plants, cultivating each one according to its special requirements, following the correct calendar of activities, fighting pests, and carrying out an infinity of tasks necessary to obtain a good harvest.

Agriculture in Indian communities is intimately related to activities other than cultivating the earth. They form a complex that should be understood as a whole. Use of the natural world includes not only agriculture, but also the gathering of wild plant foods, hunting, fishing where it is possible, and the raising of domestic animals. All these tasks imply a great range of knowledge, abilities, and practices that acquire unity and coherence through a particular conception of nature and the relation of humankind to it.

In analyzing Indian cultures, it is frequently difficult to establish the boundaries between what is economic and what is social. It is also difficult to separate what is believed from what is known, myth from historical memory and explanation, and ritual from acts whose practical efficacy has been proven time and again for generations. Therefore, along with what we would call solid empirical knowledge, we find ritual practices and beliefs that, in our effort to adjust indigenous cultural reality to our own categories, we would call magical. Our categories, of Western origin, do not exist in these cultures. In Indian cultures, the conception of the world, of nature and humankind, makes quite different kinds of actions seem equally necessary. For example, a propitiatory ceremony for a good growing season may be as important as the proper selection of seeds for planting. There is a unity of human beings and the natural world, which is the reference point for human knowledge and abilities as well as for work, the specific way of obtaining sustenance. This unity is also present in human plans, in the capacity for imagining as well as observing nature, in the willingness to have dialogue with it, in human fears and hopes faced with forces beyond human control.

Of course, this occurs in all cultures, but in Western culture there is an effort to separate and specialize in distinct aspects of a unitary reality. The poet eulogizes the moon, but the astronomer studies it. The painter re-creates the forms and colors of the countryside while the agronomist understands soils. The mystic prays . . . There is no way, in Western logic, of unifying all these things in a common understanding, as does the Indian.

It is difficult to comprehend many characteristics of Mesoamerican civilization if one does not take into account one of its most profound dimensions: the conception of the natural world and the human being's place in the cosmos. In this civilization, unlike that of the West, the natural world is not seen as an enemy. Neither is it assumed that greater human self-realization is achieved through greater separation from nature. To the contrary, a person's condition as part of the cosmic order is recognized and the aspiration is toward permanent integration, which can be achieved only through a harmonious relationship with the rest of the natural world. By obeying the principles of the universal order, human beings fulfill themselves and meet their transcendent destiny. Thus we can see that work, the effort applied to obtain from nature that which humans need, has a different meaning from its meaning in Western civilization. It is not a punishment, but a method of harmonious adjustment to the cosmic order. A positive relationship with nature should be achieved on all levels, not just the purely material one of physical labor. For that reason it is impossible to separate ritual from physical effort, empirical knowledge from the myth that provides its full meaning within the Mesoamerican cosmic vision.

This does not mean an absence of practical considerations nor an ignorance of benefits and advantages; rather, they are located in a different context. There is a practical logic in the distribution of work time and in the diversification of activities. However, that logic becomes evident only if one understands the ultimate objectives of productive activity and the necessities it satisfies. Indian cultures tend toward self-sufficiency. This tendency is seen at various levels: family, lineage, barrio, and community. Self-sufficiency today is never an absolute reality, but it is a general, well-defined orientation. The sheep provide manure, which fertilizes the land. Families therefore want to have sheep, even though they rarely eat them or sell them. The turkey, which is needed for the meal during the fiesta, for the rituals of marriage, for house construction, or for the banquet I may give as a *mayordomo*, is raised in the household rather than bought. And within the community are those who know how to deal with other necessities: the midwife, the bone setter, the herbalist, the blacksmith, the musician. The community is an intricate web of general knowledge, of diversified activities, and of indispensable specializations that allow life to be lived with autonomy.

The logic of self-sufficiency governs many actions. For this reason it is incorrect to look at Indian agriculture in terms of the theoretical value of raising only cotton or sunflowers or tomatoes instead of a diversified *milpa*. Such speculation also ignores exhausted soils, sharp drops in market prices, voracious intermediaries, technological and financial dependence, and many other problems that have brought to ruin an endless number of modernization and agricultural development projects.

What does the self-sufficient Indian type of economy have to offer? Above all, it offers basic security, a broader margin of subsistence in difficult years, even though one has only what is really indispensable. Various crops, together with wildplant gathering, hunting, fishing, and the raising of domestic animals, intermixed with some sort of handicraft production (pottery, textiles, basketry, and many other products), and the generalized capacity for other sorts of work such as construction and maintenance—all offer a broad spectrum of possibilities that can be altered or combined, according to the circumstances. No one of these possibilities alone, given the conditions of indigenous communities today, assures survival. Together, however, they offer an acceptable margin of security. For this multiple strategy to succeed, each activity must be on a small scale, producing what is necessary and nothing else.

This fact explains another general characteristic of the Indian economy: its low level of surplus and its low level of accumulation. These characteristics, from the point of view of those who argue for capitalist development in the national economy, have been repeatedly pointed out as scandalous limitations. The Indians do not buy, or they buy very little;

they do not generate capital, and they do not invest. We will analyze this question later.

Another result of an economy oriented toward self-sufficiency is that it both requires and provides the opportunity for developing individual abilities in many diverse activities. Contrast this with our own world, headed toward a greater and more fragmented specialization each day. Witness the specialist who knows more and more about less and less. The Indian in a traditional community has to know what it is necessary to know about many different things and develop abilities for many different tasks. And he or she learns differently, not in school, but through living, through contact with others, and through doing the work itself. Exercising or broadening one's abilities is the result of a process that cannot be distinguished from life itself. There is no special time or place for learning what needs to be known. One observes, practices, asks questions, and listens, at whatever time and wherever one may be. Some profound satisfaction must reside in knowing one is capable, through one's own efforts, of solving so many common daily problems and attending to basic needs.

There are also effects on the way work is organized. The family is usually extended, composed of various generations who live under the authority of the head of the family (the grandfather or the great-grandfather of the smallest ones). It functions as an economic unit. There is a division of labor between men and women, whose norms are inculcated in children from an early age. There are norms of cooperation and participation, which are generally based on reciprocity. There is an intense family home life, based on shared or complementary work, on ritual and celebration, on the sharing of domestic space. Space is conceived more in terms of continuous collective relationships than in terms of privacy. The problems and joys of work are more fully shared because their meaning and consequences are understood by everyone, on the basis of their own experiences.

Relations within the family clearly reflect its nature as a production and consumption unit. However, the family's economic function is obviously not its only one, and economic activities in themselves do not indicate the richness and the importance of domestic life. The family unit, occupant of the domestic space, is the most secure place for reproducing the culture of the Indian community. The woman's role is basic. It is her job to rear the children and pass on to her daughters all the cultural elements that will allow them to perform adequately as women. To a large extent, she is the primary link for the continuity of the language itself, and the repository of norms and values that are vital within the Mesoamerican cultural matrix. Her role is recognized socially and within the family. In the communities that have preserved their own cultures to the largest degree, the woman participates more actively and on an equal footing with men, not only in domestic affairs but also in decisions affecting the community.

One of the traits frequently noted by those who study indigenous life is parents' benevolent and respectful treatment of children. Physical punishment is rarely used to correct children. Neither are children restricted from participating in family discussions. There is a broad tolerance for premarital sexual relations that even includes, in some groups, acceptance of homosexual relations during adolescence. Communication between grandparents and grandchildren has a privileged place and provides a social space for making good use of the experience of the elderly.

Between the family and the community exist other levels of social organization that also fulfill economic functions. For example, kinship relations beyond those of the extended family can be used to organize cooperation. A larger number of individuals can thus be mobilized for certain tasks that the domestic unit cannot do for itself. Cooperation may be given in the form of labor at harvest time or for the construction of a house. It may also be given in the form of cash, for a marriage celebration, for a wake and burial, or for fulfillment of ceremonial obligations attached to holding public office in the community. Cooperation is always based on reciprocity—today for you, tomorrow for me. In many cases each person keeps an exact record of what he has given to other members of the lineage and what he in turn has received from each of them.

The barrio, or the *paraje* in some regions, is another unit of organization that functions in some economic activities. The members of a barrio may have to meet their labor obligations for some public work. They sometimes have the collective responsibility of cultivating a parcel of land to cover the expenses of the church or school, the cleaning and care of the chapel, or the collaboration in some way toward the expenses of the local fiestas. When the population lives in a dispersed fashion, the center may have only a few permanent inhabitants, but it is used periodically for meetings of a ritual, commercial, or administrative nature. In these cases the maintenance and care of the public installations is organized by *paraje*, either in rotating fashion or by permanently assigning certain tasks to each of them.

A trait that deserves special mention in the social structure of Indian communities is endogamy, that is, the tendency for marriages to be between members of the same community. On occasion endogamy is an explicit norm in customary law. Whoever violates it loses communal rights and privileges. More frequently it is an implicit norm, and

compliance is achieved through social pressure. In either case endoga-
mous marriage is a custom that contributes in an important way to the
maintenance and continuity of the Indian community, insofar as it
impedes the incorporation of "the others" into the social universe of the
group. It also contributes to the reproduction of community culture by
guaranteeing that the new couple shares it.

Settlement patterns vary. There are the dispersed communities
already mentioned, in which houses are scattered among the cultivated
fields and are separated by considerable distances. Others are centralized
communities, with contiguous houses lining streets and paths, but
always with gardens and small household *milpas* among them. And
there are communities of an intermediate order, in which one can
identify an inhabited center that disperses toward its margins. In all
cases the community has one set of authorities who are recognized by all.
These central authorities have the responsibility of organizing and
supervising the communal work projects. *Tequio*, *fajina*, and *fatiga* are
some of the regional names for this form of collective work, in which all
adult men are obliged to participate. Such *tequios* are used for public
works, such as the construction and maintenance of the roads, the
building of schools, and the repair of churches and other public buildings. Generally, a married man is considered an adult, regardless of his
age. Women are not excluded; they prepare the food to be distributed
among the *tequio* participants.

The occasions for cooperative or collective work carry with them a
fiesta spirit, an atmosphere of social sharing between the members of a
lineage, of a barrio, or of the entire community. This is an element that
encourages participation and reinforces the solidarity of these groups.
Thus, one activity can bring together in an inseparable manner social,
symbolic, and entertainment functions, as well as purely economic
ones.

The notion of salary is foreign to a large part of the work oriented
toward self-sufficiency. Work is not paid, it is returned; one acquires the
obligation of doing for others what they did for you, when the appropriate
time arrives. Communal work is an implicit obligation of being part of
a community. It is a universal obligation, without distinction. "Here, sir,
when someone doesn't go, he must pay someone else to work for him."
Taken together, these forms of cooperative work organize the efforts and
abilities of the community according to priorities that are decided by the
community itself, or by its recognized authorities. The rhythms and
requirements of basic agricultural tasks have to be taken into account,
of course, as does the fact that the systems of social organization used—
family, lineage, barrio, community—have many other functions as well.
All this, together with the worldview of each Indian culture, creates a

conception of work that is necessarily different from that of capitalist societies or of Western civilization in general. We will come back to this point.

It has already been mentioned that complete self-sufficiency is never achieved today. Interchanges occur, in different forms and of different intensities. People come together in a weekly market, which may be in the barrio itself, in the center of the community, or in the mestizo city that controls the region. Even today in some zones there is direct interchange of products, or barter, without the use of money. In general, however, all things have a price and are bought and sold with money. But the people of the Indian communities do not go to the weekly market only as buyers and sellers. Basically, they go to interchange, even though the process may require a brief monetary intervention. They exchange a small quantity of their own agricultural or handicraft products for things they need that they do not produce themselves. In a later chapter we will describe how this relationship of exchange is transformed when commerce is no longer between members of Indian communities, but, rather, through the intervention of the capitalist mercantile system.

Interchange does not happen only at the weekly market. In vast regions of Mexico there is a system of annual fairs. These are visited regularly by inhabitants of very distant zones whose products are different. In this way the movement of products from the coast and the lowlands toward the high plateau is organized, and vice versa. In some cases these are huge fairs, which in the course of a week receive hundreds of thousands of visitors, including merchants, intermediaries, and primary producers. The main motive is religious: the fiesta of a venerated sacred image whose fame is regional or national. Going to the fair, however, simultaneously accomplishes various functions. One fulfills a promise to a saint or requests a divine favor. One enjoys the dances, the music, and the fireworks. One sees acquaintances who are encountered each year, exchanges news and a friendly drink with them. One visits the doctor. Things are bought and sold. In short, one lives a time-out from the normal work year's activities. Many fairs have been celebrated for centuries in the same places. Through their presence and through ceremonial activities, people from the same distant villages reconfirm particular relationships with other villages that probably predate the European invasion.

The vast movement of products assembled from diverse regions for annual interchange in the great fairs includes the circulation of goods manufactured by specialized communities. Although the cultivation of the land is the economic base of Indian communities, and although in most cases there also exist handicraft activities on a domestic scale, there are also communities that have specialized in producing certain kinds of objects for the market. Some are handicrafts of long tradition, in which pre-Hispanic technology has varied little over the last five centuries and whose styles and decoration are practically the same. For example, there are large pottery bowls made without a wheel and fired under large stacks of firewood, blouses of *coyuchil* [a native cotton] woven and embroidered on a backstrap loom, wooden objects lacquered with techniques practiced before the European invasion, and paper made from the chopped bark of trees. Other handicrafts, of course, have suffered profound modifications from the technology, needs, and tastes introduced by the invaders. Some are also the result of much more recent innovations, but based upon old artistic traditions, such as the paintings on *amate* [bark] paper.

In any case, the frequent handicraft specialization of the communities does not contradict a basic orientation of the Indian economy toward self-sufficiency. Handicraft production does not replace the agricultural activity of the community, but it does reinforce the capacity for interchange, which becomes yet another resource in a system of diversified production. The relative specialization of some communities can also be understood as a strategy contributing to the self-sufficiency of the broader Indian world, beyond the local community. This holds true if one thinks of products whose principal market is other Indian communities.

Property rights, adjudication, and use of the productive resources of the Indian community also reflect the basic orientation of economic activity. Land, because of its fundamental importance, provides the best example. In principle, land is not private but, rather, communal, property, and mechanisms exist to assign to each family head parcels of land. These can be used by the same person for many years and even be passed to his descendants. However, they may also revert to the community and be assigned to others, according to established norms. The forests and mountains, which cannot be used for agriculture, are also communal property and all community members may use them to obtain what they need. In general, even plots that are recognized as private property are subject to certain limitations. For instance, they may be sold only to another member of the community, not to an outsider.

Land is not conceived of as just a marketable good. There is a much deeper connection with the land. It is an indispensable productive resource that forms part of the inherited culture. It is the land of the ancestors, in which they are now resting. There, in that defined space, various superior forces also manifest themselves. Some are positive but others are malevolent and must be propitiated. There are also sacred sites and reference points and dangers. Land is a living being that reacts to human conduct. For that reason, the relationship with it is not purely mechanical but, rather, is symbolically established through innumerable rituals. The relationship is also expressed in myths and legends. Frequently, peoples' image of the earth itself has reference to their particular territory, which occupies the center of the universe. Among displaced communities, the collective memory of the original territory and the aspiration to recover it remain, even when the people now have other lands on which to live. Group and territory—a defined group and a specific territory—form an inseparable unit in Indian cultures. Later we will examine the fortunes of Indian territory throughout history and the problems presented today.

It is in relation to a common territory/history and territory/culture that the group that aspires to self-sufficiency defines itself. We ourselves, those of such and such a place, or of such and such a group (since land and community are synonymous here), do such and such things, or make these objects, or have these customs. The social fabric of an Indian community includes a more complicated and varied cultural weft than one appreciates at first glance. The variety of occupations, specialized jobs, and specialized knowledge is surprising.

Medicine, for example, includes, on the one hand, general knowledge and practices that are used within the household for common problems. On the other hand, it includes diverse specialists who preserve ancestral traditions used to attend to more severe illnesses. In Indian cultures, many illnesses are explained by the intervention of superior forces. These forces act to punish conduct considered unacceptable because it constitutes a transgression of norms ensuring harmony between human beings and between humans and the universe. Thus treatment may include propitiatory ceremonies and rites prescribed by tradition.

There is also a profound knowledge of the therapeutic properties of herbs and other products, however, which results from their cumulative, systematic use in each particular culture. The therapeutic effect of medicinal products is also reinforced by using them within a symbolic and emotional context that has cultural meaning. A multiple therapy exists that recognizes the psychosomatic character of many ailments and attends physical problems as much as spiritual ones. The Indian doctor is a specialist who diagnoses and prescribes on the basis of natural, bodily symptoms, but who interprets them within a framework of broad symbolic significance. In consequence, he makes use of a large number of cultural elements to restore integral health or, when necessary, to adequately prepare for approaching death. Here again in the field of medicine, it is impossible to establish strict boundaries between social life and other areas of thought. Human conduct conditions health; the knowledge of the curative properties of plants forms part of the total conception of nature and is expressed with corresponding symbolism. What we call religion and what we call medicine are intertwined in many ways, so that the distinction is erased.

Indian communities count on other specialists to carry out necessary tasks beyond the general competence of everyone. There are people who are better than others at building houses, making agricultural implements, making ceramic or wooden objects. There are also specialists in managing the weather, who drive away storms and bring the good rains. There are singers of prayers for the dead and dance masters for the fiestas. There are musicians, storytellers, and old people who remember history. There is no room here for even a summary description of these and many other activities. The example of medicine must serve to point out that each specialty in an Indian community must be understood within the context of its culture. It is difficult and usually fruitless to isolate, to analyze, and to evaluate each activity alone, separated from the other tasks and concepts that form an integral communal life. Taken together, they create the capacity for each group's self-sufficiency. The mechanical transference of terms we customarily apply, such as "specialist" or "professional," forms an obstacle to understanding life in an indigenous community. The bone setter does not cease being a peasant farmer and he may also be a musician. This year, he may be responsible for the Virgin [as *mayordomo*], besides participating in the regular communal work projects (*tequios*) like everyone else. A brief description of communal government may help complete this picture of Indian communities.

Authority in Indian villages accompanies social prestige, which is acquired throughout life by demonstrating the capacity for community service. In the realm of public life, one gives community service by participating in a system of public posts, or *cargos*. In all groups a hierarchy of *cargos*, most of them annual, constitutes the communal government. In some cases, the fulfillment of *cargos* is voluntary, with those who aspire to them volunteering to the appropriate authorities. In other cases the *cargos* are obligatory and are filled by designation or by election. One must work up the hierarchy beginning with the lowest *cargos*. Very young men or adolescents fill the lowest posts, called *topiles* in many communities, obeying the directions of those who occupy higher ranks. Each *cargo* has defined obligations.

As one ascends the hierarchy, the public commitment increases, in terms of both the time that must be spent and the expenses required of the *cargo* holder. A *mayordomo*, for example, is responsible for the organization of the annual fiesta dedicated to one of the images that are communally venerated. He must pay the expenses of the fiesta. These will include, at a minimum, payment for musicians, religious services, food and drink for all who attend, for clothes and adornments for the sacred image, and for rockets and fireworks. To meet these expenses, which are heavy given the low income levels, the *mayordomo* resorts to various expedients. He raises household animals, which will be consumed or sold for the fiesta. He asks for cooperation from members of his lineage, building upon expectations of reciprocity for past or future contributions. He sells his own labor, usually outside the community, for some period of time. He acquires debts and saves what he can. On these occasions the ties of solidarity within Indian communities are clear, because the prestige of the *mayordomo* is also the prestige of the family and the lineage and the barrio. The spending on these ritual occasions has been called sumptuary expense. The reasons for investing resources in this manner have been explained in terms of a particular economic modality, the economy of prestige. For many it seems irrational, another proof of the Indian's lack of ability, spending on useless fiestas what he could productively invest to increase his capital. But perhaps there is a better explanation.

The *cargo* system formalizes the authority of the community, which is simultaneously civil, religious, and moral. The three aspects are indissolubly linked, and authority is acquired progressively. When an individual has occupied all the *cargos* in the hierarchy, including the highest (generally called *mayordomo*), he enters the group of *principales*. In these men resides the maximum authority of the community. This means that to acquire a recognized position, one must demonstrate for years a will and a capacity for public service, along with conduct that conforms to the norms and expectations defined by the cultural group. To earn recognized, legitimate authority implies investing time and resources throughout most of one's life to fulfill functions that the community considers necessary. As one ascends in the hierarchy, one gains experience. Thus, those who have ascended through the hierarchy are those who know how public affairs should be conducted, those who can guarantee continuity and confront collective contingencies. Their advice is of proven value, and even in the area of personal life, it is evaluated in the light of a career of recognized merit.

The organization of government briefly sketched above presupposes the convergence of individual will and conduct toward joint goals. Such a convergence can be achieved only if individuals share common aspirations and values. Personal and family sacrifices must be made to carry out a community *cargo*, and the only return is public consideration. The prestige earned is manifested in ritualized deference, but it implies no material benefit of any significance. Such sacrifices indicate an orientation toward life that is difficult to comprehend from the individualistic, acquisitive perspective of modern capitalist society. Why do people behave in this way? Why is such conduct accepted and rewarded? Of course, there are social pressure mechanisms that help enforce proper conduct. These include falling into disrepute and suffering from the negative opinions of others, exposure to ridicule, and families' and authorities' insistence on proper behavior. Whoever accumulates as an individual, instead of spending toward the sumptuary expenses of a *cargo*, as prescribed by the group, loses prestige and authority instead of gaining them. Conflict may reach the point of forcing someone to leave the community. To a large extent, this explains what happens in the case of those who convert to Protestantism and refuse to participate in the system of traditional government.

Nevertheless, social pressure itself requires some explanation. It is found in the fact that participation is an indispensable condition for being recognized and admitted as a member of the group. And it is the group that is the exclusive repository of the cultural patrimony that has been inherited. To gain legitimate access to the cultural patrimony and to be able to participate in decisions about it, one must be a member of the group. To be a member (thus closing the circle) one must prove that he accepts the collective norms. Participation in the *cargo* system, with all it implies in terms of fundamental orientation toward life, is one of the basic norms that identifies group members. This form of organization is so important that in many cases emigrants return annually to their community to comply with their obligations in order not to lose their rights as group members.

The correspondence between different aspects of Indian life that have been described so far is apparent. The orientation of production toward self-sufficiency is congruent with the economy of prestige. Both tend to equalize material levels of life, preventing the growth of wealth differences. The ties of family and neighborhood solidarity, based on reciprocity, have the same effect, as do the ways of acquiring authority. Communal property rights and the limitations imposed on private landholding are also congruent with the system. The image outlined is of a society that tries to take care of itself through diversified use of all the resources at its disposal and under its control. It organizes work capacity in such a way as to guarantee available labor, according to the magnitude of the task at hand. It puts into play a complex web of loyalties and solidarity that result from kinship and not from the work relationship itself. Full individual development is realized through community service, and the reward is prestige and authority. It is a way of life that offers and requires the development of multiple capacities on the part of each individual. All this is expressed and justified in the realm of ideas through a transcendent vision of humankind in the universe. In this conception, nature, of which humans are a part, is governed by a cosmic order to which all beings must adapt. For this reason humans do not confront the natural world; it is not an enemy or an object to be dominated, but, rather, an immediate, encompassing reality, and human life must be in harmony with it. Work is, then, a way of relating to the natural world, and the relationship, as between humans, is reciprocal. Thus service to the community, in whatever sphere it is offered, is also recognized as work.

The same principles of universal order seem to be found in the systems for classifying the natural world. Indian classifications of the plant world, to the extent they have been studied, frequently employ terms that come from an ancestral way of conceiving the world. Frequently in botanical nomenclature certain characteristics of plants are associated with the colors of the different directions in the universe, which in turn correspond to deities linked to human destiny. The classification principles are also applied, as far as is known, to distinguish the parts, organs, and elements of the human body. The classification principles thus connect with conceptions about health and illness and with therapeutic practices and their corresponding rituals. There is much yet to be learned in this area, because research has been limited. Nevertheless, it is clear that collective representations about life, the universe, and fundamental human problems exist. They ideologically sustain and make coherent the social and cultural practices of Indian communities.

The supernatural world, in this vision of the cosmos, plays a role of primary importance. The forces beyond human control, in order to be comprehensible, are embodied in a broad repertory of symbolic beings. These include the owners of springs and hills and caves; the rulers of the rain and the lightning; the animal whose life and fortune is indissolubly linked to the life and fortune of each newborn human; the winds; and the earth itself. The relationship with the natural world is symbolized through a ceremonial intended to propitiate the supernatural entities that represent it. This is a coherent way of symbolically expressing human participation in the fundamental and indivisible unity of the universe to which we belong.

Unity with the cosmos is also expressed in another transcendent dimension: time. As opposed to the Western conception, time in Mesoamerican civilization is circular, not linear. The universe proceeds through a succession of cycles that, although not identical, pass through the same stages in an unending spiral. When one cycle ends, a similar one begins. Humans fulfill their own cycle, which is in harmony with the other cycles of the universe. This necessary harmony is expressed in the rituals of the agricultural calendar that symbolize the renewal of life, in which humans must participate. Also, as we will see later, the circular conception of time is present in conceptions of history. The liberty of the past, the golden age before colonial domination, is not a dead past, lost forever, but the basis of hope, because in the cycle of time that age will come again.

I want to be clear about several questions related to the selective synthesis of Indian culture that I have presented in this section. In the first place, I want to underline that it is selective. I have not presented an ethnographic summary of all the traits of Indian culture. I have selected only certain aspects that are especially pertinent for giving a vision that clarifies what I believe to be the fundamental, determining characteristics of Mesoamerican culture.

In the second place, in this synthesis I have described traits that are common to the diverse indigenous cultures of Mexico. Nevertheless, these cultures are not completely uniform. In comparing different Indian cultures notable differences will be found. The particular form in which the general traits I have mentioned occur varies a great deal, and distinctive elements will be found that give to each culture its particular profile. In my opinion, such variations, however important they may be for a complete understanding of each culture, are not enough to call into question the common scheme outlined above. Unity exists within diversity as a result of membership in a common civilization.

Finally, and most important, this panorama of Indian culture takes into account only part of the contemporary reality of Indian communities. Contemporary reality is much more complex, and it is contradictory. Traditional forms of life coexist in conflict with new ones. Coherence is cracked and broken in the presence of new ideas, new necessities, other peoples, and other objects. The spheres of self-sufficiency are reduced and all that remain are besieged bastions. Some parents prefer that their children not speak the language of their ancestors. Emigration increases.

In the face of these patent realities, of what value is the image of Indian culture presented in these pages? I discuss these and other problems that characterize the contemporary situation of Indian peoples in the second part of this book. Here my intention has been to describe the autonomous culture of the Indian peoples, that which is based on its cultural heritage and over which it exercises control and makes decisions. It is from that autonomous culture and the elements that compose it—material items, organization, knowledge, symbolic and emotional elements—that each group confronts new situations and changes in the surrounding world. Through its autonomous culture it establishes relationships with the new world, adapting to new circumstances, resisting in order to preserve its social spaces in all areas of life, appropriating foreign cultural elements that prove useful and compatible. It invents new solutions and ideas and strategies of accommodation that allow the group to survive as a different, distinguishable collectivity, whose members have access to their own common cultural patrimony. This is only a part of contemporary reality, but within this part resides the reason for existence as Indian peoples.

# 3.

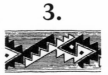

# De-Indianizing That Which Is Indian

Even though the dominant colonial ideology restricts the living Mesoamerican heritage to the population recognized as Indian, the national reality holds within itself a different truth. The effective presence of that which is Indian is found in almost every social and cultural aspect of the country. It is expressed in cultural traits of very different kinds, traits that undeniably have their origin in Mesoamerican civilization and that are variously distributed in the different groups and strata of Mexican society. The presence of Indian culture is, in some aspects, so commonplace and omnipresent that one rarely stops to think about its profound significance, or about the long historical process that made possible its persistence in social sectors that assume a non-Indian identity today.

## One or Many Ways of Life?

In all Indian cultures diversity can be observed, but within the basic unity of Mesoamerican civilization. The same is not true of the different cultural groups in non-Indian Mexico. Here, the differences are much more marked. As we will see, they are not explained fully if we try to see them as variants or subcultures of the same civilization. Behind their plurality there is a history of power relationships within the scheme of colonial domination. Let me mention something that will receive more detailed attention later: the lack of unity and coherence in the non-Indian culture of Mexico is a fact that in itself calls into question the plans for integration into a national culture postulated as "superior." There does not exist a unified national culture, but, rather, a heterogeneous grouping of different and even contradictory ways of life. One of the principal causes of this heterogeneity is the different way in which each group has been historically related to Mesoamerican civilization.

A basic causal factor in cultural diversity is the land base. Geographical variation, without being an absolute determinant of cultural differences, without doubt underlies many distinguishing characteristics of regional lifeways. This is a universal phenomenon that had great importance, as we saw, in the birth and development of Mesoamerican civilization. The diversity and contrast of ecological niches, each with different natural resources, has been the permanent framework for the cultural configuration of Mexico. Its particular importance has not always been the same, because the natural world acquires significance and is transformed into a resource for human beings only through culture, and culture has varied in the course of history.

The regions of Mexico have been studied from different points of view. The country has been divided up in terms of physical geography: soil types, relief, vegetation, climate, and similar variables. Economic regions have also been delineated, according to the distribution and characteristics of production activities. Most of these studies refer to the contemporary period. Only a few isolated studies give a panorama of the historical development of certain economic regions.

Until now, there has not been a work that includes all the cultural regions of Mexico. It is clear that this task presents additional problems. It is not reliable to delineate a region by the simple presence or absence of a certain number of isolated cultural traits. It is also difficult to deal with all the historical and contemporary information that would allow construction of an image closer to reality by taking into account that cultural regions are historical phenomena that are transformed and reaccommodated by many factors. Although we do not have a systematic panorama, the existence of different regional cultures is an undeniable fact that is easily verified simply by traveling through the country with the senses alert and a willingness to talk with the people.

A northerner differs from a *jarocho* from Veracruz and from someone from the Bajío in his habits, his manners and customs, and in all the diverse aspects of his culture. One cannot generalize about northerners, however, because the rural culture of Sonora is not like that of Nuevo León, not to mention the differences between the countryside and the city, which we will discuss shortly. Different histories have created particular social spaces and ways of occupying the land. Contingents of colonists of varied origins arrived, and their initial objectives were not the same, varying as they did from mining to ranching to commerce to establishing secure frontiers. They also built different kinds of relationships with the Indian population that occupied each region before the European invasion. In some areas Indian enclaves have survived, while in others the original population was annihilated, expelled, or de-Indianized. A few small areas are characterized by relatively recent foreign settlements, for example, the U.S. Blacks who settled in El Nacimiento, in the municipality of Músquiz, Coahuila; the French of

San Rafael, Veracruz; or the Italians of Chipilo, Puebla. The influence of African culture brought by slaves, which has been little studied, most certainly left a different imprint in each zone, according to the size of the Black population, its relative magnitude in the local demography, and the particular conditions of the relationship with the rest of local society.

Throughout the country, and in the interior of each region, there is a marked contrast between the countryside and the cities. The urban ways of life are visibly different from the rural. Here again the use of census data is misleading and of little utility. The figure of twenty-five hundred inhabitants as a criterion for distinguishing rural from urban localities does not reflect reality. Many much larger communities have a rural culture and vast sectors of the large cities also maintain, to a large extent, lifeways that reflect recent rural origins and interrelationship with the rural world. Apart from the precise quantification of the rural and urban parts of the Mexican population, it is clear that both are present and embody different cultures, helping accentuate the cultural diversity of the non-Indian sector. The major implications of the city/countryside duality will be discussed in the third section of this chapter.

Apart from the "horizontal" cultural differences between regions of the country and urban/rural sectors, the cultural panorama of non-Indian society is complicated even more by the presence of "vertical" distinctions, that is, the hierarchical division of society into classes and strata. Unlike the cultural contrasts that result from the coexistence of ethnic groups or the consolidation of culturally distinct regions, the cultural variation that results from the division into classes and strata should be understood in terms of levels. In a society with common origins, the component groups participate in a common culture to different degrees, depending on the ruling social order that gives opportunities and privileges to certain sectors to the detriment of others. In non-Indian Mexican society, the problem of cultural levels is necessarily tied to the two fundamental origins of the population, Indian and European. Ideologically it may be maintained that we have a mestizo society that harmoniously combines the racial background and culture of the two primary sources. However, the reality is different, because the majority of the popular classes and sectors have Indian origins, often very recent. In consequence, they have been able to maintain many more elements of Mesoamerican culture. On the other hand, some upper-class sectors are derived more or less directly from the Spanish colonizers and tend to conserve non-Indian cultural forms. This problem will be discussed in greater detail in chapter 7.

Thus, the cultural panorama of non-Indian society is far from being homogeneous. The presence of that which is Indian, an underlying cause of heterogeneity, is also different in different regions, in the countryside and in the cities, and in different social classes and strata. Let us explore the situation in general terms.

### The Peasant World

There are a large number of traditional rural communities that are not considered Indian and whose inhabitants do not claim to be so. Nevertheless, a close examination of traditional rural culture reveals a marked similarity with many aspects of Indian culture outlined in the previous chapter. This is true to such a degree that it may be stated that these communities have an Indian culture but have lost the sense of identity that goes with it.

The basic economic activity is agriculture, which to a large extent makes use of Indian techniques. Corn continues to be the principal crop, along with other products of the *milpa*, depending on local conditions. There may be greater use of the plow and of draft animals, a practice favored by the haciendas, which occupied the flatlands, easily cultivated with the plow. The haciendas generally promoted the de-Indianization process. In terms of land tenure, individual property coexists with *ejidos* and communal mountain land. In the organization of agricultural work people make use of family solidarity and the cooperation of neighbors, based on reciprocity. Wage labor in agricultural tasks is infrequent. Myths, stories, and legends in which the natural world figures as a living entity persist, as do propitiatory practices and beliefs about supernatural beings, all of which are clearly of indigenous origin. On the other hand, the vision of the cosmos that might give coherence and meaning to these ideas and practices appears fragmented, and collectively it is more weakly expressed than in Indian communities.

The "mestizo" handicrafts of traditional communities are not very different from those found in Indian communities. It is true that some have been lost, for example, the manufacture of *huipiles* [traditional women's blouses] and other items of clothing and some objects associated with ceremonial life. But artistic abilities are found in equal measure and are applied in the same way, that is, as a sheaf of cultural resources developed generally by community members. They all contribute to relative self-sufficiency in different levels of social organization. Here, as well, the economic orientation looks toward self-sufficiency, although in general terms the degree of commercial exchange may be greater than in Indian communities.

In the realm of communal organization, the municipal council [*ayuntamiento*] is stronger and has more authority than in Indian communities. Nevertheless, the barrios persist and have some of the functions of the indigenous *parajes* and barrios. The *cargo* system remains, although it primarily involves religious activities. The fulfillment of such *cargos* continues to be a legitimate way of acquiring prestige and social recognition. Sumptuary expenses continue to be of great importance as a goal of economic activities.

The presence of Indian culture is clearly visible in other aspects of life in traditional peasant communities. Living quarters and food habits, for example, are adapted to similar patterns, if one compares Indian and non-Indian communities that occupy similar ecological niches. To restore health people resort to various practices that form part of the indigenous heritage. It is common to find herbalists, bone setters, and midwives whose practices are difficult to distinguish from those of their Indian counterparts.

What, then, makes traditional peasant communities different from Indian ones? A first obvious characteristic is language: the non-Indian peasant speaks only Spanish. This statement must be qualified by two frequently found features. First, many times elderly people and some families remember the original Indian language, although its use is restricted and communication is generally in Spanish. Second, the number of words of Indian origin is greater than in the standard Spanish dialect of the region. Nevertheless, it is a fact that Spanish and not an Indian language is spoken in these traditional communities. However, this fact does not explain the Indianness or non-Indianness of communities that share very similar cultures. Neither is Indianness determined by distinctive clothing, which is a result and not a cause of belonging to an Indian community.

The absence of an Indian ethnic identity has much more profound significance because it reveals that a mechanism of identification has been broken, one that allowed the designation of an "us" related to a cultural patrimony that was ours alone. Indian culture persists, to a large degree, but the group that holds it and uses it no longer identifies itself as an articulated whole in relation to which only members of the group have decision-making rights. Since that rupture, traits such as language itself and a distinctive form of clothing lose one of the important functions that made them necessary: they no longer serve as elements to identify "us," a group that corresponds to an ethnically differentiated group. For some writers this change is a result of acculturation, of close contact with another society that possesses a different culture. For others, it relates to an inescapable historical process in which caste-type relations are transformed into class relations. Along the same lines, others try to see the change as a sign of proletarianization, which is also inevitable. I prefer to speak of ethnocide and de-Indianization, concepts that I will elaborate later.

De-Indianization of rural communities is a process that has occurred at a different pace throughout the history of Mexico, as will be seen in Part II. It is easy to find communities recognized today as mestizo, but that were Indian at the beginning of this century or even more recently. In these situations it is not surprising that a predominantly Indian culture has been preserved in many areas of life. Thus, the change from Indian community to traditional peasant community is not to be understood as a transformation that implies the abandonment of a Mesoamerican way of life. Rather, it is a process that occurs in the realm of ideology. Change occurs when the pressures of the dominant society succeed in breaking the ethnic identity of the Indian community.

This does not mean that de-Indianization is purely a subjective change. In fact, the pressures from the dominant society intensify precisely when the presence of groups with a distinct identity constitutes an obstacle to practical objectives. These objectives may include obtaining labor to work outside the community, or implementing a modernization program promoted by the dominant society. De-Indianization has been achieved when, ideologically, the population stops considering itself Indian, even though the lifeway may continue much as before. Such communities are now Indian without knowing that they are Indian.

The rural peasant world is not limited to traditional communities. In various regions of the country a completely capitalist agriculture dominates. The harvest from these agroindustries is destined for the market, often a foreign one. The orientation of this agriculture is not for self-sufficiency, but for accumulating profit. Its operation requires wage labor and it depends on monoculture. Many Indians and traditional peasants travel to these zones in search of seasonal work, and the contingents of workers also go to the United States. The campesino, in extreme cases, has given way to the farmer and the agricultural impresario and the wage worker. Even in this rural world so different from the one I have called traditional, many elements of Indian culture flourish. Local life includes traits that are unmistakably Indian in terms of food, medicine, and other social practices. Temporary workers do not lose contact with their cultures of origin, and they renew these contacts by periodically returning to their communities. For them, capitalist agriculture is a different world, an outside world, where one goes when impelled by circumstances. Without taking into account the background of Indian culture that wage workers carry with them, it is impossible to understand the practical way they are integrated into capitalist agriculture. This is true even though they may come from non-Indian communities.

The rural world, taken as a whole and in spite of its regional differences and different forms of agricultural production, has a strangely Indian cultural flavor. It is manifested in many aspects of life, although it varies with local circumstances. Two facts are of particular relevance. First, the rich agricultural tradition of Mesoamerican civilization represents accumulated experience and a long process of adaptation to local conditions. It is not easy to bypass successfully. That tradition, as we have seen, is a complex that includes cultivation techniques and associated knowledge within the framework of a particular conception of nature. The practice of this agricultural tradition requires a certain social environment and an intellectual and emotional perspective. It can be transformed, and in fact transforms itself constantly, but it must nevertheless maintain a certain coherence in order for the whole complex to function properly. This fact explains the persistence of many Indian traits in the rural world.

A second fact should not be overlooked. With the imposition of the colonial regime, physical space as well as society was divided into two opposite and incompatible poles. The city was the seat of colonial power and the limited geographical realm of the conquistador. The countryside, on the other hand, was the physical space of the colonized, of the Indians. This separation allowed the persistence of forms of social organization belonging to the rural Indian world, which in turn allowed the dynamic continuity of Mesoamerican cultural configurations. Between the city and the countryside relations were never those of equal to equal, but, rather, of the subjugation of the rural/Indian to the urban/ Spanish. This identification persists today, in urban sectors as well as among the Indian population and in the rural peasant communities. Within this framework, to which I will return, we can better understand the defining presence of Indian culture in rural Mexico.

## The Indian Heritage in the Cities

The city was the bastion of the colonial order. There the invaders established their privileged space of domination. Many cities were built over the ruins of ancient centers of Indian population, but others were constructed on sites that had not had permanent settlements before. Everything depended on the needs and interests of the colonization process. In some cases, the predominant urgency was to establish a center of power in areas occupied by a dense, sedentary population, thus assuring an ample labor force, services, and products that were indispensable for the consolidation and expansion of the colonial enterprise. In other cases, it was necessary to found towns and cities to exploit the mines and obtain gold and silver, the desired precious metals. When the mining areas were far inland, in the territory of the nomadic and warlike groups of the north, it was critical to found cities other than the mining centers themselves. These other centers would provide greater security on the roads, for the transportation of precious minerals, food supplies, and the necessary labor force. It is a fact that the chronology of the founding of European settlements in New Spain exactly parallels the slow development of the various enterprises important to colonization: warfare, pacification, mining, European agriculture, stock raising, and both internal and external commerce. All this required the congregation of European population centers of variable size based on possibilities and needs. They were scattered centers of power in a territory that was, outside the perimeters of the cities, still indigenous.

But even in the cities there was an Indian presence. Mexico City had barrios and neighborhoods inhabited exclusively by Indians. There was spatial segregation, which expressed the nature of the colonial order. The center consisted of the city as such, that is, the Spanish city, while the Indian barrios formed the periphery. Drastic regulations existed to assure the residential separation of colonizers and colonized. The Spaniards [*peninsulares*] were prohibited from living in Indian localities, and the Indians, for their part, were obliged to live only in the urban areas assigned to them. Material vestiges of that separation remain in Mexico City and other urban centers. They include the quadrangular layout of the central Spanish city and the names of the old Indian barrios and towns that adjoined it, absorbed today by urban expansion. They also include differences in architecture, the names of many streets, and perhaps an old sentry post, which marked the boundaries of the original city. For centuries, urban Indians lived in the city, but under different living conditions from the European colonizers. They lived segregated, on the margin of many aspects of city life, because the real city was an area of colonial power, which was off-limits to Indians, to the colonized.

The organization of the urban barrios has been brutally and systematically attacked by the excessive growth of the great cities. There has also been an erratic application of administrative measures, which demonstrates the lack of any urban policy even moderately attentive to the needs of the population. Rarely have the territorial divisions within cities been based on the spatial distribution of the forms of social organization that really exist. Rather, measures have been taken for purely administrative ends. The placement of great urban structures and of transportation systems has generally followed technocratic criteria, which ignore the social and cultural fabric that makes urban life possible. Financial speculation on urban property provokes displacement and reaccommodation of the population, always to the detriment of the poorest sectors. The old Indian barrios became desirable areas when they ceased being the periphery and were incorporated into the center of the city itself. The outlying towns, in turn, were and continue to be engulfed by voracious and uncontrolled urban growth.

In spite of these processes, some communities resist and others rebuild themselves. They are not Indian barrios, in the strict sense of the term, although historically they may derive from ancient Indian communities. In many cases they preserve features that prove their origin. In some urban zones the original indigenous languages continue to be spoken, within the family as well as in certain aspects of communal life. In various parts of the city, and not only in the periphery, which remains more rural than urban, organizations called *mayordomías* continue to organize the fiestas for the local saint. The extended family plays an important role in organizing cooperation within the domestic group. Rituals and celebrations of Indian origin, which include the ceremonies for the Day of the Dead and pilgrimages to the famous sanctuaries, continue in the very heart of the city. There are groups that, through dances and rites of ancient origin, exalt a generic Indian origin without reference to any specific group or region or community. An example is the so-called *concheros*, who recruit a large part of their membership from city inhabitants.

The urban markets, at least in the central and southern part of the country, always offer a great diversity of products that originated in Mesoamerican civilization. They include a rich variety of foods for popular consumption, foods that may be scorned by other urban sectors. There are crayfish and prickly pear leaves [*nopales*], fermented agave beer [*pulque*] and bean- or chickpea-filled pastries [*tlacoyos*], *huauzontles* [*Chenopodium nattalias*] and grasshoppers, prickly pear fruit and fleshy leaves of the agave plant. On the outskirts, distributed in an orderly way similar to that described by the chroniclers of the sixteenth century, can be found the herbalists' stands. They have remedies for every kind of problem and amulets to avoid danger. When one has the opportunity to visit markets in other parts of the world, one recognizes with surprise the profoundly Indian character of the urban markets of Mexico. And all these traits are really only a small sample of the cities' underlying cultural heritage, the living inheritance of their ancient Indian population, which today has been de-Indianized.

Approaching the old barrios of the city allows us to see in hazy outline a way of life that is the result of the adaptation of many Mesoamerican cultural forms, over a long time period and in conditions of subordination to the dominant culture, to an urban context. It is interesting, for example, to compare the old urban housing arrangements [*vecindades*] with the new, multifamily structures that have been built to replace them. In the *vecindad*, the private rooms are aligned along a common patio, where communal areas for important functions are also found: bathrooms, water taps, washbasins, play areas, and work areas. All of these tend to strengthen relations between the inhabitants and generate a group spirit. This spirit is weaker in the new multifamily structures, where the effort is to provide each apartment with all the basic requirements for daily life, and where the common areas are simply parking lots, sidewalks, commercial zones, or, at the most, sports areas. In these multifamily structures, only the very young, by playing together and through easily developed group competition with youths from other buildings or units or barrios, are able to develop some sort of group spirit in relation to the place where they live.

Here we have face to face two ways of understanding and experiencing communal life. In the case of the modern multifamily structures, the privileged area is the apartment, the exclusive space of the nuclear family. In the other, the *vecindad*, the communal patio is the axis of daily life for a collection of families, many of them extended families. Behind these facts are different cultural orientations. One corresponds to individualism, which is dominant in contemporary Western civilization. The other points toward a local society in which communal ties play a greater role, as they do in Mesoamerican civilization. This situation permits the growth of cultural forms belonging to one's own group, in a daily environment broader than that offered by the nuclear family. It is not surprising that the barrios with a larger number of *vecindades* are those that manifest a more vigorous local identity and a more solid communal organization to carry out different tasks. This became evident in the events following the earthquake of September 1985.

Although many things have happened since the founding of the first colonial cities, even today there are phenomena that make evident their dominant nature. In the refuge regions the central point is a ladino city that dominates a surrounding constellation of Indian communities. Economic, political, social, and religious control resides in and is exercised from this city. It is the center of power. Those who unrightfully hold this power are not the Indians, but the ladinos, who like to call themselves "cultured people" [*gente de razón*] and who proclaim with pride their non-Indian descent from European colonizers. In these cities the presence of that which is Indian marks every aspect of life. The majority of those traveling through the streets are Indians, as are those who go to the market to sell and to the stores to buy, those who work at the most poorly paid occupations, those who fill the jails and those who, at nightfall, stumble drunkenly back to their communities.

But that which is Indian is also present in the conduct and thought of the urban ladino. In part, this is because the ladino has adopted some traits from the regional Indian culture, as regards food, language, and certain beliefs and symbolic practices. But fundamentally it is because the life of the ladino is structured in terms of contrast with that of the Indian, by the necessity of permanently marking everything with an indelible "not Indian." In the small ladino world of these cities, that which is Indian is omnipresent as everything one is not and does not want to be. Guzmán Bockler [1970: 101–121] has written that in Guatemala the ladino is a fictitious being, because the essence of his identity is negative. Being ladino is not being anything specific of one's own, but just being "not Indian." Without the presence of the Indian, the ladino ceases to be, since he exists only through the colonial domination exercised over the Indian.

The accelerated growth of the large Mexican cities in the last fifty years is due principally to the arrival of Indian or mestizo immigrants from the rural zones. The dynamics of the process involve the impoverishment of the countryside and the concentration of economic activities and opportunities of all sorts in the urban zones. The migration Indianizes the city. In general, the new arrival can count on family or friends from the same village who have arrived before him. They facilitate his first contact with the city, helping him adapt and find work. Together they form a nucleus of people identified by their local culture of origin. In this small world transferred from the village they can speak their own language and re-create, as far as possible, their own practices and customs. Sometimes the group becomes larger, since it is easy to identify with people of the same region above and beyond the specific traits of each community. Then it is possible to establish a broader cultural environment that goes beyond that of daily domestic life. Tournaments of *pelota mixteca* [a ballgame of pre-Hispanic origin] can be organized, or a Mixe band to play the music of the home region. The fiestas of the homeland can be celebrated, with appropriate dishes whose special ingredients are either brought by the most recent traveler or substituted with something acceptable from the urban stores. At another level there are many organizations of "countrymen" [*paisanos*] now living in the city who try to do something for their native land. They may collect money for some public project, send books to create a library, take important local matters before central authorities, receive and help orient new arrivals to the city.

Contact and close relations with the home community are not lost. To the contrary, they are renewed on every possible occasion, since the coming and going of individuals makes it possible to share the latest news: who died, who got married, who left, what has happened to the communal lands invaded by the cattle rancher, or the boundary conflict with the neighboring community. In addition, whenever possible one returns to the community, even if it is only once a year for the fiesta of the patron saint. And obligations are fulfilled, both those based on *compadrazgo* [godparenthood] and those that come from having accepted a ceremonial *cargo*. In this way, extensive areas of the city are inhabited by people who live there in a transitory way. Their interest and hopes are fixed on what happens many miles distant, in the village or neighborhood of which they form a part, and which gives meaning to an emigration they hope will be temporary. They are Indians who exercise their own culture insofar as the city allows. It is not uncommon for them to hide their identity and deny their place of origin and their language in their contacts with "the others." The city, after all, continues to be the center of foreign power and of discrimination. But their identity persists, disguised and clandestine, and because of that identity their membership in their original group is maintained. With it go loyalties and reciprocity, rights and obligations, the practice of and ties with a common and exclusive culture. Without that universe of ongoing relationships, based on the existence of the Indian communities, the survival of hundreds of thousands of Indian inhabitants of Mexican cities would be impossible. A very revealing fact indicates just how true this is: *Mexico City is the place with the largest number of speakers of indigenous languages in all the Americas.*

The city is also filled with Indian workers, contingents of whom come daily from nearby Indian communities. Others come from distant places and remain in the city during the time they are working. In every part of the city are found the "Marías" with their children, installed on the corners with the greatest volume of traffic, selling chewing gum and trinkets or begging from passing cars. Many men in badly fitting work clothes labor as masons or at whatever other tasks they can find. Domestic work is more stable and employs a great number of Indian women. Between them often exists a chain of relationships that allows individuals to go from their home community to the regional city and from there to the nation's capital. These networks now extend to several cities in the United States.

The situation is different for the Indian students. They are proportionately few, but their numbers increase constantly. By necessity, they must come to the city, if they can, in order to continue their secondary and higher education. This group also includes some professionals and workers of Indian origin and has been the social circle from which have recently emerged new forms of political organization based on Indian ethnic identity. Urban experiences and contact with different sorts of ideas, information from the broader outside world, and relationships with other Indian emigrants have all made possible the formation of political groups motivated to press the demands of the Indian communities. In another section I will deal with this theme in greater detail. Here, I simply point out this new Indian political presence is an urban phenomenon, which arises precisely in the physical space reserved historically as the seat of non-Indian colonial power.

The presence of the Indian in the cities has not passed unperceived by the dominant, privileged elites. In earlier times the Indians were referred to as the masses [*la plebe*], but today another term has become established: they are "the *nacos.*" The word's connotations are undeniably negative, discriminatory, and racist. In particular, the *naco* is the de-Indianized urban inhabitant to whom are attributed tastes and attitudes that are a grotesque imitation of the cosmopolitan behavior to which the elites aspire. The behavior of the *naco* is deformed to the point of caricature by his supposed inability and lack of culture. The word "*naco,*" nevertheless, also designates anything that is Indian, any trait that recalls the original ancestry of Mexican culture and society. Any fact that evidences the Indian world present in the cities is exorcised by applying to it the simple qualifier *naco.* Thus the city protects itself from its deeper reality.

## The Bronze Race and the Beautiful People

The apparent presence of the Indian in official Mexican culture is very evident to foreign visitors, especially Latin Americans. The Revolution of 1910 has accorded to the image of the Indian a special privilege, that of serving as one of the major, official symbols of nationalism. Later we will examine the other side of the coin, government policy toward living Indians, or *indigenismo*. Here it is important to point out the ideological exaltation of the Indian, which has made his presence visible in the public sphere under State control.

Art supported by revolutionary governments, especially between 1920 and 1940, had a very nationalistic character. It was, after all, necessary to go back to our roots. The popular nature of the Revolution, much in evidence in those years, led this search for roots along the paths of history until it reached the precolonial past. Upon its return to the present, the search for roots legitimized the culture of the nation. If not all of national culture, it at least legitimized those aspects that were easily appreciated: the bucolic life of the campesino, popular handicrafts, and folklore. In music, dance, literature, and the plastic arts, the theme of the Indian provided the basic elements for shaping a vast nationalistic current under government patronage.

Hundreds of square meters of murals adorn every type of public building in many cities of the republic. Murals are in seats of government and public offices, in markets and hospitals, in schools and libraries, in factories and workplaces. In these murals, the image of the Indian is practically indispensable. Rarely is there missing some allegory about the precolonial world that frequently lays the foundation for or presides over scenes of the world of today or tomorrow. There is space to indicate the painful transition from a past that was happy and full of wisdom to the horrors of the Conquest and slavery. There is also space for some pictorial references to the dances and showy ceremonies of contemporary Indians. Brown faces with high cheekbones and almond-shaped eyes, along with the sacred political heroes, occupy the most prominent place in Mexican mural painting. The pre-Columbian codices seem to come to life again in the work of Diego Rivera, to recount history in a different way, in the terms of the Mexican Revolution. In this sense, the painters of the nationalist school play the role of a new Tlacaélel, that ancient priest who for many years occupied the position of Cihuacóatl, the gray eminence of the Aztec state. Tlacaélel ordered the ancient books destroyed in order to paint new ones that would more adequately portray the history of the glorious Mexica, the People of the Sun.

Another favored way of exalting the Indian roots of Mexico has been through museums, which exist in most State capitals and in many other cities. The best and most pristine example is the National Museum of Anthropology in Chapultepec Park, a privileged section of Mexico City. The architectural conception, in all its details, reflects an ideology of exaltation of the precolonial past. Simultaneously and in a contradictory fashion, it expresses a rupture with the present. The proportions and the sobriety of the façade, the amplitude of the vestibule and the interior plaza, and the elegant magnificence of the finishes bring to mind in some ways the characteristics of Mesoamerican cities. However, they are treated in such a way that the effect also reflects the layout of Christian temples: an entrance with choir and latticework (the vestibule of the museum), a great central nave (the patio) with lateral chapels (the exhibition rooms), culminating in the front altar (the Mexica Room, with the Sun Stone at its center).

All the rooms on the ground floor of the museum are dedicated to archaeology, but each has a corresponding upper area. The major exhibition room, dedicated to the Aztecs, is the only room that does not have a mezzanine, and it is also larger than the other rooms. The top floor is composed of all the mezzanine rooms and contains the ethnographic exhibits, the reference to the Indians of today. Many visitors do not go through those rooms, because of fatigue or lack of interest, both factors directly related to the layout of Museum space. The words the visitor sees upon leaving, carved in the huge interior panel of the façade over the entrance doors, precisely summarize the ideological message of the museum and the broader use the State has made of the precolonial past: "In the greatness of their past people find courage and confidence to face the future. Mexican, contemplate yourself in the mirror of that greatness. Foreigner, see proof here of the unity of human destiny. Civilizations pass, but humanity will always preserve the glory of others who struggled to build those civilizations."

The Indian presence as depicted in murals, museums, sculptures, and archaeological sites, all open to the public, is treated essentially as a dead world. It is a unique world, extraordinary in many of its achievements, but still a dead world. Official discourse, translated into the language of the plastic arts or of museography, exalts that dead world as the seed of origin that gave rise to today's Mexico. It is the glorious past of which we should feel proud, which assures us a lofty historical destiny as a nation, even though the logic of that assertion may not be entirely clear. The living Indian and all that is Indian are relegated to a second floor, when they are not ignored or denied. As in the National Museum of Anthropology, the contemporary Indian occupies a segregated space, disconnected from the glorious past as well as from the present, which does not belong to him: an expendable space. Through an adroit ideological alchemy, that past became our past, that of the Mexicans who are not Indians. However, it is an inert past, a simple reference to what existed as a kind of premonition of what Mexico is today and will be in the future. It has no real connection with our contemporary reality and our collective future.

Today, other aspects receive official attention designed to stimulate the growth of tourism. These include the restoration of archaeological zones and the commercialization of indigenous handicrafts. That which is Indian is sold as a unique image, which provides a touch of local color, an accent of the exotic to attract tourists. This is an Indian Mexico for external consumption.

What is "Indianness" for the elites of the country? In what way is it present among the beautiful people? In general, no one in these strata claims any indigenous ancestors. To the contrary, the usual situation is an ostentatious claim of European lineage, of descent that has been maintained without mixture over the generations. When possible, the emblems of a more or less doubtful nobility are exhibited. There are families that still conserve a coat of arms that presides over the principal living room of the house. If a family does not proclaim noble blood, it asserts a modest origin, a fortune and a social position earned through effort and talent. Although it may not be stated baldly, these characteristics are always associated with ancestors who were not Indians, just as their descendants are not Indians today. The Indians were the workers on grandfather's hacienda, and the Indian women were the domestic servants of that period. When there were lands worked by peons, enjoying social occasions together with them from time to time was inevitable. In some families of ancient oligarchical ancestry, there is a continuing love of horse racing, of ranch-style home cooking, of cock-fights, and of a certain religious flavor to domestic life. This is all part of being Mexican, and one can enjoy it occasionally on Sundays. Here one runs into that which is Indian, but only if one looks down. Looking straight ahead, at equals, the skin is white and the hair and eyes are light. No one speaks Náhuatl, but many speak French, and today, almost everyone speaks English.

In an anthology issue, the U.S. magazine *Town and Country* presented "The Mighty Mexicans," a parade of photographs and brief descriptions of the most powerful people in the country. This was, naturally, during the elation of the oil boom. In a cursory view of the life and tastes of this privileged sector, the Mighty Mexicans were presented in their daily surroundings, their homes and factories, their offices and their places of relaxation. Symptomatically, a group of young married socialites appear in their finest clothing and jewelry. In each photograph there is a decorative element that indicates beyond a doubt the model's Mexicanness. Beside her there is an Indian woman in an authentic *huipil*, a short, plump, smiling woman with brown skin and a grateful look on her face. Any one of these photographs represents an extreme synthesis of the colonial schizophrenia in which we live.

The middle classes of urban society have grown rapidly in the last five or six decades. They live daily within this schizophrenia. The old aristocracy looked to Europe for models of conduct and thought, but the middle classes of today have only to look to the other side of the northern border. The United States provides all the archetypes to configure middle-class aspirations. One's real origins do not matter—that not very distant past that remains buried in a provincial city, in a poor barrio, in a small town, or even in an Indian village. What matters are the small achievements of today, and their material manifestation in the consumption of electric appliances, smuggled clothing, and occasional trips to San Antonio and Disneyland. It is difficult to reconcile continually growing aspirations with limited possibilities in a situation that finally deteriorates into a crisis with no apparent resolution. The middle classes here are characterized by a profound cultural uprootedness. There is a will to renounce the life lived until very recently, and a feeble, poorly articulated will to reconstruct the current lifestyle. The household space is not organized according to necessities and tastes that are one's own. One buys or rents according to the bargains available, one furnishes according to the advertisements of the moment; one may decorate in ranch style. The important thing is that one's home not look like a poor, working-class abode. To make that point clear there are the imitation felt cushions, the color television in the center of the room, the electric appliances in full view, and the implausible, brightly colored prints on the walls. Traditional culture of whatever background has no explicit place here. It remains buried and comes into view only occasionally and unexpectedly, like a detail that calls into question everything that is apparent. Where all daily things are replaceable—coffee, sugar, pork cracklings, happiness, beauty—then, in fact, culture and life itself are replaceable. Can that which is Indian be here? Perhaps it is in some corner of patriotic discourse, in the interstices of an evening of "typical" folklore, enjoyed along with the new acquaintance from El Paso. Disconnected from its roots, the middle class dances to whatever rhythm is played, without any desire to remember or any impulse to imagine. If the other is the *México profundo*, this is the surface, the superficial Mexico.

## Cultural Schism

A national society composed of more than eighty million people, living in a country of widely varied geography, a society embarked on a project of capitalist development, which affects different regions, strata, and groups in a very unequal fashion—such a society is necessarily complex and heterogeneous from the cultural point of view. However, these inequalities and differences have, in the case of Mexico, a deeper background that conditions cultural dynamics. Mexico's background distinguishes it from societies that have an ancient and solidary cultural unity within which occur variation and inequalities that form true subcultures within a general framework. Here the pattern is different. The underlying opposition that determines the structure and cultural dynamics of Mexican society is the confrontation of two civilizations: Indian Mesoamerica and the Christian West.

It is not possible to understand the cultural characteristics of the Mexican population in terms of a spectrum of gradual variation, as if it were an uninterrupted continuum that links the most backward with the most developed, the traditional with the modern, the rural with the urban. What here we call advanced, modern, and urban is not the leading edge of an internal self-development, but, rather, the result of the implantation of Western civilization from above. What we call backward, traditional, and rural is not the beginning point of that development, but, instead, the underlying stratum of Mesoamerican civilization. The relationship between the two poles was never and is not today harmonious. On the contrary, it is a relationship that until now has been irreconcilable because it rests on the imposition of Western civilization and the consequent subjugation of Indian civilization. There is not a simple coexistence between the poles, which would probably facilitate reciprocal cultural interchange and might result in their unification, as proclaimed in official ideology. What exists is an asymmetrical relationship of domination and subjugation in which the majority Indian population is not conceded the right to conserve and carry out its own civilizational development. If such development occurs, it is only through the incessant resistance of the Indian groups, a resistance that takes the most varied forms. In terms of the dominant ideology, Indian civilization does not exist. The civilizational confrontation is masked by the phraseology of development, in its various modalities, which converts the imposition of a foreign civilization into a natural and inevitable process of historical advancement.

The cultural diversity of Mexican society goes back ultimately to the antagonistic opposition of two civilizations. At its extreme points the contrast and opposition are evident and total. The old, aristocratic oligarchy and its modern descendants, who promote technocratic modernity, confront the Indian communities that still preserve their own identity. In the broad, intermediary sectors and groups the situation seems less clear at first glance. Traditional campesinos do not think of themselves as Indians, even though their culture is predominantly Indian. The subordinate urban groups are not culturally homogeneous. Some keep as a culture of reference that of their home communities— Indian or mestizo. Others have forged a popular urban culture of Indian inclination, but adapted and transformed through long experience of life in the city. Others find themselves in anomie, in instability, fluctuating between urban misery and middle-class self-absorption. For their part, the middle strata have not created a lifestyle of their own; they do not possess a culture they themselves developed. In general, they consume foreign cultural products offered to them by an easily controlled market. These products vary from opinions and aspirations to foods and recreation, from idiomatic phrases to a taste for best-sellers.

Cultural diversity is not a problem in itself. In fact, it constitutes tangible and intangible cultural capital of enormous potential for the country. There exist a plurality of accumulated historical experiences, which form a vast repertoire of resources to confront the most varied situations. The problem lies in the dual, asymmetrical structure that underlies that plurality. At this point it is indispensable to return to the origin of this problem, which is none other than the colonial situation from which current Mexican society is derived. This is a past whose basic, antagonistic duality has not yet been superseded. To the contrary, it is expressed in every facet of national life. It is an original sin that has not yet been redeemed.

# PART II.

How We Came to Be Where We Are

The profound division of Mexican society expresses the unresolved confrontation of two civilizations. It is the result of a historical process almost five hundred years old. As we analyze the current situation and search for ways to overcome the problems we face, the general framework for our reflections must be the basic characteristics of that historical process. This second part deals with that topic. The attempt is not to summarize all the events of the last five hundred years, just as it was not the intention of the previous chapters to present an ethnographic compendium. What I hope to do is stimulate new reflection about our history, a different reading that will help us to better understand how we came to be where we are today. These are propositions and not conclusions, roads to travel that can barely be made out in the distance.

# 4.

# The Problem of National Culture

In the previous pages I have offered arguments that lead to the conclusion that Mexican society is composed of a variegated assortment of peoples and social groups. Each one of them possesses and practices a specific culture, which differs from that of the others. The degree of cultural divergence varies according to the cases one decides to compare. There are local variations that do not obscure the presence of a common basic culture, and there are radically different ways of life, oriented in terms of essentially different historical experiences. My argument has been that the cultural diversity of Mexico cannot be understood in terms of different cultural levels. That is, it is not a matter of expressions that differ among themselves according to the position that each group or social segment occupies, in terms of their greater or lesser access to the resources and practices of a common culture. This phenomenon— cultural differences related to social stratification—is no doubt present in the cultural dynamics of the country. However, it is not the factor that explains the cultural diversity of our society. Much deeper than such situational differences, at bottom, what explains the absence of a common Mexican culture is the presence of two civilizations that have never fused to produce a new civilizational program. Neither have they coexisted in harmony, to each other's reciprocal benefit.

To the contrary, the groups of Mesoamerican origin and the successive hegemonic groups dominant in Mexican society, with their versions of Western civilization, continue to be opposed. There has never been a process of convergence, but, rather, one of opposition. There is one simple and straightforward reason: certain social groups have illegitimately held political, economic, and ideological power from the European invasion to the present. All have been affiliated through inheritance or through circumstance with Western civilization, and within their programs for governing there has been no place for Mesoamerican civilization. The dominant position of these groups originated in the stratified order of colonial society. It has expressed itself in an ideology that conceives of the future only in terms of development, progress, advancement, and the Revolution itself, all concepts within the mainstream of Western civilization. Cultural diversity and, specifically, the omnipresence of Mesoamerican civilization have always been interpreted within that scheme in the only way possible. They are seen as an obstacle to progress along the one true path and toward the only valid objective. The mentality inherited from the colonizers does not allow perception of or invention of any other path. Mesoamerican civilization is either dead or must die as soon as possible, because it is of undeniable inferiority and has no future of its own.

The presence of two distinct civilizations implies the existence of different historical plans for the future. We are not dealing simply with alternatives within the framework of a common civilization, proposals that might alter current reality in many ways but that do not question the ultimate objectives or the underlying values that all share as participants in the same civilizational project. We are, rather, dealing with different projects, which are built on different ways of conceiving of the world, nature, society, and humankind. They postulate different hierarchies of values. They do not have the same aspirations nor do they understand in the same way how the full realization of each human being is to be achieved. They are projects that express two unique concepts of transcendence. Throughout, attempts at cultural unification have never suggested unity through creation of a new civilization that would be the synthesis of the existing ones. Rather, unity has been attempted through the elimination of one (Mesoamerican civilization, of course) and the spread of the other.

The colonial enterprise engaged in destroying Mesoamerican civilization and stopped only where self-interest intervened. When necessary, whole peoples were destroyed. On the other hand, where the labor force of the Indians was required, they were kept socially and culturally segregated. Indirectly and in a contradictory fashion, the minimum conditions for the continuity of Mesoamerican civilization were created, in spite of the brutal decline in population during the first decades after the invasion. This decline is one of the most violent and terrible demographic catastrophes in the history of humanity. Its intrinsic nature prevented the colonial regime from posing a project of cultural fusion that might have amalgamated the Mesoamerican and the Western civilizational planes The ideology that justified colonization was that of a redemptive crusade, thus revealing the conviction that the only path to salvation was that of Western civilization.

The Westernization of the Indian, nevertheless, turned out to be contradictory, given the stubborn necessity of maintaining a clear distinction between the colonizers and the colonized. If the Indians had stopped being Indians in order to be fully incorporated into Western civilization, the ideological justification for colonial domination would have ended. Segregation and difference are essential for any colonial society. Unification, on the other hand, whether by assimilation of the colonized to the dominant culture or through the perhaps improbable fusion of two civilizations, denies the root of the colonial order.

The birth and consolidation of Mexico as an independent State in the turbulent course of the nineteenth century did not produce any different plan, nothing that deviated from the basic intention of taking the country along the paths of Western civilization. The struggles between the liberals and the conservatives reflect different conceptions of how to achieve that goal, but those struggles never question it. The new nation was conceived as culturally homogeneous, following the dominant European conviction that a state is the expression of a people with a common culture and the same language and is produced by having a common history. Thus, consolidating the nation was the goal of all the groups contending for power. They understood consolidation as the slow incorporation of the great majority to the cultural model that had been adopted as the national plan.

What was the model around which the nation should unify? It was a purely Western one. It could not be otherwise, given the background of the ruling groups. Those who claimed the right to define the course to be taken by the newborn nation were the minority who inherited the orientations of Western civilization, transplanted to these lands by the ancient colonizers. Liberty, yes; greater justice and equal rights, yes; but all directed toward the transformation of Mexican society into a "modern" nation in the mold of Western civilization. The vast majority of Mexicans lived outside that mold because they belonged to a different civilization. Consolidating the nation meant, then, proposing the elimination of the real culture of almost everyone in order to impose a culture held by only a few. And the model to be imposed was not in any respect a higher level, a necessary and natural step to which the great majority would have risen had they not been prevented by the injustice and the restrictions of the colonial regime. No, it was simply a different model, a different civilization.

In the terms in which I treat the problem of national culture here, neither do the paths taken after the triumph of the Mexican Revolution signify a change of direction. Modernization and concern with "development" follow the lines of substitution of a Western cultural model, and the clearest example is now closer: the United States. In the previous chapter I discussed some considerations about the official ideological formulation of Mexico as a mestizo country, and this point will be taken up again later. Even though the paths taken may end abruptly or lead to the edge of a precipice, the efforts of the ruling sectors continue to focus on achieving goals that correspond to the paradigms of Western civilization. Faced with disaster, one is allowed to question the strategies and the procedures being followed, but never to imagine that there might be alternatives on a global level.

The only plan that at any moment had the possibility of converting itself into a national alternative—leaving aside for a moment the permanent resistance and the incessant struggles of the Indian villages—was that formulated by Emiliano Zapata's movement. Its defense of the villages, its agrarian orientation, its affirmation of the real life patterns forged through the centuries, all gave to the Zapatista movement a special, different place within the various currents of the Mexican Revolution. No doubt there were other groups that acted from the same deep sense, but none achieved the transcendence and the national significance that the southern Revolution had in its day. Nevertheless, the Revolution defeated Emiliano Zapata more than it did Porfirio Díaz. We should not deny the importance of the agrarian articles of the 1917 Constitution or the merits of the best moments of the revolutionary governments, as in the Cárdenas period, but we must recognize that the essence of the Zapatista plan was eliminated. The only parts included in the triumphant revolutionary program were those demands that appeared compatible with the goals that in the end defined the Revolution. I say those that seemed compatible, since in the course of the years, and more so each day, there have been backward steps in the initial agrarian program. This clearly indicates that the program is less compatible with the Zapatista postulates than seemed to be the case at first. In fact, only isolated demands were incorporated, but never the underlying plan that gave the demands meaning and depth.

A first conclusion is inescapable. The ruling groups of the country, those who make or impose the most important decisions affecting all of Mexican society, have never admitted that to advance might imply liberating and encouraging the cultural capacities that really exist in the majority of the population. Never has it been suggested that development might mean precisely creating the conditions in which the diverse regional and popular Indian cultures could grow and become fruitful. These cultures make life possible for the majority of Mexicans. A colonized mentality, based on a scheme of domination from which they benefit, has kept the ruling groups from considering any cultural alternative. They rigidly promote Western schemes, through inability, for convenience's sake, through submission, or, most probably, through simple blindness to reality itself.

What has been proposed as national culture at different moments in Mexican history may be understood as a permanent aspiration to stop being what we are. It has always been a cultural project that denies the historical reality of Mexican social origins. And it does not admit the possibility of building the future on the basis of reality. It is always a substitution project. The future is somewhere else, anyplace other than here, in this concrete, daily reality. Thus, the task of constructing a national culture consists of imposing a distant, foreign model, which in itself will eliminate cultural diversity and achieve unity through the suppression of what already exists. In this way of thinking about things, the majority of Mexicans have a future only on the condition that they stop being themselves. That change is conceived as a definite break, a transformation into someone else. It is never conceived as bringing up to date through internal transformation, as liberating cultures that have been subject to multiple pressures during five centuries of colonial domination.

The constitutional history of Mexico is an example that illustrates this schizophrenic posture in a striking way. In all cases it has led to the juridical construction of a fictitious state from whose norms and practices the majority of the population is excluded. If this is not the case, how do we explain evident contradictions? How do we explain the individualism and egalitarianism insisted upon by the nineteenth-century liberals, which led directly to the consolidation of the indentured servant systems on the Díaz-period haciendas? How do we explain anticlerical legislation converted into fictional dead-letter laws, followed by a tacit agreement with the Church that negates the spirit of the laws? We must admit a great dominating fiction. Otherwise, how do we explain a system of democratic elections based on the recognition of political parties as the only legitimate vehicles for electoral participation in a country in which an absolute majority of the population does not belong to any party or exercise its right to vote? One would look in vain for a single example demonstrating an intention to understand and recognize the real systems that various groups use to obtain and legitimize authority. One would look in vain for an attempt to structure a national system in which local political forms would have a place and in which, at the same time, they might encounter the stimulus and the possibilities for progressive development. There are no such examples. The country must be modern right now, made so by virtue of law, and if reality follows other paths, it is an incorrect and illegal reality.

This schizophrenic fiction, manifest in all aspects of the country's life and culture, has grave consequences, which do not seem to worry the proponents of the imaginary Mexico. In the first place, the fiction produces the marginalization of the majority, a marginalization that is real and not imaginary. The participants in "the Mexico that ought to exist" have always been a minority, at times a ridiculously small minority. The others, all the others, remain excluded by decree. Their participation in the theoretically democratic processes is reduced, in the best of cases, to a simple external formalism. It is far from their real life and is sometimes completely fictitious. The norms that pretend to govern all orders of life are conceived as lying within a cultural matrix in which only a minority of Mexicans participate. From that governing nucleus and as a function of their interests and tendencies, various efforts have been made to integrate other sectors into the behavior the model implies. These efforts have varied over time but have always been within the mainstream of Western civilization. To be a Mexican citizen in the full sense of the term, it is not enough to have been born here and not renounced the nationality earned at birth. For the majority an additional condition remains, unexpressed in the illusions of legal terminology. It is to learn a culture different from that which frames and gives meaning to one's daily, concrete existence, because one's own culture turns out to be illegitimate within the imaginary Mexico. This is not, then, a marginalization that is expressed only in reduced access to goods and services, but, rather, a total marginalization, an exclusion from one's own way of living. Many Mexicans thus have a choice: they can live on the margin of national life, related to it only by the minimal, inevitable relations between their real world and the other, which appears as different and external; or they can live a double life, also schizophrenic, changing between worlds and cultures according to circumstances and necessities; or, finally, they can renounce their identity from birth and try to be fully accepted in the imaginary Mexico of the minority.

The notion of democracy was established two centuries ago as one of the central aspirations of Western civilization. However, upon being mechanically transplanted into a postulate of the imaginary Mexico, it converted itself into a series of mechanisms of exclusion, whose effect was to deny the existence of the population. It is a curious democracy that does not recognize the existence of the people themselves, but, rather, sets itself the task of creating them. Afterward, it would, of course, put itself at their service. It is a surprising democracy of the minority, a national program that begins by leaving out the majority groups of the country. It is a project that ends by making illegitimate the thoughts and actions of the majority of Mexicans; the people themselves wind up being the obstacle to democracy.

A second consequence is also inevitable. By making reality a blank page, one chooses not to make use of the greater part of the cultural capital of Mexican society. It becomes an absolute impossibility to recognize, appreciate, and stimulate the development of the extensive and varied cultural patrimony that history has placed in Mexican hands. The old colonial blindness remains, the notion that here there is nothing with which a future can be built. If the people have to be created to substitute for the nonpeople who exist, it follows that a culture also has to be created to substitute for the existing nonculture. The elements that ought to constitute the core of the new culture are not here, and they are important: ideas, knowledge, aspirations, technology, what to do and how to do it. Once more we find the dishonest task of substituting for reality instead of transforming it.

All the capacities accumulated and refined through the centuries, all the cultural patrimony of the *México profundo*, pass without notice into the category of uselessness. It would seem as if generation after generation, century after century, our people have simply traveled a mistaken path whose end has now been reached. All of their history, according to the rules of the imaginary Mexico, was not really history at all, or even part of history. It was an aberration, something senseless. What is left of it—the living cultures that guide the lives of millions of Mexicans—is marked in red numerals. It is not only useless and foreign to the future of national culture, but also a dead weight that should be removed in order to take the correct path. The new direction starts at zero, from total innocence, without historical memory. The proposition is not even to squander what we have, but to suicidally reject it.

The perverse imaginary development scheme, for example, intends to reduce the useful activity of individuals to a single mechanical dimension: a work force to be applied indiscriminately to any task. Excluded are all the capacities that find space and conditions to develop themselves simultaneously in the communal context of indigenous and rural life. They cannot be used to advantage in this cultural model of work relations because it does not contemplate among its goals the full realization of individual and collective potential. Multiple examples can be found in all areas of national life. There is a permanent insistence on ignoring the capacities created by the *México profundo* and an absolute indifference to the challenge and the promise of a national project that would develop those capacities instead of mutilating them.

The inevitable question is, How did we get to the point at which we find ourselves? It becomes clear that the schizophrenia surrounding the debate over national culture is the current expression of a long historical process. Its origin lies in the installation of the colonial regime almost five hundred years ago. At that moment a system of cultural control was put into effect through which the decision-making capacities of the colonized peoples were limited. Their control over various cultural elements was progressively wrenched away, as it benefited the self-interest of the colonizers in each historical period.

It should be emphasized that the system of cultural control came to include all aspects of social life. It refers to the possibility of deciding, in whatever circumstance, how to put into play the cultural elements indispensable for social action. The study of the historical process that has resulted in the current system of cultural control cannot be limited to one single aspect of social activity. For example, it cannot concern itself solely with the loss of lands and material goods, or the employment of the work force for the benefit of the colonizers and, later, of their descendants in the national period. Mechanisms of economic exploitation have played a major role in the history of domination. But the system of cultural control that made them possible is more complex, more diversified, and more inclusive. Its comprehension requires introducing other analytical criteria, beyond the purely economic.

The fact that the system of cultural control is total does not mean that all decisions are made by a single group or class. Certainly, the decisions that the dominant sector considers basic, those that in some way express their reason for being and their aspirations, will tend to concentrate within one level. But the subordinate groups also have decision-making capacities within their own cultural realm. These strongholds expand or contract as the conditions and the forces making up the system of cultural control change. From this perspective, the historical dynamic may be understood as a constant struggle of the subordinate groups to conserve and extend all the spheres of their own culture, within which they have some control over the cultural elements required for social action. Facing them is the dominant society, whose intention is to broaden and consolidate its own sphere of cultural control as it relates to needs and self-interest. This process can be seen most clearly in plural societies of colonial origin, such as Mexico, where subordinate groups have a very different culture from the dominant ones. In this situation, the struggle is for space of one's own within the system of global control. The struggle thus simultaneously expresses the confrontation of different cultures and cultural goals and the conflict over greater participation in decision making within the total system of cultural control.

These ideas, presented in schematic form, are intended to orient the reader to the theoretical perspective that underlies the following chapters. I will try to present a general vision of the major events and most important mechanisms that have configured and transformed the system of cultural control in Mexico over the last half millennium. As I have said, the effort is not to make a historical synthesis, a task that would be beyond the scope of this work. Rather, I would like to point toward a way of thinking about our history, one that will put the cultural reality of Mexico at the center of attention. This reality is understood as the histories of diverse peoples with ties among themselves, but who also follow their own particular cultural determinants. More than offering results, the following pages propose a future task, a collective and increasingly broad one: the analysis, with an open mind, of how we came to be where we find ourselves, in order to decide on the best way of escaping the current situation. Beyond the related problems we face, no matter how dramatic and agonizing they may be, I propose to reflect on the matter of civilization, in hopes it will permit us to overcome the schizophrenia caused by the lack of understanding between the *México profundo* and the imaginary Mexico.

# 5.

# The Colonial Order

The genesis of the current cultural dilemma in Mexico is, then, to be found in the installation of a colonial order beginning in the third decade of the sixteenth century. It was then that a split society was created. Its dividing line marks the subordination of a group of peoples of Mesoamerican culture to an invading group whose culture was different and of Western origin. A colonial situation took form in which the colonizing society affirmed its superiority ideologically, in every area in which it might be compared to those colonized. This situation conditioned many fundamental characteristics of independent Mexico until the present. Thus, it is well to review in summary form the principal aspects of the system of cultural control implanted almost five hundred years ago.

## A New Method of Domination

The domination of one group by another is a phenomenon that was not absent in precolonial Mexico. Subjugation by military force occurred in many regions and in different periods. However, it did not always occur nor was it present in all areas. According to the available evidence, in the central Maya area during the period of Classic splendor, for example, ending at the end of the ninth century and beginning of the tenth, one cannot speak of imperial domination. Archaeologist Alberto Ruz [1981: 207] points out the diversity of local styles found in that area, a diversity that was the result of particular developments in Maya culture produced within independent states. According to Ruz, the later rise of Chichén was not based on military domination, but, rather, on commerce, which took place even over long distances. And in the central valleys, militarism became an important aspect of social organization only after the fall of Teotihuacán, at the end of the seventh or the beginning of the eighth century.

Nevertheless, at the time of the European invasion there unquestionably existed a powerful structure of domination, which subjugated many scattered peoples in the central and southern part of the country to the Triple Alliance, under the hegemony of the Mexica. Under the government of Itzcóatl, Aztec militarism was reinforced and consolidated in Tenochtitlán at the beginning of the fourth decade of the fifteenth century. Tlacaélel occupied the position of Cihuacóatl, sharing power with the Huey Tlatoani, during the reigns of three successive Mexica rulers. He seems to have played a major role as the real power behind the throne, pushing for reforms that favored the military aristocracy. Tlacaélel represented a different line from that of Netzahualcóyotl, Lord of Texcoco.

After the defeat of this city, the new allies, Texcoco and Tenochtitlán, conquered Azcapotzalco. It was then that the changes began that modified Mexica society by putting the representatives of military power in a dominant position. Friedrich Katz [1972: 146–147] points out, for instance, that the warriors received lands from the defeated Azcapotzalco, while the *macehuales*, the ordinary people, did not. Democracy in Mexica society was lost. The representatives of the *calpulli* [residential clan groups] had formerly elected the Huey Tlatoani, but the new electors now became the members of the military aristocracy.

To justify all this, history was rewritten. The old pictographic books were burned and others were painted, describing the Aztecs as the chosen ones, the People of the Sun. This all seems to have created a new situation in Mesoamerica, the possible outcome of which must remain speculative, since the process was abruptly interrupted with the fall of Tenochtitlán at the hands of the Spaniards.

Mexica rule may have been unique, making it difficult to generalize about the forms of domination in precolonial Mexico. Nevertheless, it is the best-documented case, and it may allow us to explore some traits that help explain the meaning and characteristics of domination in the precolonial world. It is clear that a primary objective was to obtain tribute. The peoples subjected to Mexica rule periodically delivered tribute, which was concentrated in the cities of the Triple Alliance. Part of the tribute might also benefit other cities in the lake region of the Valley of Mexico. These cities had the double position of subjects and circumstantial allies.

It is well to highlight one aspect of the tributary system. The goods and products required from each subject people formed part of what was produced locally, before Aztec rule was imposed. The defeated cities were obligated to produce more or to consume less in order to pay the tribute assigned to them. This extraction of wealth inevitably impoverished the peoples subject to tribute. Nevertheless, it did not imply a fundamental alteration in their productive systems. They kept on producing the same thing and in the same manner, except that now they were obligated to surrender part of the product. There may have been exceptions, in which some subject towns were forced to produce something they had not produced before, but this was not the norm. One reason was that the diversity of ecological niches occupied by the subject peoples allowed a diversity of tributary products. This fact in turn permitted the dominant cities to control a variety of goods from distinct sources, goods not found in their own region.

The fact that the goods produced by distinct peoples had significance and were desired by others who occupied different ecological niches reveals something more important. One and all belonged to the same civilization, which made the diverse local products compatible. It was not necessary to modify what we would call the production schemes of the subject peoples in order to make their products acceptable to a dominant society with different consumption needs. This suggests that when peoples share the same civilization, as in Mesoamerica, political domination does not lead to abandonment or substitution of the predominant production practices. Rather, it may lead to the impoverishment of the subject population, or to increased production on their part, to compensate for the tribute extracted. No situation of initial incompatibility exists between what is produced, which is part of the culture itself, and what is paid as tribute.

To reinforce this point, it is well to remember that one of the general obligations the Aztecs imposed on all regions under their domination was the organization of regular markets in which local products could be traded. In distant provinces, such as along the border with the Maya, subject peoples did not have to pay tribute; their obligation was to provide men for the garrisons, to feed the troops, and to facilitate opportunities for commerce. Merchants had great importance in Aztec society. Besides their main activity, they also carried out a form of espionage, transmitting information of a military (and also, no doubt, commercial) nature. I am not familiar with any study that has compared the products entering Tenochtitlán in the form of tribute with those from commerce. Nevertheless, merchants were socially important and the routes they covered extended far beyond the frontiers of Aztec domination. These facts allow us to assume that in economic terms commercial activities were at least as important as tribute. It seems reasonable to suggest that many wars of conquest sought openings for commerce, as much as or more than they did the imposition of tribute. In any case, the undeniable importance of commerce also demonstrates the point I made above: peoples who belong to the same stratum of civilization are compatible in terms of production.

In areas under Mexica control the military presence also had characteristics that help explain the nature of precolonial domination. In some sites there were permanent garrisons, but in many there were not. It was necessary only to send the *calpixque,* an official in charge of collecting tribute. Some peoples participated in the military campaigns of the Triple Alliance by providing men for war, in return for which they received part of the booty. Mechanisms for indirect political control also existed. That is, local officials and the internal structure of authority were maintained, with certain restrictions imposed. Katz [1972: 190] summarizes these restrictions as follows: new leaders had to be approved by the Mexica state; declarations of war or peace treaties were also the prerogative of the Aztecs; and in cities along the lakes, the Mexica made all decisions about irrigation works. A frequent way of consolidating Aztec domination was marriage alliance between members of the respective governing elites. Thus were established new loyalties based on a relationship different from military power. It should also be pointed out that the Aztecs did not establish permanent colonies in the areas they dominated. The only exceptions, according to Katz, were along the Tarascan and Maya borders.

For a complete understanding, the religious implications of domination should also be mentioned, since in the Mesoamerican world that dimension had an intense presence in all aspects of life. There was no religious aspect to the wars of domination in the sense that there was no effort to impose the victors' religion on those conquered. Even Aztec religion, following the reforms of Tlacaélel, was flexible and capable of including the deities of subject peoples in its own pantheon. There was a religious way of symbolizing the domination that had been imposed: an enclosure in the great temple of Tenochtitlán where the sacred images of defeated peoples were preserved. It was rather like a prison for captured divinities. Local cults were neither prohibited nor prosecuted, nor was the existence of local gods denied, although the Aztecs did insist on expressing the superiority of their own deities. Even so, there was nothing like a missionary spirit seeking the conversion of the dominated to the religion of the Aztecs. The only exceptions were some late attempts to introduce the cult of Huitzilopóchtli, the most characteristic Aztec god, as one more representative in the polytheistic pantheons of other peoples.

This way of dealing with religious differences and the process of domination becomes clear when one takes into account that all Mesoamerican religious systems are the result of the same process of civilizational development. Over centuries and millennia, there was constant contact and mutual influence. Thus, we can recognize the same deity among different peoples and in different epochs. Well-known examples include Tlaloc and Quetzalcóatl from the central plateau, who become Chac and Kukulkán among the Maya of Yucatan, and an older god of fire, who appears in diverse cultures. There are common patterns beneath the conceptions and religious systems of Mesoamerican peoples, which make them compatible rather than mutually exclusive. Perhaps it is in this context that we can better understand a complex of practices that have to do with religion and warfare, and that are always mentioned to demonstrate the "barbarity" of Mesoamerican civilization. I refer, of course, to the so-called war of flowers and to ritual human sacrifice.

The very idea that two peoples could come together periodically to battle for prisoners in order to sacrifice them for religious purposes makes sense only if one does not look at it as an isolated fact to be explained, but, rather, as part of a complete cultural system shared by all the peoples involved. Different groups had to share similar conceptions about the universe and about the transcendental human obligations necessary for maintaining the continuity of the cosmos in order to participate periodically in a ritual that culminated in the sacrifice of some number of their best men. Otherwise, the "war of flowers" would have been to the death, since death on the battlefield would have made more sense than death in the enemy's temple. The common background of Mesoamerican civilization provided the shared ideas that made acceptable what today, from the outside, seems incomprehensible.

Let me make two additional points to conclude this general description of the forms of precolonial domination in Mexico. One refers to the fact that there were no qualitative differences in military technology between different Mesoamerican peoples. The arms used were similar, and the advantage was given by the number of men who fought on each side, rather than by the potency of their armament. Based on a certain level of demographic size and on favorable geographic factors, peoples of the region could maintain sufficient military strength to resist the invasion of any outsider. This is demonstrated by the persistence of autonomous kingdoms in the interior of the territory dominated by the Aztecs right up until the time of the Spanish invasion.

The second point has to do with the linguistic policy practiced by the Mexica relative to subject peoples who spoke a language other than Náhuatl. There was no attempt to impose the language of the victors. "Náhuatlization" was not one of the objectives of domination.

From these facts, as in the case of religious policy, one finds a notion of "the other"—other peoples, enemies or allies, subjects or not—that does not involve a conception of natural and absolute inferiority. Even further, the cultural differences between peoples are not used to justify domination. Had this been true, there would have been efforts to "civilize" those defeated. What we see is in fact an acceptance of the others' ways of life, of their productive systems, of their religious beliefs, of their forms of government, and of their languages. None of these things have to be eliminated or excluded; all are compatible with the system and objectives of domination. A common civilization makes possible the subjugation of a people without implying the negation or illegitimacy of their culture.

The colonial system established by the Spaniards was of a completely different nature from the forms of domination known up to that point in Mesoamerica. The dominant Western ideology was accentuated in the case of Spain, which came fresh from the experience of the wars of reconquest against the Moors. It conceived of the subjugation of peoples with non-European cultures as an undeniable right derived from the obligation of disseminating the Christian faith to all peoples. During the invasion period, this missionary impulse gained new vigor in Catholic countries as a result of the schism in Christendom that resulted from Luther's reforms. In various ways the papacy encouraged enterprises of conquest, which were understood as redemptory crusades. In this climate, the conception of "the other" was naturally that of an inferior being. It reached the point of questioning or even denying the humanity of the other, which in the terms of the time meant questioning the possession of an eternal soul.

This ideological conception fit well with the less spiritual interests of colonial European expansion. It was a way of arguing that presented Christian civilization as the only possibility for salvation, but included under the same mantle the desire for precious metals, spices, territory, and a labor force, all of which would rapidly enrich the economies of the metropolitan regions. The natural superiority assumed by the colonizer was not limited to his conviction that he possessed the only true faith. His religious convictions necessarily became an affirmation of superiority in all other areas of life. Material aspirations, the way of understanding progress and human duty, the criteria for distinguishing good from evil and the desirable from that to be rejected, the correct and incorrect ways of thinking and doing things and behaving—all constituted a whole that was postulated globally as superior. It was a unique way because it was the only true way.

Within this ideological context, a technology of war and domination more efficient than that employed by Mesoamerican peoples was put at the service of a program radically different from that of precolonial domination. It is thus clear that the structure of power imposed by the Spaniards and the consequent system of cultural control implanted by colonial society constituted a new form of domination, unknown to that point in these lands in terms of both procedures and consequences. The difference from previous situations was radical.

The colonial order was by nature exclusive. It rested on the cultural incompatibility of colonized and colonizers. The purposes of colonization were fulfilled only to the extent that those colonized changed their ways of life to adjust them to the needs and interests of the colonial enterprise. These required changes, however, did not lead to the assimilation of the colonized into the dominant culture, but only to their adaptation to their new role as conquered, and colonized, peoples. The difference between the two groups was maintained because upon it rested the justification for colonial domination.

Exclusion meant that the dominated culture was not recognized as having any value of its own. It was a culture denied, one that was incompatible. Those colonized were not subjugated in order to take away what they made or produced, but to force them to make or produce something different. Here we see the profound difference between the colonial order imposed in the sixteenth century and the previous forms of domination. In the new subjugation "the other" was denied. His culture and his cultural vision of the future not only were incompatible, they did not exist. Exclusion was evident in the system of cultural control imposed, itself a result of the imposition of a different civilization.

### The Creation of the Indian

Before the European invasion, each one of the peoples who occupied the territory that today is Mexico had a particular, clearly identified social and ethnic identity. No conception existed of the subjugated peoples as inferior or intrinsically different, even during the last decades of the Mexica expansion. The nomads of the north, known generically as *chichimeca*, were distinguished as a category of people, and the term *chichimeca* was undeniably pejorative. Nevertheless, even in this case, the fact that the Aztecs themselves were of nomadic origin made it difficult to conceptualize the *chichimeca* as naturally inferior.

The Indian is the product of the establishment of the colonial regime. Before the invasion there were no Indians, but individually identified peoples. Colonial society, on the other hand, rested on a categorical division between two irreconcilable poles: the Spaniards, the colonizers; and the Indians, the colonized. In this scheme of things, the individuality of each of the subjugated peoples passed to a second level and lost meaning. The only fundamental distinction was that which made all of them "the others," that is to say, those who were not Spaniards. During the early years of the colony, New Spain was conceived as a society with two republics, that of the Indians and that of the Spaniards. Each one was subject to different orders, which established and codified what should be its internal life, and the ways in which it would relate to the other republic. The relationship, of course, was not between two equal republics, but between a dominant society, which believed itself superior in all ways, and a republic of Indians, which was therefore defined as inferior. The Viceroy, Don Luis de Velasco, wrote in 1559:

> The two republics of which this kingdom consists, that of Spaniards and that of Indians, experience great repugnance and difficulty in their relations with each other, in terms of their government, their growth, and their stability. The maintenance of the first always seems to involve the oppression and destruction of the second.

The "natural order" postulated by Saint Thomas fit perfectly as an ideological justification for inequality, subjugation, and exploitation of the "miserable serfs," the colonized or the Indians. Since its beginnings the category of Indian has been shameful, denoting a natural and irremediable inferiority. In the ideological climate of the times, what was "natural" could only be understood as the inscrutable will of divine providence. The Indian, Cazcán or Maya, Otomí or Aztec, was necessarily inferior to the white, Christian European, and that inferiority destined him to a subordinate position in society. They would be "the humble but necessary feet of the Republic." At the shock of discovering "the other," the first debate was about his humanity. Once this was admitted, the norms began to be elaborated and the practices accumulated that would turn the presumption of inferiority, postulated ideologically, into a real social inferiority within the colonial world.

In certain fundamental ways the Indian was perceived not just as inferior, but as the incarnation of evil itself. This is particularly clear in relation to Indian religious conceptions and practices, which were attributed to the direct intervention of the devil. This was either because he had always reigned in these lands far from the hand of God, or because in his astuteness he had managed to corrupt the achievements of an early evangelical mission, attributed to the apostle Saint Thomas, who was tentatively identified with the figure of Quetzalcóatl. In any case, the "idolatries" expressed evil itself and not just natural inferiority. On the one hand the king had the paternal obligation to look after the Indian as a vassal, but on the other, the Indian ruled by the devil had to be fought, persecuted, and punished. This double condition attributed to those colonized allowed every possible method of coercion to be used to force the new protagonist, the Indian, into the role destined for him in colonial society.

The indiscriminate incorporation of diverse Mesoamerican peoples into the common category of "Indian" led to a series of processes that effectively reduced many of their differences. In the end the result was a greater uniformity among Indian cultures than had existed in precolonial times. The higher levels of Mesoamerican social organization were destroyed, including those that corresponded to the state, the kingdom, and the ethnic groupings beyond the community level. The ruling groups, the priests and wise men and political and military leaders, were all eliminated, in many cases, quite literally. Only in the restricted confines of the local community could some former patterns of authority persist, now put to the service of the colonizers. During the first decades, the territorial units of the Aztec "empire," defined as a head community and its outliers, were still used to collect tribute and to organize forced labor parties through the *repartimiento*. They were also used to fix parish boundaries. Later on, these divisions lost significance, and the local community was left as the only social space where the continuity of Mesoamerican civilization was possible.

Little by little the ancient social stratification of the Indian world dissolved in a social universe newly leveled downward, toward the level previously occupied by the *macehuales* and the *sub-macehuales*. It is true that the *caciques* and *principales* of many communities remained, converted into intermediaries of the colonial power. They were recognized as legitimate authorities with privileges that many used for their own benefit and for their personal enrichment. However, historically, this group suffered one of two fates: either it became Hispanicized, adding to the ranks of the mestizos who had renounced their Indian identity; or it lost importance as an intermediary group and thereby lost its internal authority, incorporated itself into the mass of other Indians, and shared their condition. The tendency for social leveling of the Indians was inevitable within the colonial order.

Many aspects of Indian policy were aimed at achieving that leveling. Prohibitions and obligations were established, at least in terms of the letter of the law, in general form for all Indians: tribute, obligatory work, boundary markings, resettlement of populations, community organization, clothing, religious duties, and so on. In practice, different realities imposed themselves, but the aspiration of colonial society was undoubtedly to create a uniform, well-defined whole, which included all those of the social category that through error or ignorance was called "Indian."

Colonial society was conceived as a simple duality. One group, the Indians, served the principal function of serving and enriching the others, the Spaniards. However, from the beginning unforeseen groups were present. First were the Black slaves brought from Africa, who became a problem when they escaped and became outlaw groups living in *palenques* [remote, self-governing communities]. They came out only to ravage the highways, putting travelers and commerce at risk. Soon afterward came the mestizos and the *castas,* that inconvenient but necessary mixed group who formed the common people of the cities. They also wandered all over the land, without destination and living apart from the rule of law. In spite of the elaborate attempts to classify the *castas* and assign to each one a clear position in the stratified order of colonial society, those who were neither Spaniards (*peninsulares* or *criollos*) nor Indians never found precise placement in a society that rested on the rigid dual order of colonized and colonizers.

Even though the *castas* were formally defined by the percentage of different blood they carried—American, African, and European—in reality it was social criteria, not biological, that defined the different groups. Undoubtedly, a large number of racial mestizos who were born and grew up in Indian communities were considered Indians. In the same way, many racially pure Indians passed for mestizos when they left their communities of origin and became serfs or free laborers. Some mestizos were taken for creoles, and the passage from one group to the other had less to do with relative "purity of blood" than with other social factors, among which wealth was especially important. The miserably poor Spaniards formed part of the common people, intermixed with the *castas.* In the haciendas, mines, and workshops, the mulattoes and mestizos were frequently the bosses and overseers in charge of supervising and enforcing the work required of the slaves and Indians. In a detailed analysis, which has still not been done, it would be possible to place the members of the *castas,* according to regions and time periods, within one or the other of the two fundamental universes composing colonial society: the Indians and the Spaniards. This does not imply ignoring the real social and cultural differences that separated the *castas* from both sides. Rather, it implies understanding their participation in the new Hispanic society, beginning from the fundamental, inescapable dichotomy of colonial society. The nonexistence of a new "mestizo society" representing the fusion of the societies of Mesoamerica and the West is a point to which I will return in the pages that follow.

## The Initial Violence

The Conquest was a violent invasion. This violence—physical, bloody, brutal violence—was not an initial episode; it has been a permanent marker of relations with Indian peoples from the sixteenth century until the present. The subjugation of Anáhuac was achieved through blood and fire, as would be the occupation of the rest of the territory. The slaughters at Cholula and in the Templo Mayor are at the beginnings of our era: "Just so were they treacherously slain, deceitfully slain, unknowingly slain" [Anderson and Dibble 1975: 29–30].

From the material point of view the violence was imposed by the deadly superiority of Spanish arms and tactics of war. Diego Muñoz Camargo relates that the Tlaxcaltecans sent by Cortés to Cholula to ask that the Spaniards be received peacefully said that "if the Spaniards were angered they were very ferocious, brave, and daring people, who carried superior weapons, powerful steel weapons." The same chronicler comments:

> They said this because [the Cholultecans] did not have iron but only copper, and the Spaniards also brought firearms and fierce animals on leashes tied with cords of iron, and they wore clothes and shoes of iron, and they carried powerful crossbows, and lions and leopards that ate people, as they called the mastiffs and greyhounds that our people did in fact bring, and that were very effective. [Muñoz Camargo 1947: 226]

Firearms, horses, armament, helmets, iron swords and lances, attack dogs—these elements defined the military superiority of the Spaniards against the Indians. That superiority was carefully maintained and employed whenever necessary during the three centuries of the colony. Military force meant superior killing ability, and it was the pillar that sustained the colonial order, the ultimate and unopposable basis of domination.

However, arms do not kill by themselves, and those who use them must have motives for killing. The venturesome conquistadors had a primary motive, which was gold, silver, and quick riches; these would give them the honor they had not achieved in Spain. But this motive required other acceptable justifications for the violence with which it was achieved. The invaders considered the use of violence legitimate because the ideology of the Conquest and colonial domination offered pertinent arguments. They were fighting against idolatry in the name of a king named as patron of the Indies by the pope himself. War was just because it led finally to the salvation of the conquered. In this temporal world the Indians, vassals of the king, could not elude the violence directed against them when it was carried out because of the superior and indisputable interests of the Crown. And the interests of the king were necessarily the interests of his loyal vassals as well.

During the first half century of domination there were conflicts between missionaries and *encomenderos*, who had been given rights to Indian labor, over the violence with which the latter treated the Indians. One of the most angry voices of protest was that of Fray Bartolomé de las Casas:

> Oh, if one could only make others understand a hundredth part of the afflictions and calamities that those innocent people suffer from the wretched Spaniards! May God give understanding to those who could and should rectify this situation. Santiago and after them! they shout, and with naked swords they begin to open those naked and delicate bodies, and to spill that freely given blood. [Las Casas 1953: 49]

The opposition of the priests weakened beginning in the last third of the sixteenth century, when the *encomienda* lost importance and the religious orders themselves found their place in the colonial order. They became more concerned with the defense of their own interests and privileges than with the well-being of the Indians.

The mortality of the Indian population during the first century of the colony provoked the most brutal demographic catastrophe in history. S. F. Cook and W. Borah [1977: 11] have arrived at the following estimates of the Indian population of central Mexico: 1518—25.2 million inhabitants; 1532—16.8 million; 1568—2.7 million; 1605—1.4 million. Other estimates indicate that the population of the Valley of Mexico decreased from approximately 3 million inhabitants in 1519 to only 70,000 by the middle of the seventeenth century. The first years after the fall of Tenochtitlán left a horrifying balance, since by 1524 only one-third of the original inhabitants were left. The Indian population began growing slowly, beginning in the middle of the seventeenth century, but it was well into the present century before Mexico reached a population similar to that inhabiting the territory in 1519. These are the facts.

To military violence must be added other causes, other forms of violence that help explain a genocide that is otherwise inconceivable. There were epidemics caused by diseases brought by the invaders and unknown in the precolonial world and to which the Indians had no resistance. The epidemics began at the very start of the Conquest, among the defenders of Tlatelolco, and continued during the whole colonial period, causing a terrible mortality among the Indian population. *Matlazáhuatl*, probably exanthematic typhus, attacked only the Indian population and occurred at least thirty-two times during the colony. Population declines, the loss of farmland, and the immoderate tribute requirements impoverished the communities, lowering and unbalancing the original food supply, and leaving the population even more vulnerable to disease.

The new conditions of life and work imposed by the colonizers also brought death. The initial slavery, which was maintained as a legal practice for the "rebellious" Indians of the north, the forced labor in the *encomiendas* and, later, in *repartimientos*, all subjected Indians to an implacable and withering decline. The massive relocations of the colonized peoples referred to as *reducciones* and *congregaciones* profoundly altered life habits. They upset the Indian universe in ways that were often intolerable. Alcoholism became widespread. "Few peoples in the whole of history were more prone to drunkenness than the Indians of the Spanish colony," concludes Gibson [1964: 409], in his study of the Aztecs under Spanish domination. Collective suicides, systematic abortion, and conjugal abstinence denote, as Alejandra Moreno points out, an indifference, a lack of interest in life because "these Indians are imaginative, and seeing themselves uprooted, they go to the hills and die from pure pain and sadness" [Moreno Toscano 1976: 63].

Colonial violence also included the struggles induced between the Indians themselves. Cortés assaulted Tenochtitlán with 900 Spaniards and 150,000 Indian "allies." Muñoz Camargo indicates the manner in which the Tlaxcaltecans were convinced:

> There was in this city such killing and destruction as to defy imagination. Thus our friends learned of the courage of us Spaniards, and thenceforward they did not consider committing greater crimes, all guided by divine order, and our Lord was served by this land being won and rescued from the power of the devil. [Muñoz Camargo 1947: 225]

Afterward, the armies that were employed to extend the frontiers of the colony were formed of Indians giving *encomienda* service, or of Indians from communities forced to provide service, even if it meant death. The conflicts between villages over boundaries and water, which have been a constant source of violence in rural Mexico, originated in the erratic colonial policy that established boundaries and assigned lands. It is not beyond the realm of possibility that this policy was conscious and was destined to provoke divisions and confrontations that prevented any eventual unification of Indians against the Spaniards.

Corporal punishment was the norm, not the exception. It was applied to Indians by *encomenderos*, *hacendados*, foremen of mines and workshops, Indian *caciques* themselves, and the clergy. The stocks and the whip were a common experience of those colonized, and there were also more drastic punishments up to and including shameful murders. The violence against Indians reached such extremes that it disgusted even the conquistadors themselves. Alejandra Moreno [1976: 35] points out that quite a number of them ended their lives secluded in monasteries. One soldier, Lerma, who gave his name to the river, preferred to go away with the Indians (a new Gonzalo Guerrero), and nothing more was ever heard of him.

Violence in all its forms was present in the colony. It was not an abnormal, an unusual, or an avoidable occurrence, but, rather, a necessary condition. It was the only possible way to subjugate the Indians to the rule of the whites. Violence was omnipresent and total, like the colonial situation itself. This persistent, deep-rooted violence has stained the life of independent and contemporary Mexico. Violence and colonization were inseparable and mutually reinforcing.

## With the Sword, the Cross

If violence was the primary and ultimate recourse for assuring domination, religion was its inseparable companion. This was so partly because of the ideological justification religion offered for conquest and colonization. In addition, the clergy and the ecclesiastical hierarchy played a major role in exercising control over the Indian population. The Church had a much more important colonizing task than the army, at least until the last decades of the eighteenth century.

Historians customarily distinguish a first period of missionary activity in New Spain, which concludes about 1570. It was the epoch of the "spiritual conquest" carried out by the mendicant orders—the Franciscans, the Dominicans, and the Augustinians. The clergy took in their hands the tasks of pacification and disputed among themselves, and with the military and civilian colonizers, over control of the Indians. A profound contradiction became apparent between the spiritual goals of the Conquest and its material goals. The friars waged the battle on different fronts. They tried to keep the Indians isolated from morally pernicious contact with the Spaniards; they denounced the abuses of the *encomenderos;* they founded schools to prepare a new, obedient, and Christian elite from the surviving children of the Indian nobility; they even aspired, as Robert Ricard [1947: 394–419] has shown, to found a new indigenous church, with its own priests and bishops. Some of them wanted to create a Utopia here, a true kingdom of God on earth.

Nevertheless, none of this made their evangelizing mission a process that tended to negate the essence of colonization. They did not represent an alternative, but, rather, different modalities and different hierarchies of values in the exercise of colonial domination. For them as well, the

Indian was an inferior being, an eternal minor, a soul to be saved in spite of himself, if necessary, and by whatever means available, including violence. Any means were legitimate to achieve such lofty ends. The first young people who were Christianized were obligated to denounce the "idolatries" of their own people, and they formed bands to destroy the idols.

The priests needed effective control over the Indian population for the success of their mission as much as did the conquistadors, who were anxious to derive more tangible, immediate, and earthly benefits. The communities were nominally subject to the power of the king, but in reality they were much more directly beneath the control of the priests. The sense of property that the priests developed in relation to the Indians became absolute. On occasion they employed "their" Indians as a frontline force to expel friars of another order who had had the temerity to establish themselves in what the first group of priests considered their private hunting preserve—a preserve, of course, for hunting souls. These internal struggles also involved other, less pious motives, such as access to tithes and to the various personal services provided by the Indians. To enjoy the benefits of that century, the priests were not averse to the use of violence. In 1539, for instance, the Ecclesiastical Board felt it necessary to prohibit priests from seizing or beating Indians.

The work to which the missionaries put the Indians involved very different activities. New crops and agricultural techniques were introduced, as they were practiced in Spain, and various trades were introduced that were necessary to the life of the colony and unknown until then in the Mesoamerican world. A first task given to the Indians was to build churches and convents, which multiplied rapidly across the face of New Spain. There were stronghold convents in the interior of Indian territory, and sumptuous churches in the cities and mining towns. Accusations among the various orders and between the orders and the secular clergy were exchanged regularly. In 1563 Father Maturino Gilberti accused "Tata" himself, Bishop Vasco de Quiroga, of, among other things, being involved in the construction of a sumptuous cathedral that would be impossible to finish and that would be to the detriment of the Indians of the Michoacán lake region.

Indians in fact rebelled against the excessive work on religious buildings. Gibson [1964: 111] relates that in 1557 the Indians of Teotihuacán burned the image of Saint Augustine and reacted violently against the Augustinians, who wanted them to build a convent that would require as much labor as had Acolman. The Indians demanded and achieved the return of the Franciscans, who were apparently less grandiose in their architectural ambitions.

To organize work, collect tithes, ensure that doctrine was taught, and watch over the conduct of the new Christians, the priests intervened heavily in the internal life of the communities. They established systems of annual posts [*cargos*] for service in the churches, which were based to some extent on earlier forms of local organization. They established the *cofradías* [organizations devoted to the worship of particular saints], which were quite different from those in the Spanish communities. In Mexico they did not correspond to trade guilds, but, rather, had responsibility for the financing of festivities and offered their members some financial security. For example, they paid the costs of Christian burial. Frequently, the priests were in control of the community treasuries, where tribute from the Indians was collected and disbursed, and reserved a small amount for emergencies and internal fiestas. It should not be surprising, given the priests' constant interference in community affairs, that they should become the true local authorities. They had almost unlimited powers to designate or remove Indian officeholders in the civil organization as much as in the organizations dedicated to religious affairs. Behind their authority stood the Holy Office, that is, the Inquisition, established first in 1536 and then permanently in 1571. It should be pointed out that in the society of New Spain this tribunal had a much wider sphere of activities than its ecclesiastic nature would suggest.

In the best moments of the first phase of evangelization, a convergence between the achievements of Mesoamerican and Western civilization seemed possible. Ricard [1947] points out this possibility in his analysis of the educational and research efforts of the Franciscans and their Indian disciples in the School of Santa Cruz de Tlatelolco. Nevertheless, faced with the hostility of the Crown and of many spokesmen of the mendicant orders themselves, this enterprise was soon abandoned. As with the project of creating an indigenous church, the possible dialogue between civilizations was aborted. The council of 1555 prohibited the ordination of Indians, mestizos, and Blacks. It would not be until the middle of the seventeenth century that the first Indian priests appeared, sporadically, without any mission of their own, and without access to the ecclesiastical hierarchy. The imperious reality of the colonial order imposed itself, making no concessions whatsoever.

Another fact that should be remembered is that Christianization was quite superficial. According to Father Pedro de Gante, between 1524 and 1536 five million Indians were baptized in New Spain. Motolinía alone insisted that he had baptized four hundred thousand. The consequences were foreseeable and did not go unperceived by the more perspicacious. Father Bernardino de Sahagún says:

Even after having preached to them for more than fifty years, if they were now left by themselves, I believe that in fewer than fifty years there would be no trace left of the preaching they have received. [Quoted in Lafaye 1977: 212–213]

The poor results of evangelization seemed to apply even to the Indians who had had the best and most lasting religious instruction. A celebrated *cacique* of Texcoco, a former student of the Tlatelolco School, was condemned to death by the Inquisition for propagating idolatry and obstructing the triumph of the holy faith.

In the tasks of evangelization, the priests were not operating in a simple world. Rather, they worked in societies that had a formally established religion, deep-rooted over the centuries and profoundly interwoven into all aspects of their lives. There were formal similarities between certain Mesoamerican and Christian ritual practices. Some priests saw in these similarities the remains of an early evangelization, fifteen hundred years before the arrival of the Spaniards. Others, Sahagún among them, totally rejected this supposition and dedicated themselves to the total uprooting of Indian religious ideas and practices, however similar they might seem to Catholic ones. This was the position that finally predominated. But there was no way to avoid recognizing, in practice, the presence of the Mesoamerican religions. The attempt was to manipulate them as a shortcut toward true conversion. The temples and idols that could be seen were destroyed; in 1531 Zumárraga reported the destruction of five hundred temples and twenty thousand idols. But frequently the new Christian temples were built on the sites formerly occupied by the ancient *cues*, or temples, which had been leveled, or on top of pyramids. Many of the great sanctuaries that thousands of pilgrims visit today are built on the exact spots where Mesoamerican temples stood that also attracted pilgrims from all directions and from great distances. This is the case with Tepeyac, Chalma, Amecameca, and Cholula, to mention only a few. "Idols behind altars" is more than an apt rhetorical phrase.

In another area, the friars had to permit the use of the dances and songs that formed an indispensable part of Mesoamerican ritual. They changed the words, of course, and introduced new instruments, rhythms, and melodies, but the *mitotes* [ritual dances and songs] continued (and still continue) as an obligatory ingredient in religious celebrations.

During several decades the priests learned and employed the Indian languages in their evangelizing tasks, in spite of the fear of some who saw in that practice the danger of continuity in prior beliefs and a twisted interpretation of the Christian message. Náhuatl was the preferred tongue, and its teaching was proposed as a general method of facilitating preaching in all of New Spain. To a large extent the "Náhuatlization" that can be observed in many parts of the country resulted more from missionary action than from Aztec expansion. In addition, the use of Indian languages facilitated another sort of goal. It gave the priests exclusive control, since they were the only ones who knew the languages of the conquered. The ability to communicate was converted into a means of control and domination.

In addition, territorial demarcation of the regions converted to Christianity, and the general work of evangelizing, was frequently based on the territorial units that existed before the European invasion. This made possible the continuity of local forms of social organization within small regions, as long as the missionaries could find a way of using them for their own purposes. Even particular Mesoamerican religious traits, such as the existence of local deities, found a place in the new order. Each barrio, cattle ranch, or village came to have its own patron saint. The shrines built to venerate these tutelary images were important reference points for maintaining the communal identity of the Indian people, and they gained importance with the decline or destruction of broader social units.

The slow abandonment of the initial missionary spirit in the last third of the sixteenth century makes the Church in New Spain appear plainly as an agent of domination. In Ricard's words,

> what was founded, before all and above all, was a Spanish Church, organized on a Spanish model, directed by Spaniards, and where the indigenous people played to some degree the role of second-class Christians. In summary, a Spanish Church was superimposed on an indigenous Christianity. The Church in Mexico appeared finally, not as something emanating from Mexico herself, but as something coming from the metropolis, something from outside, a foreign framework applied to an indigenous community. It was not a national Church, but a colonial Church, given that Mexico was a colony and not a nation. [1947: 31]

The Jesuits, who arrived in 1572, brought with them the spirit of the Counter-Reformation and concentrated their attention on the creole population. The secular clergy displaced the early missionaries, and the mendicant orders were sent off to facilitate and consolidate the colonization of the huge territories in the northern provinces. It was not unusual to find friars who became rich, hung up their habits, and returned to Spain. The Church quickly became the major landholder in New Spain, and in that role the Jesuits were particularly conspicuous until their expulsion. Slowly the image of the missionary stopped being that of protector of the Indians, or the least harmful option. The rift between priests and Indians reached the point of rupture and open hostility. Nevertheless, there were uprisings against the expulsion of the Jesuits, which were put down and punished with more than customary violence. The Church, in its different ways of operating, maintained itself until the end of colonial times as a basic institution for the control of the Indians.

### The Indian: A Useful Object

Colonization was an enterprise of exploitation. The extraction of material riches was the colonizing society's primary and permanent goal. The priests' pursuit of spiritual objectives in the early period was not opposed to material enrichment, but was, rather, an additional endeavor. It never really challenged the colonial enterprise and ended by being an ideological argument used in certain circumstances to defend existing oppression. It never altered in the least the daily exploitation.

The objects of exploitation were the colonized, the Indians. The definition of their role in the society of New Spain, above and beyond the interminable legal discussions, was that of "miserable subjects" of his Majesty. They were obligated to create the wealth that would be enjoyed by the colonizers, here and on the other side of the Atlantic. The social, economic, political, legal, and ideological organization of New Spain was an immense and complex apparatus that responded, ultimately, to one simple goal: it ensured the exploitation of the Indians. The Indian was useful to the extent that he was converted into an object of exploitation. He was a hostile enemy when he tried to evade exploitation or threatened its success. He was treated indifferently or ignored when he remained on the margin of the occupied, the useful, the exploited Mexico. In this case he was only someone with the potential to be colonized.

There were two principal mechanisms for the utilization and exploitation of the Indians: tribute and work. Both rested ultimately on the physical and intellectual efforts of the Indians. However, the distinction is convenient because "work" was employed on Spanish projects in which each Indian counted individually, as a unit of physical labor. "Tribute," on the other hand, was extracted from the wealth generated in the communities, using all their resources: their land, their forms of organization, their knowledge, their abilities—all of their culture. This difference is important because it has implications for the continuity of Mesoamerican civilization, as we will discuss shortly.

Tribute was imposed from the very beginning, although its forms and amounts changed over three centuries. Legally, it was founded on the presumption that the "discovered" lands belonged to the Crown. The original inhabitants were then Crown subjects who, through tribute, compensated the king for his generous concession in allowing them use of the lands. During the first decades of the colony the conquistadors were compensated by granting them *encomiendas*, which meant the right to receive the tribute and work of a larger or smaller number of Indians, and the obligation to protect them and instruct them in the Christian faith. At the outset, each *encomendero* fixed the amount of tribute according to his own judgment. Usually it was done by calculating the harvest and estimating the minimum the tributaries needed for their subsistence during the year. Everything left over constituted the tribute. Later, laws were established that tried to define with more precision who the tributaries were and to establish uniform rates for tribute payments. Payment in labor was also prohibited, obliging the tributary to pay in money and not in kind. The attempt was thus to involve the Indians in the monetary economy of the colonizers.

The tribute belonged originally to the Crown. The king gave *encomiendas* to those he judged worthy of them, but the division was not equal. The military captains of the Conquest received the greatest number and passed some on to their favorite subordinates. Other conquistadors received smaller *encomiendas* and some none at all. Hernán Cortés was conceded a vast domain to which he even had legal property rights, unlike the *encomenderos*. The *encomienda* did not imply owning Indians as property, thus distinguishing the *encomendados* from slaves. However, in practice it was difficult to recognize the distinction, and the Crown finally decided to abolish the *encomiendas*. Crown rights over Indian vassals were reaffirmed, thus avoiding the danger that the royal colonies would be transformed into small kingdoms in which the only real power would be exercised by the *encomenderos*. The tribute returned to the king.

Tribute enriched the metropolis and maintained the colony. Before the different charges imposed on the Indians were unified into a single tributary quota, they had to be paid separately to the Crown and the *encomendero*, to the priests in charge of evangelization, and to local political leaders and *caciques*. All this was in addition to contributions to the community, and to assessments and special tribute required for all sorts of purposes. When the Crown finally decided to directly assume the costs of evangelization and civil administration, it did not signify any improvement whatsoever for the tributaries. They now paid one tribute quota that included all the same charges as before and others that were incorporated as the years went by. In many cases, payment did not exempt them from the obligation to pay special assessments and costs, frequently organized through underhanded arrangements with

*corregidores* and *alcaldes mayores* [local colonial officials], governors
and judges, with *caciques*, and with other functionaries of every imaginable stripe. In any case, tribute provided the funds to finance the civil
and religious government of the colony, the growing wealth of civil and
religious bureaucrats, and the European wars of the Spanish king.

When tribute began to be collected in money and not in kind, the
Indians were obligated somehow to obtain the necessary funds. Paid
work outside the community was one possibility, as was the sale of local
products, or the rental of communal lands. The individual tributary
amounts were deposited in a community treasury [*caja de comunidad*],
which at the beginning was administered by the priests. From these
treasuries most of the funds went to pay tribute, and a small remaining
portion was left for community expenses, especially for financing
religious fiestas. Local governors and members of the Indian councils, or
*cabildos*, were given sinecures and privileges that were also derived in
part from the tribute. They were also given responsibilities. At the end
of the sixteenth century the tributary debts of the community were
considered personal debts of the local governor and council, and they
were hereditary.

In order to avoid such risks, Indian authorities resorted to measures
that were contrary to Spanish norms but corresponded to ancient
practice. For example, instead of charging all the tributaries equal
amounts, they established different taxation according to the rank of
each individual and the lands he possessed. In this way the income of the
community was linked to and reinforced its internal social organization.

The other mechanism of exploitation, as mentioned above, was work.
Obligatory work existed in the precolonial period and fulfilled similar
functions, but it had different characteristics. Gibson [1964: 220] points
out  that before the invasion work was a collective obligation whose
nature was gratifying and enjoyable, as opposed to the European conception in which the implications of coercion and slavery were prominent.
It was from this latter perspective, evidently, that work obligations were
imposed on the Indians.

The Indians worked for the colonizing Spaniards. The methods varied.
In the early decades, as indicated, the *encomenderos* and the *corregidores*
exacted work in addition to tribute. By the middle of the sixteenth
century the decrease in Indian population made it necessary to seek
other alternatives to make use of the scarce labor force. *Repartimiento*
was a system controlled by the civil authorities of the viceroy. It
distributed Indian labor for the benefit of a large number of Spaniards,
thus limiting the privileges of the *encomenderos*. Taking advantage of
ancient Mesoamerican customs, work obligations were established in
rotating fashion for the communities, in accordance with the territorial

units that existed before the Conquest. Work through *repartimiento* was officially designated for works "of public utility," but this definition was sufficiently lax to cover all the particular necessities of the Spaniards, in return for modest wages. The Indians on *repartimiento* built the cities, served as porters for heavy burdens, worked in the mines, cultivated the haciendas that were beginning to cover the countryside, took care of the cattle, served as domestic labor, and died in battles in the name of their masters or in drainage works to save them from floods.

*Repartimiento*, unlike the precolonial *cuatequitl* [obligatory communual work], did not recognize or make use of the work specialization existing in the communities. At the beginning all did the same work, which was whatever was required. The channels of communal organization were used to recruit the workers, who were then used individually and according to the needs of the moment. In their compulsory labor, the Indians were only a mechanical force applied to tasks indiscriminately. The objectives and interests to be served by the tasks were determined exclusively by Spaniards.

There was also free labor, although for the Indian that "freedom" was a forced option, limited by many circumstances of colonial domination. The Spanish haciendas required a labor force that *repartimiento* could not satisfy, above all, given the drastic decrease in the Indian population. The *hacendados* hired farmhands and became involved in conflicts and arrangements with the Indian governors and with *corregidores* and *repartimiento* officials to ensure that their peons were not obligated to work in some other place. The textile factories and flour mills also required permanent workers. There the work conditions were so bad that it was necessary to bring prisoners to work off their sentences in the mills. Domestic service employed slaves and also free workers, called *naboríos*. In the mines and plantations Indians worked for wages, almost always under the direction of foremen who belonged to the *castas*, preferably mulattoes or mestizos. The Indian *naboríos*, like the peons of the haciendas, very quickly became tied to their employers for life. They were never able to repay the debts they owed for loans their employers made to them.

In Mexico City the Indians quickly learned the Spanish trades. They exercised them with dexterity and incorporated them into their own forms of social organization. Trades were taught within the family and each barrio maintained its own specialty. The Indian workers' competence was such that Spanish artisans defended themselves by organizing guilds from which Indians were excluded or within which, at least, they could never reach the level of master.

The impoverishment and excessive exploitation of the communities resulted in many Indians' leaving them and trying to make a living as free

workers. The tribute and forced labor requirements, the special obligations imposed arbitrarily, and the frequent mistreatment by Spanish and
Indian authorities went along with the loss of community lands coveted
by the haciendas and with low prices for marketable products. The
community, which continued to be the major arena for Indian continuity, saw its capacity to maintain all those born within it reduced.

The loss of lands was the limiting factor for the communities of
occupied Mexico, the Mexico useful for colonial exploitation. The
haciendas were the principal instrument of exploitation. They were first
devoted to the products brought by the colonizers: wheat, sugarcane,
cattle, and others of lesser importance. Soon, however, they expropriated
from the Indians several of the major Mesoamerican crops, such as corn
and maguey. They finally controlled the market for those products as
well. The huge extensions of land that the haciendas accumulated were
of course taken from original Indian holdings. Faced with the voracity of
the haciendas, the communities' lands were demarcated, but very
strictly and without taking population increase into account. By the
middle of the seventeenth century the Indian population began to
recuperate, meaning that the new arrivals were more likely to be born as
peons on the haciendas than as communal farmers. In addition, even the
lands formally assigned to the Indians were coveted by the *hacendados*
and were frequently taken away through violence or with the complic-
ity of Indian governors or *caciques*, some of whom became large
landholders themselves. The rapid increase in cattle raising also affected
the communities. Conflict over damages to Indian fields caused by
herds of cattle has been incessant from the sixteenth century to the
present day.

The land changed owners and also destinies. Wheat replaced corn and
*milpa* products on the best land. Irrigation water went to Spanish
cultivation and not to Indian agriculture. Cattle, horses, sheep, and goats
occupied lands that had been agricultural and the hillsides, which were
rapidly deforested. Erosion increased on the central plateau, along with
Spanish occupation, which had an insatiable appetite for wood. It was
used for construction, firewood for households, scaffolding for mines,
and fuel for various purposes. Many hacienda lands were left unculti-
vated, as a symbol of the honor and wealth of the large landed estates.
Great extensions were used only for planting magueys. *Pulque* was
drunk by Indians but produced by the haciendas, since in 1749 planting
magueys on community lands was prohibited. Grapes, olives, and indigo
were introduced, but had little effect, except in small areas.

The advance of the haciendas and the desire to avoid the most direct
ties with colonization led many communities to retreat to distant and
inhospitable zones, which Aguirre Beltrán [1967] has appropriately

labeled "refuge regions." Even there, with the passage of time, the Indians found their lands besieged and threatened.

The priests, who had opposed the *encomienda* system (in part because they were prohibited from being *encomenderos* themselves), never tried to stop the growth of the haciendas, which was so detrimental to the Indian communities. The Church was the major landholder in New Spain, and the Jesuits were the most prosperous and enterprising *hacendados*. The flock of Indian souls under their care in turn took care of the flocks of cattle and the crops of their spiritual pastors.

Commerce was also a means of exploiting Indians. In the early colonial years, they were supposed to provision the cities with agricultural products, not only through tribute in kind, but also by selling necessary food items. In 1579, each Indian family was required to raise twelve hens and five turkeys to guarantee a supply of eggs and fowl for Spanish consumption. Fruit and vegetables produced on the *chinampas* in the southern part of the Central Valley were destined for consumption in Mexico City. The *alcaldes mayores* [local-level Spanish officials] made their fortunes advancing paltry sums of money to Indians as payment for crops still in the field, which the *alcaldes* then resold after harvest at their true price. They also trafficked in Spanish products needed by Indians, or even in products that Indians did not need but were obligated to buy. One case is known of an Indian who had twelve pairs of new shoes he had been forced to purchase. The introduction of a monetary economy was an objective that colonial authorities pursued diligently. It added another instrument to the ample repertory of exploitation, since mercantile exchange always worked to the benefit of the Spaniards. And in case some doubt should arise to disturb the conscience of the colonizers, there were always people like López de Gómara to pacify their spirits:

> They were given beasts of burden so that they did not have to carry things themselves; wool to wear; and meat to eat, all of which they lacked. They were shown the use of iron and oil lamps to improve their lives. They have been given money so that they may know what they buy and sell, what they owe and what they have. They have been taught Latin and the sciences, which are worth more than whatever gold and silver was taken from them, because with learning one is truly human, and silver was little used by them and not by everyone. Thus they were freed by being conquered, and even more so by becoming Christians. [Quoted in Zavala y Miranda 1954: 111]

# 6.

# Forging a Nation

Independence turned us into the *gachupines* of the Indians.
—*Guillermo Prieto* [quoted in González Navarro]

## Creole Independence

At the end of the seventeenth century the colonizing society of New Spain was self-sufficient, with regional markets in which local products circulated. The countryside was dominated by haciendas and ranches, which had displaced Indian agriculture. They were in the hands of creoles and rich mestizos, as shown by Enrique Florescano and Isabel Gómez Gil [1976]. The useful Mexico, the only one to which I am referring, was controlled economically by the Church and the merchants, in alliance with the owners of mines, agricultural enterprises, and textile mills. The eighteenth century brought a new bonanza in mining, which had favorable repercussions in other activities. But the climate of well-being did not hide the grave contradictions whose unfolding would lead to independence.

The creoles' discontent fed the growth of a different social conscience in that group. At the beginning of the nineteenth century they totaled a million inhabitants and represented 16 percent of the population of New Spain. Their unhappiness had several causes, some ancient and others of more recent origin. Always, and above all else, the creoles were second-class Spaniards in the land in which they were born. The highest posts of the colonial administration were closed to them. There was never a creole viceroy, and they had to struggle hard to achieve a system in which they alternated with Spaniards in the highest posts of the religious hierarchy. They were a minority in occupying other administrative posts, since there were many *peninsulares* who came across the Atlantic with royal appointments. The most fortunate creoles enjoyed sinecures, and the most audacious found ways of rapid enrichment, even buying titles of nobility. But the *true* nobility remained in Spain, not in the Indies.

The Bourbon Reforms brought New Spain under greater control and made it more of a colony. Gálvez, the *visitador* [inspecting official] sent by the Crown to put the Reforms into effect, tightened the screws, thus affecting creole interests in all areas. There would be more *peninsulares* in positions of control, farewell to the privileges of the *el consulado de comerciantes* [merchants' organization], gone the *alcaldías mayores* [local posts], which brought such riches to those who bought them, more fiscal accountability, and more remittance of money to Spain, because the king was at war. Everything favored the growing nationalist aspirations of the creoles.

They bore the stigma of having been born here and not there. They were from this continent scorned by Europe, a continent thought inferior in its natural environment and in its people. In the Old World they thought that nothing original or of value had been produced in America, a debased continent. The creoles were included. The creole response was based on two ideological pillars, *guadalupanismo* and the appropriation of the Indian past.

In 1648 Bachiller Miguel Sánchez made it known that the dark-skinned Virgin venerated by the Indians in Tepeyac since 1531 was, in reality, a miraculous image that had remained as a direct testimony of the appearances of the Virgin herself to an Indian named Juan Diego [Lafaye 1977: 332–346]. In her appearances she asked him to transmit to Bishop Zumárraga her desire that a sanctuary be built for her in that place. There is no record of anyone else's mentioning her appearances before Bachiller Sánchez. Nevertheless, the cult of the Virgin of Tepeyac had spread widely, and pilgrims, mostly Indians, came from all directions to the same site at which they had previously venerated Tonantzin. It is a fact, pointed out by Lafaye [1977: 378], that the name Guadalupe was unknown to the majority of the Indian pilgrims who arrived at Tepeyac, even in the middle of the eighteenth century. Even so, the history of the appearances was immediately accepted in New Spain and the cult of the Guadalupana [the Virgin of Guadalupe] spread rapidly. For the creoles, the indisputable fact was that the Virgin Mary had chosen this land among all others. She had not appeared personally in any other nation, leaving behind her image and requesting a cult in her honor. This was the strongest and most irrefutable proof of the legitimacy and even superiority of Mexico, of America—and of the creoles themselves—in relation to Spain and Europe. This conviction turned out to be incompatible with the position of second-class citizens assigned to them by their own homeland.

New Spain was becoming the homeland of the creoles. Clavijero, at the beginning of his work, identifies himself as a Mexican. Farther on in the text, as noted by Lafaye, the Mexicans are only the Indians. The revival of the Indian past, now assumed as the past of the creoles themselves, we owe in large part to Clavijero. This expropriation, like *guadalupanismo*, was an ideological process that was necessary to destroy the assumption that domination by *peninsulares* was legitimate.

Of course, reviving the Indian past and defending the rights of contemporary Indians were very different things. Even Father Servando Teresa de Mier did not argue for any principle of equality, nor did he argue for the abolition of slavery or of the *castas*. In 1811 the consul of Mexico to the court in Cádiz described the Indian thus:

> lazy and languid, stupid by nature, without inventive talent or the power of thought, drunk, sensual, insensible to religious truth, without discernment of social duties, and indifferent to his fellow beings. [Quoted in Zavala y Miranda, 1954: 110]

The capacity for dissociating the Indian of yesterday from the Indian of today is a mental alchemy that endures to the present.

Creole discontent was able to crystallize as a national project thanks to the conjunction of a series of internal and external factors. Among these, the French triumph over Spain and the fall of Fernando VII had an explosive effect. The legitimacy of the ties between the American kingdoms and the Spanish king could be considered broken in these circumstances. Within New Spain, the creoles could count on the permanent discontent of the Indians and of significant groups among the mestizos and the *castas*. In fact, it was mestizos and creoles of the low-ranking clergy, priests to the Indians, who initiated the rebellion and kept the flame of independence alive until 1821. It was not they who finally assumed control of the new nation, but, rather, the rich creoles who during the years of struggle had kept themselves carefully on the sidelines, never openly embracing the insurgent cause and on occasions fighting on the side of the royalists.

Independence did not bring with it an in-depth transformation of the brand-new Mexican nation. Perhaps only the project of Morelos, expressed in the Constitution of Apatzingán, contained elements that might have upset the colonial structure inherited by independent Mexico. It had this potential to the extent that it proposed forming the basic political unit from the parish, which would have made possible real participation by the majority of the population. Of course, it would have been within the framework of an exclusive Catholic orthodoxy, which

Morelos apparently defended out of fear of the social anarchy that his ideological anarchy might provoke. Faced, however, with the conflicts that broke out immediately after Independence, such intentions remained in the realm of planning. These conflicts continued for half a century, until Porfirio Díaz established an imperial peace.

In many ways the goals of independent Mexico did not differ very much from those postulated in the Constitution of Cádiz in 1812. It decreed the abolition of Indian tribute and the disappearance of the *castas* as categories for establishing different social rights and obligations. Also, in accordance with the liberal spirit of the time, it set forth that wealth should be privately owned, a proposition that the reform would convert into national reality. In these and other points, the influence of the Spanish Constitution of 1812 made itself felt as the years passed. This influence was as important as, or perhaps more important than, the constitutional models provided by France and the United States.

On the other hand, the situation of national independence signified a fundamental change compared with New Spain's previous status. Independence created a new sociopolitical entity, Mexico, or "Anáhuac," as was suggested at one point. Its citizens became the owners and exclusive beneficiaries of all the patrimony and all the wealth contained in the national territory. The new identity of "Mexican" implied precisely that, to accept oneself and be accepted as a member of a collectivity with rights to control and use the national patrimony. This patrimony included the land, with its products and riches; the profits from industry and commerce; the ways of ascending the social scale and the guaranteed rewards which that signified; the common defense against outsiders; a right of national pride, based on the glories of the past, the present, and the future; and the commitment to share a common destiny. All this made it necessary to define a national enterprise, which would first specify who the Mexican citizens were and what qualifications they should have to be able to exercise their corresponding rights. Second, it would specify the ways in which those Mexicans would control and administer the national patrimony, which was their exclusive possession. The turbulent history of the nineteenth century and, in reality, all the history of Mexico until the present may be understood as a succession of confrontations between social groups. In this confrontation each group has struggled to impose its own vision of the above rights and responsibilities upon the others, or to defend itself from some other, dominant vision, which was imposed on them against their will and their self-interest.

This has been a difficult situation to resolve, inasmuch as Mexico grew out of a colonial society in which social differences, polarized by the presence of two different civilizations, have been employed to justify the successive domination of different minority groups over the majority.

## The Promised Land

The territorial definition of the new nation was a primordial question for its first citizens. In principle, they inherited a land divided into five provinces since the last years of Spanish domination. That could have been the territory whose riches and potential constituted the patrimony of the Mexicans. Very quickly it was reduced by the independence of Central America and a short time later by the loss of more than half of the remaining territory, lost to the military power and the greed of the United States. The defense of the borders, especially the northern border, was a constant headache and led to measures that are reflected in many of the characteristics of modern Mexico.

The concern with colonizing the north was present from very early times in New Spain, and it grew constantly. Quite varied methods were attempted to draw the population concentrated in the central region toward the North. Thousands of Indians were taken there by force. The *gente de razón* were offered advantages they did not have in other areas. Nevertheless, the North remained barely populated. The Liberals took a step forward, encouraging the formation of landholdings of gigantic size. In that land where no one lived, there were only Indians. Since they were savage Indians, used to making war on intruders, and good horsemen, they seemed to be everywhere. Small numbers of them needed large extensions of land to survive, and they defended those lands. They were a constant worry for the *gente de bien* [good people of means], a continual menace that defused the enthusiasm for colonizing the north. War and extermination were the responses during the nineteenth century.

The free Indians of independent Mexico were not recognized as independent nations. Such recognition was out of the question, since it implied renouncing control over the enormous extensions of land they occupied. They were either Mexicans who had to submit to the laws of the country, or they were rebels who threatened the national sovereignty and, therefore, were enemies and traitors to the homeland. Building a nation in the North was a new conquest, a new armed invasion with more powerful weapons and up-to-date arguments. The Indians had to defend themselves from both the Mexicans and the North Americans. Those who fled from this side were exterminated on the other, and those who crossed the border heading south were pursued and engaged here, to the extent that Mexico's military power permitted. Every means was

used against them. Moisés González Navarro [1954: 139] lists the
rewards earned by Indian hunters. In Chihuahua in 1859, 200 pesos were
paid for a dead warrior, 250 for a prisoner, 150 for a live woman or child,
and 100 for a dead one. Prices were still the same in 1883, 250 for a
prisoner and 200 for a scalp. Live Indians were priced somewhat higher,
because there were always North American adventurers to buy them.
Reluctantly, some treaties were signed. For example, a treaty with the
Comanches in 1843 spoke of alliance and protection. In 1850, the
government of Chihuahua signed another with the Apaches. As part of
the Treaty of Guadalupe, there were negotiations to try to require the
United States to stop Indian invasions from the north. The Indians who
stayed on the northern side of the new border from that point forward
became North Americans. The agreement did not last long, since Santa
Anna eliminated this provision in the Treaty of La Mesilla.

Some peoples resisted in spite of everything. The Yaqui and Mayo rose
up in 1825 under the youthful leadership of Juan Banderas, and did it
again from 1885 to 1905, under the command, first, of Cajeme and, later,
of Tetabiate. Don Porfirio sent many Yaqui to Yucatan in chains, for
being "obstinate enemies of civilization." There they escaped from the
henequen plantations to begin their return on foot to their own land,
thus writing one of the most prodigious epics in the struggle for liberty.
It was only one episode among dozens in the same country and during the
same century.

At the other end of the national territory, royal privilege had allowed
Yucatan to maintain the *encomienda* system during the whole colonial
period. Yucatan reached the middle of the nineteenth century converted
into a cluster of haciendas whose full potential had been realized through
henequen exports. The Maya Indians, peons who worked and lived in
absolute serfdom, kept the government in check during the rest of the
nineteenth century and into the beginning years of the twentieth.
Confronted by the Maya, liberalism did not hesitate to apply measures
that violated its own principles, even selling Maya as slaves to Cuba,
crudely disguising the arrangements as "voluntary contracts."

The disarticulation of independent Mexico resulted from the existence of provinces and, later, states that contained the seeds of self-rule
and that were prone to autonomy. They were the cause of the bloody
conflicts suffered by the country during the first decades of national rule.
The struggles between federalists and centralists were formally won by
the first group but in reality by the second. The *México profundo* was
involved only insofar as it was Indians and serfs who died in the
skirmishes and battles. The argument was not with them. It was really
a confrontation to see if the wealth of the country, in all its various
expressions, was to be for all Mexicans (referring to the dominant group),

or whether each province, each region, and each local boss should enjoy first rights to it. The Indians served only as a pretext, and as cannon fodder.

The larger problem for the Indians was the struggle against breaking up the communal lands. The Liberals, beginning with the Bourbons, made private property sacred. For them the true citizen was a property owner, and land was the basic kind of property. A modern, civilized nation was a society in which each individual had a piece of property, large or small according to the abilities and virtues of the owner. There was no other road toward the greatness of nations, the Liberals thought (or, rather, copied from others). Individual work was based on individual self-interest, which in turn was based on private property. This being the case, the communal ownership of land in Indian communities became an obstacle to be removed immediately.

The Laws of Cádiz were already a step in this direction, and the movement took form very quickly in independent Mexico. In Mexico City in 1824, it was decreed that the communal lands of San Juan and Santiago, which had survived the whole colonial period, be broken up. However, the resistance was so great that the objective could be only partially achieved: allotments were not made to individuals, but only to villages and barrios. In 1827, the government of Michoacán decreed the division of communal lands, and soon other states tried to do the same. Later the Laws of the Reform were passed in order to divide communal properties throughout the country. But the matter did not proceed as desired. In Veracruz, for instance, by 1882 only four or five communities had divided their lands, and that into large groups of co-owners. When the Revolution broke out in 1910, more than 40 percent of villages had conserved their communal lands, in violation of the law. As Gibson has very well put it, "In Mexican history significant changes have rarely occurred as a consequence of law. Law provides an approximation of historical happening, or a commentary upon it" [1964: 235].

Nevertheless, the Liberal policies of the imaginary Mexico had disastrous effects on the *México profundo*. The large landholdings grew at the expense of the communal lands, in a process that either flaunted the law or was protected by it. The growing numbers of Indians without land had no alternative except peonage on the haciendas. They were a source of cheap labor held by debt or by force. The Indian was supposed to face all of this as an individual, cut off from his communal lands and organization, with no resources other than his own strength. It was an imposed way of becoming a modern, liberal citizen.

Legal equality was another fallacy of the Liberals' imaginary Mexico. The Indian was forsaken even more by removing the few prerogatives conceded during colonial times, the most important being the communal ownership of land. The interminable rosary of Indian rebellions in defense of their communal lands will be dealt with in greater detail later. There were many of them, all over the country, and they were violent and at times long-lasting.

The nation that was desired had to imitate the European model and, soon, the model of the neighbors to the north. "For the Liberals," Luis González points out, "there was an insuperable antagonism between the historical antecedents of Mexico and her future greatness" [1976: 178]. The Indian was a dead weight. Breaking with the past was considered a patriotic obligation. "The semifabulous glory of the Aztec kings refers to a period and a civilization that can be of interest only to the antiquary," wrote José María Vigil [quoted in Luis González 1976: 178]. Juárez's opinion about those relatives who shared his own origins is painted by Justo Sierra, who indicates that the greatest wish of the *Benemérito* [worthy national hero] was to

> remove the indigenous family from its moral prostration, from superstition; from mental wretchedness and ignorance; from its physical abjection, its alcoholism, to a better condition, even though it might have to occur slowly. [Quoted in Luis González 1976: 178]

Curiously enough, there were other opinions. For Maximilian, "the Indians are the best people in the country; the bad ones are those who call themselves the decent folk and the clergy and friars" [quoted in González Navarro 1954: 127]. He created a mixed commission of Mexicans and Europeans to study the life conditions of the Indians. There was no result. The empress decreed the abolition of corporal punishment on the haciendas, reduced the work day, and established limits on servitude for debt. Neither was there any result.

A country so full of Indians (more than 60 percent in 1810) could not seriously aspire to modernity and progress, the Liberals seem to have thought. The Indians' tendency to sell little and buy only what was indispensable made them enemies of the panacea of the time, free trade and free enterprise. Their clinging to ancestral techniques was the negation of the new god, embodied in technology. Some sensed an impending tidal wave. Manuel Castellanos thought that the Indians were "inert before intellectual progress through aversion to those they called conquistadors" [quoted in González Navarro 1954: 137]. In any case, the vision of the role Indians might play in the national society was not far removed, in essence, from the view of the *encomenderos* and, later, the seventeenth-century creoles. The Indians were a disgrace to the homeland, an obstacle to being completely French or North American, which seemed the only imaginable ways of being Mexican.

Something had to be done, and there were occasional attempts to do it, when the internal and external wars left time for it. What was necessary was to attract immigrants to improve the race and to provide the impulse the country needed. Some had arrived on their own to fill the void left by the *gachupines* who left precipitously when independence was achieved. Frenchmen, Englishmen, Germans, and "gringos" hurried to find their place amid the juicy new business opportunities. But those who came were few. The insecurity of a new country with a reputation for being barbarous and unhealthful kept them away. All possible facilities had to be offered to them, and Mexico had to be announced as a land of conquest and rapid enrichment. During Porfirio Díaz's first term it was possible to import more than ten thousand immigrants, including Italians, Cubans, Canary Islanders, Chinese, and Mormons. In spite of all efforts, the people with blond hair and blue eyes did not come, but, after all, it was better than nothing. One had to take into account the matter of security, of being constantly threatened by Indian rebellions. The solution suggested by the extremely liberal Dr. Mora was to admit all the foreigners who wanted to establish themselves in Mexico

> under whatever conditions and without hesitating about the methods to achieve this end. Once they have established themselves as indicated, it is equally necessary to give them government support, with preference to immigrants of all the classes of color, in every way that is not an open violation of justice. [Quoted in González Navarro 1954: 153]

Years later, some citizens, worried about the fate of the Indians and organized in the Sociedad Indianista Mexicana, expressed themselves in the following terms:

> Sociology teaches us that crossing with others is the best way of waking peoples composed of relatively pure races from their torpor, when they still have within themselves material that can be modified. The mixture of ethnic elements produces progress. I do not know of a single case of civilized individuals of the bronze races who choose similar partners. They all tend instinctively to better their own race. (Francisco Escudero, 1911)

Mixture, on the other hand, should not be indiscriminate:

The mixture of the Chinaman with the Indian gives as a result the most degenerate type, physically and morally, that can be imagined. . . . Let foreign capital come quickly, and especially Englishmen, to stimulate with their impulse our grateful regions, which will receive them with open arms and give them all possible guarantees. But do not bring Chinamen, for the English themselves would not receive them in their beloved Home. (José Díaz Zulueta)

The national patrimony was, after all, the patrimony of only a few, who would have preferred to share it and increase it with white foreigners and not with brown Indians. Governor Enrique C. Creel of Chihuahua thought that one hundred thousand European immigrants were more valuable than half a million Indians. With the white man, it was affirmed, came technology, the spirit of enterprise, good manners, and progress. With the Indian came only lethargy, sly hatred, and treachery when one's back was turned. They were undesirable fellow citizens, even though they were the majority. And they pretended that their lands, which were part of the patrimony of "all" Mexicans, were theirs alone and were not for sale. The two civilizations were marching along different paths.

### The Indian as Enemy

What happened to the imaginary Mexico throughout the nineteenth century? It was a country that wanted to be rich and modern. Wealth was understood as the natural result of individual work and found expression in private property. Differences in wealth were justified by the greater or lesser effort that each individual put into producing it. This was a personal matter, which should not be influenced by previous conditions, such as having been born in one or another *casta* during the period of Spanish domination. Now all Mexicans were equal and each one was responsible for his own destiny. The cultural patrimony of the country, which included its natural resources, was common property to be exploited by each person in his own way, competing freely with the others, without privileges for any particular group.

The modernity of the imaginary Mexico was an imported product. Technological advances were to play an important role. "The iron rails will resolve all the political, social, and economic questions that the self-sacrifice and blood of two generations have not been able to resolve," thought Manuel María de Zamacona. The customs of the advanced countries, including their political customs, their styles, their public entertainment, should be imitated. Legislation was repeatedly passed to construct the modernity of Mexico according to the French or North American model. Both models struggled to be dominant and resented the wars and invasions that took away their prestige during particular periods.

The *México profundo* turned out to be the radical denial of the imaginary Mexico. The struggle over land, for example, involved one side, which wanted free trade and individual property, while the other side protested that land was communal and inalienable. This was the most evident proof of an irreconcilable difference. But there was not just the problem of land. Everything that was Indian was seen as the enemy of the imaginary Mexico.

From Independence until the Revolution,

> in accordance with the ideology of the time, the government's concern with the Indians, almost exclusively, was first to put an end to their ancient institutions, and second, to repress them during their rebellions. [González Navarro 1954: 147]

The free Indians of the North; the Indians who defended their lands in the rest of the country; the Indians who were incited to take part in foreign struggles; the communal Indians fighting among themselves over the boundaries of their neighboring lands, which had been maliciously ambiguous since colonial times; these sorts of Indians, which included almost all of them, constituted an intolerable threat to the peace and tranquillity demanded by the imaginary Mexico. Force was employed to put them down. Military recruitment was utilized, since "the barracks civilize the Indian" [quoted in González Navarro 1954: 162].

This was the manner in which Manuel Bolaños Cacho conceived the problem, writing in no less a source than the *Boletín de la Sociedad Indianista Mexicana*:

> the solution, then, is the forced adaptation of the Indian. Between his current manner of being, which is close to bestiality with liberty; and the hope of improvement within relative tyranny, we opt for the latter. . . . Against the landholders the Indians have occasionally risen up, although weakly. They have not even tried to oppose the recruitment ordinance, and they have watched impassively as the *jefe político* [local political boss] draws lots to choose recruits. They also watch impassively as families march away, to return who knows when, if ever, or as the head of the household leaves, or the brother, or even the son. And when the recruit returns, he is superior to any of his countrymen, in spite of

all the vices he may have acquired. Thus, in reality, the truth is that military recruitment has been an indirect method, although poor in the numbers affected, of improving the intellectual and moral condition of the Indian.

"To civilize" is a key expression. In Mexico, civilizing has always meant de-Indianizing, imposing the ways of the West. Since the Indians were here and were the majority, the solution in a modern country was to civilize them. In part, this meant to pacify them, domesticate them, end *their* violence. "We should not rest content until we see each Indian with his ox-goad in his hands, behind his team of oxen, tilling the land," warned Don Porfirio [quoted in González Navarro 1954: 162]. The best solution, and the surest, would have been to whiten the population with the civilized contributions of European immigrants. It was the formula for resolving a problem that was understood as racial. During the nineteenth century even advanced Liberals like Mora accepted the "racial inferiority" of the Indian. But immigration failed. There remained schooling as a redemptive force, the new panacea for de-Indianizing Mexico. Many talented people of the time put their efforts into education.

There was an initial problem—linguistic diversity. Ignacio Ramírez even proposed that Indian languages be used in Indian education, but majority opinion finally triumphed, straightforwardly rejecting that possibility. Francisco Pimentel, arguing with Altamirano over the path that Mexican literature should take, tried to write the epitaph for the Mesoamerican languages. "Castillian is, as a matter of fact, the dominant language in the Mexican Republic. It is our official language and our literary language. The Indian languages of Mexico may be considered dead" [quoted in José Luis Martínez 1976: 321]. There was nothing left to do with the spoken languages of the Indians except bury them, along with everything else Indian.

The most basic problem was not the diversity of languages but something of even greater significance within national reality. The rich, modern, imaginary Mexico was to be found only in certain corners of the larger cities. Programs of education were begun and made notable achievements, but they did not cross the colonial barrier, the urban perimeter. They rarely made it to the rural areas and were hardly attempted in the Indian communities. When they were, they sometimes encountered open and even violent opposition from the Indians themselves. The Kickapoo, for example, had received permission from President Juárez to locate in Coahuila. In 1909 they burned the school that had been built for them on the same day it was to be inaugurated. Other such rejections occurred in other parts of the country.

In Mexico City the San Gregorio School lasted for some time. It had been founded by the Jesuits and its original mission was to train Indian priests. Following Independence, in 1824, a revealing debate about the school took place. If the Indians were citizens equal to all the others, there was no reason they should have an exclusive school. It would signify continuation of the discriminatory and paternalistic practices of the Spaniards, which had contributed so much to the degradation of the Indian race. In discussing the matter, Dr. Mora proposed that the term "Indian" not be used to refer to a sector of society. Thus, by law, "Indians should not continue to exist." Finally it was agreed that the San Gregorio School would remain open, although little by little changes were introduced in its methods of operation, and it was finally transformed into an agricultural school for non-Indians in 1853. Thus concluded the only experiment in special education for Indians. The greatest effort had been expended by some graduates of the school itself, such as Juan Rodríguez Puebla.

On the Conservative side things were even worse. Lucas Alamán thought that teaching the Indians was dangerous, since if they knew how to read, subversive materials might fall into their hands, increasing their level of discontent and rebelliousness.

If schools did not function and the Indian did not become civilized, he at least had to be hidden so he would not be so visible. His overwhelming presence questioned in a categorical and daily way the progress of modernization in Mexico. Within the cities *pulquerías* [popular drinking establishments] were prohibited or they were allowed only on the outskirts, in the Indian barrios. In Tepic and Jalisco European-style trousers were made obligatory, to replace the traditional white cotton pants [*de manta*]. That which was Indian took refuge in the communities, the barracks of the haciendas, and the urban slums. There it remained, facing new persecution.

The Indian countryside became more impoverished. The population grew and more lands were lost. The work offered on the haciendas was hard and the pay was miserable. The situation became so grave that in 1896 the free distribution of lands to poor workers was ordered. The liberalism of the imaginary Mexico grudgingly recognized the opposing existence of the *México profundo*.

Creole identity gave way to the ideology of mestizo Mexico, but the deeper content did not change. There was a formal distancing from Spain, even anti-Spanish feeling in the early years, and the old metropolitan area, the homeland of the creoles, never regained its position as a model for Mexicans to follow. Little by little the laws left behind by the colonial system were replaced, even if only to imitate other kinds of legal systems. Octavio Paz is incisive: "We mestizos destroyed much of what the creoles had created and today we are surrounded by ruins and severed roots. How can we reconcile ourselves with our past?" [1977: 18]. Mestizo, imaginary Mexico, even though it distanced itself from Spain, never broke with the West, or even tried to do so. Aspirations for the future were to be found in another part of the West, and imitation was the path to follow. Ignacio M. Altamirano says it with nationalistic optimism:

> In Mexico, *all* of us have still not dared to give the Cry of Dolores in *all* matters. We still receive from the former metropolis our commercial, industrial, agricultural, and literary precepts, with the same fear and reverence with which our ancestors received royal edicts in which despotic kings named viceroys, forbade fiestas, or gave interesting news about the queen's pregnancy. [Quoted in José Luis Martínez 1976: 317]

Amado Nervo, years later, would summarize approvingly the efforts of the imaginary Mexico:

> and consider, finally, that everything good we have in the country is artificial and opposed to its surroundings, and achieved, therefore, in spite of popular opinion. It is with the palpable disgust of the masses in the country that we have a Liberal constitution; with the open repugnance of the people and the rich classes that we established the separation of church and state, and secularized public education; and with the patent opposition of the Mexicans that we have railroads and telegraphs and . . . even the republic. [Quoted in José Luis Martínez 1976: 327]

# 7.

# Our (Revolutionized) Modern Times

## The Tribulations of a Decadent Revolution

It is 1940, the last year of the presidential regime of Lázaro Cárdenas. Thirty years before, the Revolution that would overthrow the petrified Porfirian regime had erupted. In 1917 the new Constitution was promulgated, setting the legal framework within which Mexico would develop. This Mexico emerged from the armed conflict, from the first great revolution of the twentieth century. The factional struggles and the parallel or divergent political interests that surfaced during the period of armed conflict have been reconciled or eliminated by now. At the least, they have been forced to work together within a new, unified scheme of national power, after twenty-five years of ongoing, bloody struggle. What, then, is the new structure of cultural control created by the Revolution?

First of all, the principal groups that held power during the Porfiriato were displaced. The old landowning oligarchy had felt the impact of the agrarian reform, which had intensified without precedent during the last six-year term. The regional political bosses, who sustained centralized power, had still been evident, although perhaps under different names, at the point of triumph of the Revolution. By 1940 most of them had been destroyed or incorporated into the new political apparatus, the new official party created by Calles. The army of the poor masses ["*los pelones*"] had been replaced by the new revolutionary army, which, in turn, had lost its preeminence and was under the control of the civil authorities. The foreign interests, which directly controlled basic sectors of the Mexican economy at the beginning of the century, had been seriously affected, if not eliminated. The last blow was the recent expropriation of the oil companies. The ideological advisers of the old regime, the *científicos*, had been replaced by a new band of intellectuals who assumed the task of constructing and justifying the revolutionary project.

The process of excluding the Porfirian power groups was based, at first, on the rebels' successful use of armed force. During the armed struggle, this force depended on the support and direct participation of the majority of the country's population. Shortly afterward, the Revolution-turned-government also used the force of law to restrict or suppress the cultural elements and the resources that the defeated groups considered their own. Now they would be put at the service of "the nation," that is, of the new regime.

Who replaced the old Porfirians in power? The first group was the generals and leaders of the revolutionary armies. Among them the struggle for domination continued. At least, the struggle continued to preserve the privileges they considered their own, earned through participation in the armed conflict. These privileges included personal and group benefits, programs and demands, and authority within some particular region. In the new struggles between the victors, many were physically eliminated. Others were relegated to the rear, and some were rewarded in the final unification, the last round between the winners to determine who would emerge victorious. But the generals could not remain alone or last for very long as leaders in an institutionalizing country, one that required the presence of other groups and other talents. The new groups gained power within a complex political mechanism to which they had access in corporate fashion. The workers joined through their unions and central offices, which were both faithful to and recognized by the government. The campesinos participated through their unified organizations, controlled from above. The army quickly lost its representation as a separate sector of the political apparatus. The "popular sector" had room for everyone and ended up being the most important group, with the greatest influence over decision making.

Along with these groups there was a growing bureaucracy with power of its own. There was also a private enterprise sector for which the government provided every advantage: energy production, highways, training of workers, financial incentives, market protection, and so on. These were provided in exchange for not opposing government policy and for participating in national development projects that were seen as imminent and unstoppable.

Of course, participation in decision making and the rewards of cultural control were not distributed equally or unconditionally. To be in the game, one had to accept the rules. One of them—obedience to the highest decisions, which were concentrated overwhelmingly in the person of the president of the republic—became increasingly rigid through time. Compliance and loyalty were basic premises of participation in the new order. In return, there were corporate and individual rewards, on the basis of "every rascal gets his just reward" but also "it takes money to make money." With time, the inequalities grow larger instead of diminishing. The biggest fish, if they did not eat the smaller ones, at least drove away all the food supply.

The new groups in power had to make decisions over a larger and more varied collection of individuals and cultural resources in the country. That had been, of course, one goal of the Revolution: to break the economic, political, and social ties that restricted national development in the Porfiriato and to establish a different distribution, broader and more democratic, of the goods that constituted the cultural patrimony of the country. Thus material resources that already existed, land, oil, railroads, and the like, came under state control. So did new productive enterprises that the government founded and that made the public sector grow, along with the social sector controlled somewhat indirectly by the state. A process of this kind requires control not only over material resources, but also over all the cultural elements that make them productive and meaningful within the overall plan. Thus governmental action encompassed, to a greater or lesser degree, other areas of Mexican life and tried to expropriate or create the cultural elements indispensable for formulating and implementing the national plan.

A first goal gave a new face to an old Liberal longing: Mexico should be a culturally homogeneous society. On what basis could that unity be achieved? Once again, the option was *mestizaje*. It was thought that Mexico *was* a mestizo country and that the remnants that were not should integrate themselves as quickly as possible. This was taken as an obligation by the revolutionary governments, and became converted into an important ideological element to reinforce their legitimacy and underline their originality. There were immediate antecedents.

In 1909 Andrés Molina Enríquez had published *Los grandes problemas nacionales*. One paragraph summarizes the author's vision of the heterogeneous composition of Mexican society:

> The fundamental and undeniable basis of all work dedicated in the future to the good of the country has to be the continuity of the mestizos as the preponderant ethnic group and as the political class directing the population. [Molina Enríquez 1909: 308]

For Molina Enríquez only the mestizos were in a situation to achieve integration. He saw the Indians as divided, disorganized, without internal cohesion, and occupied only with their own subsistence. The creoles no longer counted as a historical group capable of embodying Mexican nationality. Since the Liberal triumph of 1857, that ideological role had been played by the mestizos, who were always seen as the product of the enriching confluence of two races and two cultures. Those who assumed themselves to be mestizos did not want to be creoles, much less Indians. They attempted to be something new, something whose contents were never satisfactorily defined.

Why was it declared that the Revolution was a mestizo project? Those who went to *"la bola,"* as the Revolution was popularly called, came from all strata, groups, and regions, although not in equal proportions. Neither did they have the same possibilities of incorporating their specific demands into the programs of the multiple contingents who rose up in arms all over the country. Within the masses of combatants the majority were Indians or de-Indianized campesinos. The military and ideological commanders, on the other hand, were people who came from the urban middle classes. These people had been politically marginalized during the Porfirian peace. However, not all groups were dominated by urban middle-class leaders. The agrarian movements, especially the Zapatistas, accepted the participation of urban intellectual sympathizers, but did not lose control of their own forces, or give up their own demands, until their final defeat.

During the armed phase of the Revolution, both the imaginary Mexico and the *México profundo* participated, each for its own reasons and seeking its own objectives. Later, the revolutionary groups joined together, through the elimination of some and the subjugation of others, and an official version of the Revolution was created. These events have made it possible to ignore or underestimate the fact that the Revolution consisted of a great diversity of uprisings, which responded to a large degree to very particular local and regional conditions. Of course, all of these were the result of forms of domination that crystallized in the last third of the nineteenth century and the first decade of the twentieth. But in no way were they uniform or of equal strength in all regions of the country, or in different strata of the population. A single lit fuse blew up very different powder kegs. Motives for participating in the struggle were varied and, in some cases, perhaps, antagonistic. The personal accounts that have been collected in recent years from people who lived through the Revolution show clearly that many parallel histories led to the defeat of the Porfirian regime. Those histories have not unified. Some triumphed over others in the struggle for power, some obtained rewards, and the rest remained as they were. The formal unity achieved at the end of the 1920s represented the confluence of the victorious currents, but not the integration of all the interests and demands that had converged in the revolutionary movement.

The victorious plan that defined the policies of revolutionary Mexico was not the agrarian program of Zapata and other groups, which had risen up for the same reasons and with the same objectives in various parts of the country. They fought with very clear ideas, which John Womack summarizes thus at the beginning of his book on Zapata and the Mexican Revolution: "This is a book about country people who did not want to move and therefore got into a revolution" [1969: ix].

Obviously, these were not the wishes that predominated in the national goals formulated by successive revolutionary governments. Nevertheless, the real participation of the *México profundo* in the revolutionary process made it indispensable for incorporating campesino demands, especially demands for the restitution and distribution of the land. But the revolutionary program did not identify itself with the deeper purposes of the Indians and campesinos. To put it differently, they wanted to maintain their own culture, exercise greater control over it, and on that basis develop it. They did not want to substitute something else for it. They did want to enrich it by recovering the levels of cultural control that four centuries of domination had taken away from the villages and communities. The agrarian reform had only one meaning for the campesinos: recovering a territory that was an indispensable physical resource, but at the same time a social space, full of symbolic and emotional meaning. It meant the possibility of survival, but also of continuity. For the revolutionary planners and leaders of Mexico, the agrarian reform had another meaning: it was indeed a way of carrying out social justice, but above all it was a way of making the earth produce, through the new projects of national development. This plan did not support the continuity of the *México profundo*, but, rather, its incorporation—and its negation—in what was going to be a new society. For this reason Mexico had to be mestizo, not plural, and especially not Indian.

The ideological conception of the mestizo Mexico of the Revolution was not, and has not been, an easy one. Schematically, the predominant version may be stated thus: the deep roots of our nationality are in the Indian past, the point at which our history begins. It was a glorious past, which was brought to a halt by the Conquest. Since then the real Mexican, the mestizo, has arisen. He triumphs over his history through a series of struggles (Independence and the Reform), which are linked harmoniously until they lead to the Revolution. The Revolution is the final event in the struggle of the Mexican people, the mestizos. It is a necessary fact, foreseen and anticipated by history. After the Revolution, the full incorporation of the Mexican in universal culture will be possible.

This ideology was expressed in many ways in the artistic and cultural production sponsored by revolutionary governments until 1940, and with less emphasis and more sporadically since then. The Indian roots were always recognized. The murals glorify precolonial Mexico, and Indian symbols preside over all the allegories about the history and destiny of the country. Nationalistic music tried to revive instruments and rhythms that sound pre-Hispanic. Architecture, at certain points, even included Aztec and Maya ornamentation. Archaeology was seen as a patriotic and nationalistic task, which should finish restoring the great temples and filling the exhibit cases of the museums, the new temples of nationality. Cuauhtémoc is the original hero, the first Mexican to symbolize the eternal struggle for national sovereignty.

Resounding formulations to this effect are not difficult to find. The Manifesto of the Union of Technical Workers, Painters, and Sculptors, from 1923, affirms: "The art of the people of Mexico is the greatest and most wholesome spiritual manifestation in the world, and the country's indigenous traditions are the best to be found" [quoted in Monsiváis 1976: 351].

Unlike creole nationalism, the nationalism of the Revolution could not ignore the living Indian. Indian faces invaded the great panels of the Mexican school of painters, the engravings resurrecting the powerful heritage of Posada, and illustrations filling the textbooks. There are Indians with bronzed faces, slanted eyes, and high cheekbones dressed as campesinos or dancing in their ceremonial costumes during the village fiesta. Sometimes they are shown in an allegory, fraternally embracing a soldier who is also an Indian, or a mestizo worker dressed in blue, or some engineer with blond hair and blue eyes. Popular art and handicrafts were highly valued and served as symbols for affirming the special nature of mestizo Mexico. The *México profundo* showed its real presence for a moment, and it was not possible to close one's eyes to it:

> And in an optimistic stupor we became aware of unsuspected truths. Mexico existed as a country with capabilities, with life, with its own problems. . . . It was not just a transitory or perma-nent geographical location of the body, with the spirit living elsewhere. And the Indians and the mestizos and the creoles were living beings, humans with all the corresponding attributes. . . . Mexico and the Mexicans existed. (Manuel Gómez Morín, quoted in Monsiváis [1976: 331])

But if the Indian really did exist and the *México profundo* was real, if Indians possessed positive and preservable values, then revolutionary Mexico proposed to "redeem" them, incorporating them into national culture and, through it, "universal" (that is, Western) culture. In addi-

tion, revolutionary Mexico tried to appropriate all the symbols of the
*México profundo* that could be used to construct an image of a mestizo
country.

José Vasconcelos's education program is the absolute expression of
these ideas. He sponsored mural painting and put Quetzalcóatl next to
Christ and Buddha. But he rejected teaching in Indian languages and was
opposed to any educational efforts especially designed for the diverse
Indian regions, as proposed by Manuel Gamio. He argued that "first they
are Mexicans, and then Indians" [quoted in Monsiváis 1976: 347]. Daniel
Cosío Villegas summarizes the objectives of that historical moment in
these terms:

> The poor and the Indians, traditionally bypassed, should be a
> principal and visible support of this new society. Thus it was
> necessary to exalt their virtues and achievements: their dedication
> to work; their good judgment; their withdrawal; their sensibility,
> as revealed in dance, music, handicrafts, and theater. But it was
> also necessary to push them into the stream of universal culture,
> giving them great literary works to read: Plato, Dante, Cervantes,
> and Goethe. [Quoted in Monsiváis 1976: 344–345]

The matter, of course, passed the bounds of literature. Pushing the
Indians and the poor into "the stream of universal culture" was the
intellectual project that corresponded to the other levels of the revolutionary global plan. It was about integrating all sectors of the *México
profundo* into a society that had set out on the path of Western
modernization. To achieve this it was necessary to reduce the distance
that separated those sectors from the groups leading modern Mexico.
Misery and the most obvious social problems, the result of an incessant
process of domination and exploitation for four hundred years, had to be
eliminated. But the objective was not to create the conditions for the
civilization of the *México profundo*, of Mesoamerican civilization, to
flourish. Modern Mexico did not accept the difference. That is, it did not
admit that the national plan could include a permanent Indian population with its own culture, different from the rest of Mexican society. In
fact, the difference in civilization was not recognized as such, as we will
see in the next section. It was seen as the result of inequality, as an
inferior level of historical development within which the Indians had
been obliged to remain. If inequality could disappear, or at least be
attenuated, cultural differences would disappear at the same time.

Insofar as the Indian population and all the sectors that compose the
*México profundo* are concerned, the revolutionary plan set out condi-
tional responses to their problems. The benefits to be provided to these

Mexicans would be at the same time the instruments for their integration, that is, for their de-Indianization. Lands that had been usurped for four centuries would be returned, but to modernize traditional agriculture and put it at the service of the country's economic development plan. Schools would be built in the countryside and in the Indian communities, not to stimulate and systematize people's knowledge of their own culture, but so that they would learn the elements of the dominant culture. Medical services were extended, but there was no permanent effort to learn about and develop Mesoamerican medicine. The campesinos' dedication to hard work was recognized and appreciated, but the goal was to apply their work in another manner and to other ends, foreign to the work orientation of the *México profundo*. Some parts of Indian and campesino culture were appreciated, for example, handicrafts and artistic expression, but they were considered as isolated activities, outside their own context. There was no intention of providing support to stimulate the integral cultural development of the communities. The rights of equality were recognized, but not the right to be different. Once more, the civilization of the *México profundo* remained excluded from the national enterprise.

## The Redemption of the Indian through His Disappearance

Faced with "the indigenous problem," the Revolution-turned-government institutionalized a political project for the Indian villages and sought a theoretical basis in accord with the times. This process gave rise to *indigenismo* [a movement in defense of Indian cultures]. The figure recognized as the father of *indigenismo* is Manuel Gamio, the first professional Mexican anthropologist.

In 1916, Gamio published *Forjando patria*, a work that spells out the fundamental direction of *indigenismo*. These ideas have guided *indigenista* policy until very recently. During those years, Gamio shared the viewpoint of cultural relativism, a North American school that was introduced very early in Mexico. Its major exponent, Franz Boas, took part in the founding of the International School of American Archaeology and Ethnography, created on the occasion of the Centennial. According to the theoretical perspective of relativism, cultural manifestations of different peoples cannot be placed in a single and unique hierarchy of values, as unilineal evolution had required. Rather, each one should be understood and evaluated within its own context and compared with others, without using in these comparisons standards of superiority or inferiority.

Gamio's relativist convictions did not match many of the opinions then in vogue: the racial inferiority of the Indian and the strident denial that Indian cultures had any value whatsoever, which implied the absolute superiority of Western culture in all aspects of life. Simultaneously, however, Gamio admitted the greater development of "universal" (i.e., Western) culture in positivistic science and its resulting technology—and in regard to the Catholic religion. He accepted the backwardness of Mesoamerican cultures at the point they encountered European ones, but at the same time he affirmed the existence of "positive values" in Indian cultures, values that should be respected and even incorporated into national culture.

Gamio recognized the cultural diversity of Mexico at the same time as he postulated the unavoidable necessity of creating a homogeneous society in order to forge a true nation. However, his proposal included a kind of transition stage. It would allow space for the cultural peculiarities of the diverse groups and facilitate their firm and less conflictive integration into the new nationhood. Thus, he had no hesitation in recommending that ethnic groups be represented as such in legislative bodies, in the same way as unions, professional associations, and other groups with defined interests. The new state was foreseen as corporate. He insisted on recognizing the regional differences among Indian peoples, which implied that federal policy could not be rigidly uniform. He suggested that many Indian customs, even their internal forms of government, were not incompatible with the creation of a true and unique nation. The minimal requirements were loyalty and participation in a single national enterprise. He insisted on the urgency of training professionals who would be capable of studying the ethnic characteristics of the Mexican population. "It is axiomatic that anthropology in its broadest, truest sense, should provide basic knowledge for carrying out good government, since through anthropology one understands the people who are the raw material for governing, and for whom one governs" [Gamio 1960: 15].

But the ultimate end was not in doubt. *Indigenismo* did not contradict in any way the national plan that the triumphant Revolution had been crystallizing: to incorporate the Indian, that is, de-Indianize him, to make him lose his cultural and historical uniqueness. The question was how to do it more effectively. For Gamio the path was clear:

> In order to incorporate the Indian, let us not try to Europeanize him all at once. To the contrary, let us Indianize ourselves a little, to present to him our civilization, diluted in his. In this way he will not find our civilization exotic, cruel, bitter, and incomprehensible. Of course, one should not carry closeness with the Indian to ridiculous extremes. [1960: 96]

As can be seen, Gamio recognized his own affiliation to Western culture ("our civilization," the non-Indian one). He wrote as the spokesman of the imaginary Mexico.

Manuel Gamio's thesis was to continue inspiring Mexican *indigenismo* during the following decades and to guide the course of *indigenista* work in other countries of Latin America. The language and the theoretical dressing changed with the years, as they were brought up to date and refined. But the conception of *indigenismo* as a theory and practice, designed and put into place by non-Indians to achieve the "integration" of Indian peoples into the nation, continued. The definition of what is "good" and "bad" in Indian cultures, what is useful and what should be discarded, was not, of course, a matter in which the opinion of the Indians themselves counted. It was a matter, like all *indigenista* policy, in which only the non-Indians, the "nationals," those who exercised cultural control in the country and hoped to extend it further, had a voice.

Analyzing *indigenista* efforts from 1916 to the end of the 1970s, one can confirm the constancy of Gamio's strategy. An integral plan of action was postulated, which would simultaneously attack all the aspects of the "indigenous problem." These included economic development, education, health, political organization, ideology, and so on. This multiple effort was to be based on scientific research, which would reveal deficiencies, problems, and possibilities so that the necessary "cultural change" could be carried out with the least possible conflict. Thus, for example, it would be necessary to study indigenous languages and even create writing systems and didactic materials for them, but not with the aim of stimulating the further development of those languages. Rather, they were to be used as efficient, transitory instruments to facilitate learning Spanish and becoming literate in it, as their permanent language.

In 1922 the rural school system was created. In 1925 the cultural missions were set up. In 1931 Moisés Sáenz headed the team that would carry out the pilot plan for indigenous education in Carapan, Michoacán. In 1936 President Cárdenas created the Autonomous Department of Indian Affairs [Departamento Autónomo de Asuntos Indígenas]. In 1940 the first Congreso Indigenista Interamericano was convened in Pátzcuaro. In 1948 the National Indian Institute [Instituto Nacional Indigenista] (INI) was created. These dates reveal the continuity of educational efforts by revolutionary governments in relation to the Indian population.

The goal never varied: to give education to those who did not have it. Which education was it to be, and with what content? Why, of course, it was to be education in terms of national culture, which was in turn a variety of Western culture. At the beginning and for some time those entrusted with carrying this "civilizing message" were non-Indians, carriers by birth of Western civilization. The effort was a failure. They did not understand the Indians and the Indians did not understand them. It was necessary to find another solution and it was decided to turn to the Indian youth themselves. The best would be picked, removed from their communities, and taken to "civilized" surroundings—preferably in the cities, longtime centers of *the* civilization. There they would be submitted to a brainwashing, as a result of which they would recognize the inferiority of their own culture and the superiority of national culture. Finally, they would be returned to their places of origin, now converted into "agents of change." The longed-for transformation that would lead to progress would be achieved more easily from within. "Fight fire with fire" seems to have been the motto. Some young Indians could be used as convenient tools for de-Indianization, in the same way the Indian languages could be used for teaching Spanish. The vicissitudes of this project and the sometimes contradictory results will be analyzed briefly in the next chapter.

In the other areas of "integral indigenous action" [*acción integral indigenista*] the plan was essentially one of substitution. It was true that in some cases impetus was given to the study of the culture and life situation of populations that inhabited the regions served by the Indigenous Coordinating Centers. These corresponded to the systems defined by Aguirre Beltrán as "refuge regions." However, these investigations were not destined to found programs for the development of medicine, agriculture, or any other aspect of Mesoamerican knowledge. Rather, they were to establish diagnostic information for finding the best ways of introducing into Indian communities the corresponding practices from national, modern, Western culture.

There was continuity with the sense of Sahagún's monumental work: "understand to better destroy." In the case of the friars the effort was to find the devil who was always hidden away, masked by apparently innocent practices. In the case of indigenous action [*acción indigenista*], it was to discover the factors that prevented the integration of the Indian. These factors, which made him an Indian and not the straightforward Mexican desired by the Revolution, which gave him his particular identity and image, could then be removed more easily. This point is very clearly expressed in one of the fundamental theses developed by Gonzalo Aguirre Beltrán. The Indian should pass from the situation of "caste" in which he lives to a situation of "class," so that from this new position he might contribute to the overall transformation of national society.

This is not the place to give a detailed account of the theoretical and political basis on which indigenous action was supposed to be based. The topic was widely debated from the end of the 1960s onward and there is a vast literature about it. The important point here is to single out the significance of *indigenista* policy in terms of the system of cultural control that the Revolution tried to establish. *Indigenismo*'s outstanding exponents included Aguirre Beltrán, Julio de la Fuente, Alejandro Marroquín, Ricardo Pozas, and Alfonso Caso. In setting forth their ideas, in spite of differences of tone and emphasis on certain questions, the conviction is always evident that the integration of the Indian is a desirable goal. It is the only path for achieving national unity and assuring development. Integration is seen as a natural and inevitable process, which in the case of Mexico had been obstructed by historical factors of two kinds. On the one hand, there was the domination exercised regionally by the "ladino" groups (non-Indians), from the enclave cities in the refuge areas. It was to their benefit to keep the Indian marginalized. On the other hand, there was the resistance to change generated by the Indian cultures themselves. The Indian lived in a narrow, parochial communal universe, which was impermeable to any sort of modernization. His language, beliefs, habits, and practices tended to isolate him from the new winds blowing in the world. This closed world had to be opened wide and the Indian tossed into the complex turbulence of modern society. "I would trade a hundred *indigenista* speeches for a road," Alfonso Caso once said, while he was director of the INI.

To achieve this goal it was necessary for the Indian to abandon his own culture and adopt a new and different one. The new society did not admit special cultural privileges. That is to say, it did not admit exclusive cultural patrimonies over which control was exercised by members of groups who reserved to themselves the right to decide who were and who were not members of the group. And this was precisely the situation that had allowed Indian peoples to survive and to defend themselves over almost five centuries. They had conserved a complex of cultural elements that were their own, restricted and precarious though they might be. They included natural resources, forms of organization, communication codes, knowledge and symbols over which they demanded the exclusive right to make decisions. Indigenous action tried to break that exclusivity and impose control from outside, thus deciding which part of the cultural patrimony of Indian peoples was useful and for whom, and which other part should be eradicated and by whom. In summary, the attempt was to annul what was left of the decision-making capacity of Indian peoples after the constant attacks of colonial domination. Indians were to be fully integrated into a system of cultural control in which decisions would be made in places foreign to the Indian communities themselves. Having achieved this, the revolutionary task of *indigenismo* would be complete.

Indigenous action has been slowed down and frequently canceled out by factors other than Indian resistance. The official government organization assigned to carry out the program, the INI, was placed in a difficult position within the federal administrative apparatus. It became a coordinator of such activities as health, public works, and education, which were already carried out by other branches of the government. This was in a country in which coordination between administrative units is always a declared aim but has only exceptionally been put into practice, and then in a limited way and for a short period. In addition, there were local and regional interests that indigenous action, in its best moments, necessarily threatened as it attempted to change power relations in order to accelerate integration. The interests of intermediaries, political bosses, priests, moneylenders, employers of Indian labor, and others, were always a difficult obstacle to overcome. One reason was because these groups maintained close and not always mentionable relationships with state and federal authorities. After the first missionary impulse had passed, INI personnel to a large extent lost their enthusiasm and conviction and a bureaucratic attitude gained ground.

In the mid-1970s a new *indigenista* discourse was heard in official circles. Proposals that favored a policy of respect toward and stimulus of ethnic pluralism as alternatives to forced integration were popular in the national and international sphere. They were adopted in governmental discourse, but not without contradictions and ambiguities. Indigenous action, meanwhile, extended its scope, thanks to a federal program called COPLAMAR, which gave broader decision-making power to the INI. In practice, the path followed was not that of the new discourse, but, rather, the well-worn path of integration. Pluralism as an admitted possibility, "participatory *indigenismo*," *etnodesarrollo*, and even the necessity of converting Mexico into a true "Federation of Nationalities" (announced by Lic. Miguel de la Madrid during his presidential campaign), already formed part of official *indigenista* language. However, the reality of indigenous action did not take note.

### The New Face of the Imaginary Mexico

After 1940, the Mexican Revolution as national project was finally defined, marking the path followed by the visible part of the country until the present. The mutual accommodation of the revolutionary forces had reached its end. A new model of development was imposed in which the *México profundo*, agrarian and popular, was not the beneficiary, but, rather, a source from which resources were taken. These resources made possible the growth of the other Mexico, whose outline was industrial, modern, urban, and cosmopolitan. It is worth reviewing quickly the processes that delineate the new face of the imaginary Mexico.

An important factor was the industrial takeoff that occurred as a benefit of World War II and that was initially based on import substitution. Thus began a process that brought together tendencies whose final effects were still being suffered by Mexicans in 1987. One result was technological dependence and a constant loss, through royalty payments on foreign technology, of the earnings produced by industry. Another was a growing debt from importation of equipment and parts not produced by national industry. Progressive technological stagnation occurred and Mexican products came to have scant competitive ability in the international market—the results of policies that protected the internal market by assuring generous profit margins with little effort and low-quality products. Industry was concentrated in a handful of cities, which grew rapidly and chaotically. Ironfisted control was exercised over the demands of labor, through unions that responded, in the final analysis, to government decisions. To summarize the whole process in a few words, it represented the expansion of a savage, predatory capitalist system, which had no long-term vision. It was supported in a thousand ways by the public sector within the framework of the so-called mixed economy.

In the sphere of agrarian activities, official policy and the predominant tendencies were consistent with the preference for accelerated industrial development. Traditional agriculture was relegated to the background, and an effort was made to discourage diversified cultivation oriented primarily toward consumption. On the other hand, credit, infrastructure, fiscal advantages, certificates of inaffectability [to the agrarian reform] and police force when it was needed, all stimulated a system of monoculture for export or for industrial consumption. Cattle raising, mostly for export, was also stimulated. Agrarian reform was halted. "Guaranteed prices" were established for basic foodstuffs, but in such a way that what those prices guaranteed was that urban populations could buy the agricultural products they consumed at low prices. This meant that salaries could be kept down, to the advantage of industrial enterprises.

The technological modernization of the countryside was attempted in various ways, including mechanization and the introduction of seeds, fertilizers, and insecticides that the campesinos did not produce. This practice therefore increased their dependence on the dominant society and its scarcely concealed international interests. The experiments at collective agriculture attempted by Lázaro Cárdenas were abandoned. Rural Mexico remained, contrary to its own trajectory, subjugated to industrial Mexico.

The cities grew. According to the criteria of official statistics, the country rapidly became urban. The cities expanded without foresight or plan, like mushrooms after a rain. Along with them grew the "lost cities," the belts of misery, transportation difficulties, lack of public services, pollution, unemployment either disguised or plainly apparent, conflicts, and crime. In smaller proportions, "the beautiful Mexico" also grew. It included the beautiful people, each generation taller and blonder, and the exclusive suburbs that range from the colonial Sirio-Lebanese style to the new fortresses of the Pedregal of San Ángel. Nightspots proliferated, as did expensive restaurants and a commerce in insolent luxury. A snobbism began with the "third Mexican empire." It was maintained for years by a precious group of the filthy rich, nostalgic for nobility and anxious to rub elbows each week with a few of the sad figures among the handful of European aristocratic refugees in Mexico during World War II. Snobbism extended to the insulting ostentation of the "Mighty Mexicans" of the satiny pages of *Town and Country* magazine. Thus inequality grew, not only between city and country, but also in the daily life of the city streets.

Many, very many, of the Mexicans who are urban, according to the census and their place of residence, do not form part of the imaginary Mexico. They are people who participate but who do not belong. They participate in the miseries and difficulties of the city, they work there when they can and in whatever way they can, and they inhabit a narrow space, which they endeavor to make their own and to make different. They are there more through expulsion from the impoverished and abandoned countryside than from attraction to the imaginary shimmer of the city. They do not break their ties with the rural world from which they came. In fact, they reproduce it as far as they can in their new environment by raising pigs and chickens, preparing regional dishes, celebrating their fiestas, and forming a social circle with people who share the same nostalgia and the same problems. Urbanization depends on them, but they do not belong to the urban world.

Others do belong, or at least want to belong and appear to do so. They are the middle class of whom I spoke in the first part, blinded, torn from their roots, and often farther and farther from reaching their goals and achieving their dreams. The Revolution gave a great impetus to this social class. Its growth is another of the processes that give shape to the new face of the imaginary Mexico. It is the palpable proof that the Revolution is achieving its objectives. It has a level of schooling higher than that of most Mexicans, it enjoys social benefits, it lives in apartments or single-family dwellings, it consumes as much as its budget allows, and it has ambitions and the conformity congruent with the reigning model and system. It has no higher goal than social climbing, or at least maintaining the position it holds. With the cooling of official nationalism, the middle class also abandoned the symbolic ties that united it with the *México profundo*. It saw its chauvinism as tacky and gauche and began substituting for it the aspiration of being, or at least seeming to be, gringo. Its patterns of consumption and behavior, whether real or only desired, were oriented in that direction.

In 1968 profound disagreements that exploded in the student movement appeared within this middle class. The underlying cause should be sought in the fact that the growth of the middle class had not been accompanied by new or broader avenues of participation in the political decisions affecting its life and self-interests. The political apparatus already gave signs of a dangerous hardening of the arteries. The economic expansion of the imaginary Mexico, the only framework for middle-class expectations, already showed portentous fissures and contraction. Almost twenty years later we can understand the 1968 movement as a clarion call, a warning signal of danger. The Echeverría period opening and the quick and ephemeral oil boom muffled it to the point of inaudibility. At any rate, something fundamental broke down in 1968. A vast sector affiliated with the imaginary Mexico's confidence in its own future ended.

There is another phenomenon whose importance cannot be minimized: the growth of the mass media of in-formation. I write it thus, "in-formation," to distinguish it from the root word "formation," to become informed or educated. Much has been said about the media, but not enough. One must distinguish carefully. The press, the radio, and television, to mention only the major media, are all different and have different effects. To go further, one cannot even generalize about the press. How can we judge in the same way the newspapers and magazines devoted to political opinion, to sports, and to fashion? For many, the radio continues to be the medium with the widest coverage. However, television, because it is primarily an urban medium and because of the kind of audience it reaches, is more disturbing and attracts more critical analysis. I will not enter deeply into these questions, since my purpose here is simply to give a broad outline of the system of cultural control in Mexico. For this purpose, some general considerations are sufficient.

The media of mass in-formation bring their message in different ways to different sectors of Mexican society. The media are more important to those who participate in the imaginary Mexico, since they are basically designed for that part of our world. They are essentially one-directional, centralized, and urban. Their concerns do not include the

*México profundo.* The latter, rather, appears as something outside, unfamiliar, and picturesque, but, above all, dangerous, threatening, and profoundly disturbing. Mesoamerican civilization, for the media, does not exist. It is simply a reference point for tourists. The captive audience to which the media are directed is the one that participates in or believes in the imaginary Mexico, and to them go the news, opinions, images, and sounds. They suggest a way of understanding and living, a culture, that is not within the reach of everyone ("everyone" is not all the people, of course), but to which all should aspire.

The media, above all, consolidate a vision of a Mexico that does not exist. They incite those imagining to believe, contrary to all evidence, in the reality of the world presented, in the solidity and viability of the project. The messages reach farther, without a doubt overflowing the boundaries of the imaginary Mexico. But, what must a Tarahumara think when he sees a video clip?

Industrialization, urbanization, middle class-ization, in-formation, and other derived or convergent processes of the last several decades would seem to point toward substantial changes in domination and in the system of cultural control in Mexico. Is this really the case? This question should be seen through the eyes of the oppressed, from their underlying reality. The changes, however important they may seem from the perspective of those who rule, may not seem so to those dominated.

The frontiers of expansion have varied and multiplied. They threaten and covet the territory that is the heart of the *México profundo.* The communal and *ejido* lands and the small properties of the peasants continue to be stripped away and to face pressure, today, as for the last four hundred years, from the unceasing voracity of large-scale cattle ranching. But there are new interests, which also covet those lands. They include urban sprawl, the expansion of the oil industry, the development of tourist sites, and even the establishment of environmental protection zones. Such areas are of course understood from the point of view of the imaginary Mexico. Differences unquestionably exist between the frontiers of territorial expansion. Some require local labor to a greater extent than others. Some pay better salaries than others, even though this may be an illusion that lasts only a few months. Cattle raising, city growth, and oil expansion have different ways of destroying vegetation and altering ecological niches, whereas reserves attempt to preserve them. But beyond those differences, all types of expansion threaten and mutilate the peoples' and communities' lands. They reduce the spaces available and prompt various kinds of defensive responses from the *México profundo.*

The policy of changing crops does not in principle affect territorial integrity. But substituting monoculture for diversified agriculture has the same destructive effects on Mesoamerican civilization. It attacks the productive system on which the self-sufficient economy is based, subjecting the peasants to dependence, credit, the market, technology, and even management in areas that were formerly under their own control. The same can be said, of course, of programs for modernizing and mechanizing agriculture.

The conflicts generated by the struggle for land result, with greater frequency than is noted in the press, in the rule of violence. Neither independence nor the Reform nor the Revolution have allowed the relationship between the imaginary and the *México profundo* to escape the dominating presence of violence. This violence is real, bloody, and death-dealing, whether it involves gangs of cattle rustlers, bands of paid killers, or regular army and police. The central conflict is the land, but violence comes into play as well, as a last (and sometimes only) resort to settle electoral conflicts, problems between communities, religious antagonisms, and power struggles of any sort. The *México profundo* is always faced with the final prospect of murder, prison, arson, or torture in accordance with the law or outside the law.

The bayonet continues to be accompanied by the cross. There continue to be untrustworthy priests who jealously guard their dominions, which are earthly and hidden from view rather than celestial. The fanatics who close minds and humiliate bodies continue to be present. There are obviously others as well, and always were, a minority of priests who identify with the *México profundo* and sometimes suffer its same fate. There are clerics who cross the barrier and go over to the other side, not without conflicts inside and outside the Church, and inside and outside the communities they want to serve. There are also new characters in the struggle for souls. They include Protestant missionaries, many of whom are foreigners. In indigenous areas they have provoked bloody divisions within communities. Their individualistic vision blinds them to the reality of communal organization. Their aspirations for life anywhere on earth have as their only, undisputed model any small town in the North American Midwest. Individualism, thrift, and moderation (as they understand them) are the supreme values they try to impose. They are foreign values, which necessarily come into conflict with the worldview and social practices of the *México profundo*.

Also on the scene are the atheistic missionaries, the activists, those who are committed to "consciousness-raising among the masses." This is the other side of the same coin. Like the others, they consider themselves the only owners of absolute truth, those predestined to save and redeem the people. Neither do they understand or think it worthwhile to try to understand the *México profundo*. Right now, in the present, it is a mistaken reality to be changed. They do not fight for souls, but for minds, and their doctrine is not religious but "revolutionary." Some die in the struggle, but many more indoctrinated neophytes die. Without offering any judgment about the personal motivations of the different missionaries, one thing is clear. The conscience of the people of the *México profundo*, their convictions and beliefs, continue to be denied. They are seen as a blank page upon which each outside group has the right and the obligation to write its own particular message.

The elementary school has reached almost every corner of the country. This is considered a triumph, another achievement of the Revolution. Without a doubt, the right to an organized education is a legitimate and unquestionable right of all Mexicans. But what sort of education, with what content, and for what? One cannot defend the school for its own sake, without taking into account the degree to which it responds to the aspirations and the real needs of the population that attends it. The effort has been to create a uniform school system, even though there have been some attempts at special education for certain groups and sectors of the population. A homogeneous education has been the goal, following the constant ideological premise that uniformity is required to strengthen the nation. The result could not have been otherwise. School instruction ignores the culture of the majority of Mexicans and tries to replace it rather than developing it. It is an education planned and decided upon from the center, from the seat of power in the city. It is an education in terms of the imaginary Mexico, at the service of its interests and in agreement with its convictions. It is an education that denies what exists and creates in the student a schizophrenic dissociation between his real life and the hours he spends in the classroom. This tendency is explicit, since the conviction that the school is the path of redemption is built upon a more profound conviction: what you know is useless, what you think is senseless; only we, who participate in the imaginary Mexico, understand what you need to learn to make you into someone else.

The distance between education and the *México profundo* increases as one advances to higher educational levels. The models or paradigms of university education, as well as its content, come from the outside, from more advanced centers of Western civilization. The possibility of any organic link with the wisdom of Mesoamerican civilization is rejected. This wisdom is denied even though it is not understood. The architects are unfamiliar with traditional systems of construction and the meaning and function of space, insofar as they do not correspond with the aspirations of the middle and upper urban sectors. The physicians ignore and scorn the popular use of medicinal plants. The lawyers do not have the faintest idea of customary law, which regulates the daily lives of the majority of Mexicans. The agronomists do not take into account the knowledge of peasants who continue a seven thousand–year–old agricultural tradition, since they first invented agriculture itself, right here. The economists, because they do not understand it, forget what happens in the "informal sector" through which millions of Mexicans carry out the majority of the economic activities that allow them to survive. And the list of examples could be extended indefinitely. To put it crudely: the immense majority of Mexican professionals are not familiar with the country in which they live. Here as well, the plans are not for development, but for replacement.

The political order created by the Revolution excludes the direct participation of the majority of Mexicans. Not even half the citizens have ever voted in a federal election. On occasion, the proportion of effective suffrage has been ridiculous to the point of alarm. In municipal elections, the norm is to not take into account the opinion of the local citizens in the selection of candidates. Rather, they are named from above, as a result of power struggles and pressure groups that have nothing to do with local realities and needs. And if this results in disagreement and strong reaction, the recourse is force.

I am not stating anything new in this regard; we all know this. The most serious problem is the rationalization given for this situation and the solutions that are suggested. In the imaginary Mexico, the democratic formalities developed in the West as a result of the French Revolution and the U.S. Constitution have replaced the true and profound meaning of democracy. The attempt is to impose a foreign model as the only legitimate form of participation in the political life of the country. This is a leveling mechanism, which ignores the methods and criteria through which one accedes to power and through which authority is legitimated in the real life of local groups throughout the country. The exercise of electoral rights, as established in the imaginary democratic system of Mexico, implies participation in a specific political culture that is foreign to the real political culture of the majority. The conceptions of authority and representativeness, the criteria and mechanisms for designating who should occupy posts in the structure of power, the networks of social organization that enter into play in these processes, the language codes and the intellectual and emotional motivations for participation, all are different in the Mexican Constitution and in the reality of the *México profundo*. The marginalization of political life, then, not only results from the manipulation and confrontation of interests within the dominant groups, but also derives from the explicit decision of these groups not to recognize or admit the mechanisms of authority established historically in the *México profundo*. There is no room for them. As with all other aspects of Mesoamerican civilization, no project exists to create the conditions for liberating the existing authority systems from the structures of external power that oppress and distort them. There is no project to develop these systems. If there were, they might be compatible with the national requirements of a country whose plural nature is accepted as a basis for democratic political organization.

From the point of view of the promoters of the imaginary Mexico, large sectors of the country's population turn out to be too "immature" to accept the democratic system imposed upon them. They may even be openly hostile—enemies of democracy. They do not vote, they are not active in political parties, they do not send letters to their representatives, and so on. The real people are transformed, through this ideological alchemy, into the obstacle to achieving democracy.

In summary, the national project resulting from the Mexican Revolution also denies Mesoamerican civilization. It is a replacement project that does not propose the development of the existing culture of the majority, but its disappearance, as the only path for generalizing the culture of the imaginary Mexico. It is a project that ideologically affirms *mestizaje*, but in reality allies itself completely with only one of the components, the Western one. That which is Indian remains as a past—expropriated from the Indians—that is assumed to be the common patrimony of all Mexicans. However, what was expropriated has no profound content and is converted into a vague ideological pride in what was done by "our" ancestors. What is left of the Indian cultures of today, after the passing of the nationalist fervor of the first decades, is only a folkloric vision and a multiple feeling of uneasiness about what backwardness and poverty might mean. Above all is the unadmitted perception that out there, the imaginary Mexico is denied daily by the *México profundo*.

# 8.

# The Paths of Indian Survival

Five centuries of colonial domination have provoked disastrous effects in the culture of the Indian peoples of Mexico. The social and political units of precolonial Mesoamerica, the states and kingdoms that encompassed large territories and a vast population, were destroyed. The *México profundo* was confined to the sphere of small, local communities. This reduction of social space had negative consequences for Indian cultures because it limited many aspects of development that require levels of social organization broader than the local community.

The total and systematic negation of Mesoamerican civilization and the permanent aggression to which it has been subjected have provoked cultural effects of different and varying intensity in different Indian groups. In all cases it has involved changes that reduce the cultural spaces available, that is, the capacity for decision making and the number and quality of cultural elements necessary to carry out any self-directed social action.

In spite of this long history of domination and the transformations imposed on the cultures of Mesoamerican ancestry, Indian peoples remain. They form the basic substratum of the *México profundo*. It is important to review briefly the mechanisms that have made possible the survival and the continuity of Mesoamerican civilization, the complicated paths of resistance.

## The Warriors

If violence has been the permanent instrument of domination, Indian peoples have also resorted to violence in rejecting subjugation and demanding liberty. History registers an unbroken chain of wars of defense against invasion and of uprisings against colonial oppression. These wars and uprisings tell the story of the failure of conquest, of rebellion, and of the historical affirmation of Indian peoples and their will to survive.

The processes of completely occupying the territory and the incorporating of Indian peoples into the system of domination were not finished
during the colonial period, nor even by the nineteenth century. Armed
resistance prolonged the wars of conquest in various parts of the country
for almost four hundred years. Even the fall of Tenochtitlán did not
signify the immediate submission of many peoples who were subjects of
the Mexicas. In 1531 the Yopes of the lowlands of Guerrero replied thus
to a message from the conquistadors asking them to submit peacefully:

> That they had never wanted to obey or serve Moctezuma, who
> was the greatest of the Indian lords; then how were they asked to
> obey the Christians now? They had always had wars and they were
> ready to die and prove who they were.

Some resisted to the point of collective extinction rather than accept
defeat and subjugation. The Chiapas, cornered in the gorge of El Sumidero
in 1528, opted for suicide:

> Those who remained with others who had joined from another
> place, fought until they could no longer lift their arms. Seeing
> themselves lost, with their women and children they hurled
> themselves into the river from an extremely high place and were
> lost. [Herrera y Tordesillas 1947]

As the invasion advanced, many peoples abandoned the areas in
which they lived, moving off into areas of more difficult access where
they could continue to live freely for a longer time. The nomads of the
north resisted the invasion most successfully. They were protected by
their constant mobility, which was much increased by adopting horses.
Some preserved their liberty until the end of the last century.

The peoples who were subjugated by colonial domination resorted to
intermittent rebellion when the circumstances seemed favorable or
when the oppression increased to the point of requiring a drastic
reaction. During the colonial period, there were dozens of Indian rebellions of great magnitude, in all parts of the country. There were certainly
hundreds that did not go beyond the local level and about which the
documentation is scarce. Nevertheless, with the information available,
it is possible to explore some of the characteristics of the armed Indian
rebellions.

Among the immediate causes of rebellions stand out the imposition
of higher tributes; mistreatment by *encomenderos, hacendados,* and
government officials; seizures of lands; forced work; and religious
persecution. In the cities, above all in the capital, there were great

mutinies during times of famine, particularly when corn was scarce.

Many of the rebellions about which we have the best information seem to have had a strong religious content. In different ways the ancient gods assured victory for the rebels and announced the imminence of liberty and a return to the times before the invasion. The leaders of the rebellions presented messianic profiles and appealed to revelation as an argument for recruiting followers. Some were specialists in ancient cults that were practiced clandestinely. Others adopted Christian symbolism and presented themselves as priests or ecclesiastical authorities bringing the message of a new, unique, and true religion, distinct from the perverted religion of the invading clergy.

In connection with the rebellions, many aspects of Indian cultures were re-elaborated. Historical memory was converted into a fundamental resource, which kept alive the offenses and misfortunes suffered. It also labeled the stage of subjugation as temporary and reversible, a stage that would end definitively with the triumph of the rebellion. The return to the past was converted into the project of the future. The realization that there existed a recoverable civilization permitted the subversion to be firmly articulated.

During the rebellion, many resources that had remained latent in Indian culture were put into play. Forms of organization and communication that had existed clandestinely were activated. Appeal was made to implicit loyalties. Symbols that had seemed to be forgotten were revived. Recourse was also made to cultural elements from the dominant culture, which had been appropriated by Indian peoples who were now in a position to use them in the service of the uprising. This was the case not only with European armaments, but also with the ideas and images used to justify the rebellion and endow it with symbolism. The Maya spent half a century fighting in the so-called War of the Castes. During this period they adopted an internal political organization that included military titles taken from the ranks of the Spanish army. They also developed the new cult of the talking crosses, which incorporated Christian traits, traits taken from the Maya tradition, and elements created on the spot to articulate a new religious system strictly tied to the requirements of war. Other uprisings of narrower scope and lesser duration almost certainly did not unleash processes of cultural transformation as intense as those provoked by the War of the Castes.

One of the dominant characteristics of the armed struggles of Indian peoples, from the invasion to the present, is that they have been local and isolated. Movements that achieved some regional dimension were rare, and rarer still were those that involved groups of different ethnic affiliation. One of the permanent goals of the apparatus of colonial domination was to isolate communities and mediate relations between them. The success in achieving this goal is shown by the limited extent of the armed uprisings that occurred.

## Daily Strategies

In military terms, Indian resistance was finally conquered in every case. However, defeat may have occurred only after centuries of permanent struggle. Conquered by force, Indian peoples have nevertheless resisted. They remain as differentiated social entities with their own identities, based on particular cultures in which only members of the group participate. Almost five centuries of brutal and subtle aggression against Indian cultures have not managed to prevent the survival of the fundamental nucleus of the *México profundo*. The paths of resistance form an intricate web of strategies that occupies a broad space in the culture and the daily lives of Indian peoples.

One can speak of a culture of resistance in characterizing Indian cultures' orientation toward permanence. They do not demonstrate immobility, but, rather, the adoption of those changes that are indispensable for survival. The dynamics of Indian cultures and, more broadly, of the cultures of the *México profundo*, can be understood only within the framework of colonial domination, which limited and distorted the possibilities for growth while imposing foreign cultural elements opposed to the group's requirements for survival. Faced with these dominant forces, the creation and reinforcement of mechanisms of resistance became a strategy of vital importance.

The three primary processes that have made possible the persistence of Indian cultures are resistance, innovation, and appropriation. The process of resistance is oriented toward the preservation of those cultural spaces maintained by the group in spite of the pressures of colonial domination. These spaces are those realms of life in which the group has decided to put into play elements of its own cultural patrimony in order to achieve its own goals. Before colonial domination, the group's cultural space obviously embraced all aspects of social life. In every aspect the group had the power to make decisions and could count on its own cultural elements to carry them out. But the colonial order usurped decision-making abilities, reducing the cultural patrimony of the subjugated peoples. The area of relative autonomy within which the group could exercise its own culture was constricted and limited to a smaller number of actions, since the colonizers made the decisions in all the rest. In spite of this reduction, the group's own culture sustained its identity and was the indispensable basis for its continuity. For this reason, preserving the spaces of autonomy was seen as necessary at any cost, and the mechanisms of resistance were crucially important.

One of the most common ideas about Indian cultures is that they are conservative and reject change, even when change might constitute a significant improvement. This is a prejudiced image within colonial ideology, which sees those colonized as causing their own colonization. Cultural resistance is a real fact, but it has a meaning very different from that attributed to it. Some examples may help to better understand this phenomenon.

In an Indian or campesino community, when one asks why certain rituals or other things are done, a frequent response is, "That is the custom." If one tries to probe deeper, he will probably find that many of the participants cannot explain the significance of the ritual, which gives the impression that one is dealing with formal actions that have no real meaning for the participants. It is then easy to see them as absurd practices, expressions of an irrational traditionalism. Within the scheme of colonial ideology, they can be used as one more proof of primitiveness, and of the essential inability of Indian cultures to exist as contemporaries on the threshold of the twenty-first century.

Nevertheless, within the context of colonial domination, the attachment to traditional practices should be understood in a different way. This is true even in situations in which the participants cannot verbally formulate their reasons for doing things. The cyclical exercise of these practices is, on the one hand, a periodic affirmation of the existence of the group, a collective manifestation of its permanence symbolically expressed in the fulfillment of *las costumbres*. On the other hand, it is an action that stays within the realm of the group's own culture. These celebrations put into play cultural elements that are resources of the group, and the decision to carry out *las costumbres* (whatever they might be) is also the group's decision. It is a show of autonomy that preserves space for the activity as a part of the reduced universe of social life over which the group maintains decision-making rights.

Finally, these traditional rites acquire new meaning and fulfill functions that may be very different from those they had in previous periods. This process adds contemporary reasons to reinforce other, more profound, justifications for maintaining them. I think of the annual fiestas, the collective rituals, the dances that are carried out. Their importance may be as moments that renew the identity and sense of permanence of the group, and thus the existence of the community itself. Participants may not be aware of this fact at a conscious level and may, rather, explain their participation in terms of fulfilling a promise, or entertaining themselves, or simply because it is their turn to do such and such a thing in the course of the ceremony. These may be the forms in which the decision to participate is verbalized. They may be better understood if one takes into account the clandestine habits that were necessary to

continue certain prohibited and persecuted practices within the dominant cultural order.

In this area of underlying meanings, contemporary reality presents
varied situations. Some groups maintain a collective memory about the
meaning of many rites. In others, only the traditional specialists and
their initiates have a more or less structured understanding of the
symbolic content of and justification for ritual norms. In others, memory
and understanding are diffuse, with varied interpretations by members
of the group and a tendency to use explanatory models imposed by the
dominant culture. These differences follow the specific conditions of
domination: its intensity, historical duration, and continuity. They also
have to do with the form that responses to domination have taken, since
each case has generated its own processes of resistance, innovation, and
appropriation.

Resistance is frequently manifested in another area: the rejection of
innovations from outside, in areas of practical life in which the superiority of the new elements seems evident. The specialized literature is
full of examples. In one place improved seeds are not accepted, in another
fertilizers and insecticides are rejected. In such and such a place the
children are hidden to prevent their vaccination. Over in another place
they do not like the houses that have been built to relocate the community, or they use the houses improperly: once again the hearth and
*metate* are put on the floor and the bathroom is converted into a chicken
coop. The list is interminable.

Explanations for this resistance, leaving aside the supposed "irrationality" of the inhabitants of the *México profundo*, generally resort to two
sorts of analysis. In one, a sort of culturalist perspective tries to show the
incompatibility of the element being introduced with preexisting elements of local culture. The innovation does not function because local
culture has no space for it, thus requiring a task of prior preparation,
almost always in the way of education. The second interpretive current
emphasizes social factors. The proposed change runs counter to local
interests, those of the priest, the merchant, the political boss, the "witch
doctor." These individuals are seen as having sufficient power to mobi-
lize the population against the proposed change. Without a doubt, in
many cases these two phenomena occur and such explanations have a
certain degree of validity. But a deeper analysis requires not losing sight
of other factors related to the process of resistance.

In the first place, the historical experience conserved in the collective
memory indicates the dangers of changes promoted from the outside,
dominant, foreign world; such changes have systematically provoked
effects contrary to community interests. The outsider, the colonizer, is
thus a generic danger and what he proposes or intends to do should be

evaluated, on principle, with radical suspiciousness. There is always a hidden agenda. This is a generalized attitude in the *México profundo*, and is expressed in different forms according to the circumstances. The stranger is avoided, or attacked when it comes to that. One dissimulates in front of him, or he is listened to and made to think that his proposals will be discussed "a little later."

Resistance also has a deeper explanation. Innovations of the kind we are discussing, and the changes implied by their acceptance, generally mean a reduction in the group's autonomy. The improved seeds, the fertilizers, and the insecticides might really increase agricultural production. But they would imply a greater dependence on the exterior, because they are products that must be acquired and cannot be produced locally. They are unlike the native seeds, which come from the harvest itself, and unlike the other resources, material or symbolic, that the campesino has at hand to protect and ensure his traditional crops. One must understand the orientation toward self-sufficiency and the need to preserve the limited spaces of cultural autonomy in order to understand why external innovations in traditional productive activities are rejected. In other areas similar mechanisms operate. Vaccination seems by its manner of application to be a direct, dangerous form of aggression from the dominant world. It also generates dependence because it is not part of the cultural elements the community uses to deal with problems of health and illness. Vaccination is not within the repertoire of resources the group produces and controls.

In all cases, then, we are dealing with constant struggle over the control of cultural space, over who decides—us or the others—and over which aspects of life decisions are made. Conservatism, in the case of oppressed peoples, is also a struggle of resistance aimed at maintaining rights over decision making and over control of one's own cultural elements.

A second process of cultural resistance is appropriation. Here, the group takes as its own cultural elements that were foreign and that come from the imposed, dominant culture. For the appropriation to take place, it is necessary for the group to take control over those foreign cultural elements, so that it can put them at the service of the group's own ends and its own, autonomous decisions. I have already mentioned the case of horses among the nomadic peoples of the north. The number of examples that illustrate this process is very large, and it will be sufficient to mention a few others, of a different kind. One would be that of popular religion, that is, the complex of norms, beliefs, and practices through which subordinate groups organize their relationship with the supernatural forces and powers that form part of their cultural universe. Nominally, the majority of the Mexican people profess to be Catholic.

Nevertheless, it is apparent that their conceptions and rituals differ in many ways from the dogma and ritual of the Catholic Church. A "popular Catholicism" has been described, and the term "syncretism" has been used to refer to popular Catholicism's mixture of Christian elements with those of diverse, but basically Mesoamerican, origins. If the phenomenon is analyzed from the point of view of the diverse groups that integrate the *México profundo*—Indian communities, traditional campesinos, subordinate and marginalized urban groups—instead of from the perspective of dogmatic purity, the panorama may be very different. One may see those concrete religious systems as the result of a long history of domination and imposition in the realm of religion. Thus, the so-called syncretism may be understood not as an indiscriminate amalgam of elements from different backgrounds, a sort of devotional collage, but, rather, as the product of a complex process of appropriation. Diverse Indian societies have taken the signs, symbols, and practices of the imposed religion and made them their own by reorganizing and reinterpreting them within the core of their own religious beliefs. Thus, although the colonial situation required the acceptance of these ideas, they have been subordinated within a framework that is not Christian and that has its origins in Mesoamerican religion.

This framework is not nor has it ever been immutable. It changes and is restructured over time, especially when it is the patrimony of oppressed groups. But there is a profound difference between considering popular religion as a mechanical mixture of traits from different religions and understanding it as the product of profound modification of an original religion over which one continues to have control. The ways in which the inhabitants of the *México profundo* manage their religious life offer many examples of how they have appropriated Catholic rites and images and given them a meaning different from their original one. They can imbue them with new meaning because they control them from their own religious perspective, which is not Christian but derived historically from an original Mesoamerican religion.

In other cases, the core of popular religion is of Christian origin. Even so, it is common to find that there has been a process of appropriation, because religious practices are controlled to a large extent by the community itself and not by the ecclesiastical hierarchy outside the community. The individuals who carry out the annual religious *cargos* within the local religious hierarchy are those holding such posts as *mayordomo* [individual pledging a year's service to a saint], *fiscal* [treasurer], and *topil* [messenger]. They exercise real control over many aspects of communal religious life. They have the keys to the church and are responsible for church property, they organize the fiestas in accordance with tradition, and they decide upon ceremonial expenditures. The *principales*, those who have passed through all the *cargos*, enjoy a special moral authority. Priests have only a supplementary function. Their presence is required for certain rituals, but in all else they are expendable. Again, the situation varies greatly within the contemporary reality of Mexico, but it is difficult to question the fact that a great deal of popular religion consists of elements over which the population has control, and it exercises that control in daily life.

One can find examples of cultural appropriation in any other area. In some cases the community acquires the capacity to produce, reproduce, or maintain the cultural elements it has appropriated. Those elements then cease to be foreign and become one's own, as in the religious examples mentioned above. In other cases, the group does not have that ability and can only use the foreign elements for its own purposes. As examples of cultural elements that were originally foreign but that subordinate groups have made their own, we can mention the wooden plow, domestic animals, crops of non-American origin, many handicraft techniques introduced in the colonial or later periods, some medical beliefs and practices, and certain kinds of social organization (for example, some types of godparenthood). Other items, such as motors, firearms, and cassette tape recorders, continue to be foreign, since the communities of the *México profundo* cannot produce or reproduce them. However, they appropriate them in certain circumstances and control them for their own benefit, for work or transport, for hunting or fighting, for recording or listening to music of their own, as the case may be. Through the appropriation of these foreign elements the communities increase the cultural repertoire over which they have control, and over which they make autonomous decisions.

Given the above ideas, I want to point out a fact that is frequently misunderstood: the presence of cultural elements of foreign origin does not in itself indicate weakness or loss of authenticity within Indian cultures. The problem does not consist of the proportion of "original" traits as opposed to "foreign" traits exhibited by a culture at any given moment. Rather, the question is who exercises control over those traits: those who participate in the culture, or the members of the dominant society. At the same time, it is necessary to determine whether the traits are organized around a cultural project that is one's own, or whether it is foreign. The project may relate to the group's basic scheme of orientation, its cultural matrix, or it may be derived from a dominant, foreign, imposed matrix. In terms of these criteria, a cultural element such as a wooden plow, brought by the invaders, is today as legitimate and "authentic" a part of many Mesoamerican cultures as are corn and tortillas. Thus, for this purpose, the origin of the element ceases to be important. The plow, it will be remembered, is not Spanish, but, rather, Egyptian in origin.

The third process that has made possible the continuity of Meso-american cultures is innovation. The colonial situation required con-tinual internal changes in the culture of the oppressed peoples. Changes were necessary for adjustment and resistance to new forms of domina-tion and to take advantage of the chinks or cracks within which the sphere of one's own culture could be broadened. This constant dynamic makes use of previously existing culture and of external elements that can be appropriated by the people, but also requires the constant creation of new cultural elements invented by the group. These are not spectacu-lar inventions, but modifications, at times almost imperceptible, in the habits, knowledge, practices, and beliefs of the community. There may be innovations in the realm of material culture, for example, such as the reuse of industrial products. These are almost always worn-out pieces, used for completely different purposes than those for which they were fabricated. Oilcans are converted into flowerpots or lamps. Automobile tires are transformed into soles for sandals [*huaraches*]. Bicycle sprock-ets and chains are used to sharpen knives, and so on, with many other different examples. In all these small acts there is technological innova-tion and creativity.

Innovative initiatives also occur in the area of social organization. An example is the proliferation of reasons beyond the traditional ones for establishing fictive kinship with *compadres*. Baptism and marriage are not the only occasions for establishing *compadrazgo* ties. Others in-clude the beginning and completion of a house, the debut of a dancer's costume, induction into a *cofradía*, and many other different sorts of events. Through this strategy, one is able to broaden and consolidate the web of loyalties and reciprocity that constitutes a security system for millions of inhabitants of the *México profundo*. It would take too long to try to illustrate the forms of cultural innovation that can be found in all aspects of community life. Without much difficulty, the reader can add other examples simply by looking beyond the boundaries of the imaginary Mexico.

An aspect that deserves special attention is linguistic resistance, since the preservation of one's own tongue has a fundamental importance in maintaining the deeper codes that express one's way of seeing and understanding the world. Few aspects of Mesoamerican culture have been attacked so brutally and systematically as languages. Nevertheless, the number of speakers of indigenous languages has increased continu-ally in the last sixty years. The mechanisms that assure linguistic continuity have been poorly studied. However, one of the factors that seems to play a major role is the use of the maternal language in domestic life, and the related importance of women as transmitters of their own languages. Very shortly I will discuss the other side of the coin: the major pressures that work against the survival of Mesoamerican languages.

In summary, let me reiterate that the existing cultures of Mesoamerican civilization have been able to survive thanks to the will of those who carry them. This will is expressed first of all in a tenacious resistance, in attempting to preserve their decision-making capacity and their cultural patrimony. Second, it is expressed in a constant and selective appropriation of foreign cultural elements that are useful in surviving domination. Finally, it is expressed in an incessant creativity, which allows the forging of new cultural elements and the modification of older ones. These innovations allow subtle cultural adjustments to changes in the framework of oppression and aggression within which Mesoamerican peoples exist. Contrary to the superficial and prejudiced image maintained by colonial ideology, the cultures of the *México profundo* are not static. They live and have lived in a permanent tension, transforming themselves, adapting to changing circumstances, losing and gaining territory of their own. That permanent change does not imply rupture but, rather, dynamic continuity. Communities with their own collective identities continue to exist, based on the existence of historically forged cultural patrimonies. These patrimonies acquire particular, well-defined meanings because they are connected with the cultural matrix of Mesoamerican civilization.

Intermittent violence and daily resistance should be understood as two aspects of one reaction to colonial domination. They are not disconnected phenomena, but tactics that form part of a single survival strategy. Armed rebellion can be understood only within the historical context of permanent resistance, a resistance that takes on distinct modalities with the changing circumstances of colonial domination. As we will see shortly, it may alternate with different forms of political struggle that have gained ground in recent decades.

## The Presence of the Imposed Culture

In the first part, I tried to draw a profile of current Indian cultures, and in the previous section I tried to show the mechanisms that have made possible the survival of these cultures. But thus far I have made reference to only part of the reality experienced by Indian peoples. I have taken into account only what I have called "their own culture," that is, the part of their total culture or the cultural elements over which Indian peoples have decision-making power. But in the daily life of Indian communities other aspects, which are not under their control, are also present. These constitute "the imposed culture." Now is the time to discuss this topic and complete the panorama.

The life of the communities never takes place solely within the sphere of their own culture. The extension of this sphere varies greatly from group to group. Some groups, such as the Huichols, conserve a broader space for their own culture, because of their relative isolation. Some have suffered domination in a more intense and permanent way than others. For these groups, the realm of their own culture is now restricted to the spaces of domestic life, some productive activities, some occasions for communal enjoyment, and very little else. All the rest of their life takes place in spaces dominated by the imposed culture.

We may review briefly the situation prevalent in many Indian communities. Traditional authorities have been relegated to the background and civil authority is exercised through institutions and procedures foreign to the local culture. Only in certain ceremonial activities is authority held by individuals who have acquired prestige and responsibility by participating in the traditional *cargos* involving service to the community. Customary law is applied first of all, but the imposed legal formalities are necessary to impose sanctions over a broad range of actions. In economic activities the orientation toward self-sufficiency and reciprocity persists, but many people are obliged to sell their labor power inside or outside of the community. Pressures for commercialization increase. Some industrial products gain ground over local products. Plastic cups replace ceramic ones, mass-produced cloth and clothing replace local textiles, cement and prefabricated materials replace adobe and wood and tiles, bottled drinks and canned products replace locally produced foods, and so on. Consumption needs that do not correspond to the requirements of the culture itself are thus created, and these in turn generate new mechanisms of exploitation and dependence.

Inside the community economic inequalities grow, and those differences weaken the mechanisms of reciprocity and solidarity. The agents of the imaginary Mexico occupy permanent spaces in local society. They are the teachers, nurses, priests, buyers of local products, moneylenders, government employees, and representatives of commercial firms. Some of them are originally from the *México profundo*, but through different routes and motives they have enrolled in the imaginary Mexico's scheme of interests and demands, and they act in its name within their own communities. They try to imitate urban forms of life in their appearance, in certain tastes, in surface behavior. They aspire to not live in the Mexico where they do live (which they despise while extracting everything possible from it) in order to be the respectable people in the community, *la gente de razón.*

The material presence of the imposed culture has a double symbolism in the communities of the *México profundo*. On the one hand, it offers the somewhat diluted image of the hoped-for progress, the long-yearned-for development, finally arriving in those forgotten corners. One can travel easily to places that used to be inaccessible. There one almost always finds a school and even a rural health clinic. There is often electricity and in the small local stores one can find cigarettes, beer, bottled soft drinks, and canned food. These symbols, given their precarious and deteriorated condition, do little more than accentuate the material misery of the immense majority of the Indian communities. Here, ultimately, the imposed culture is converted into misery. Whatever the criteria employed to measure the material conditions of life, Indian peoples remain on the lowest level, at the very bottom of the country's economic pyramid. The exploitation of local resources and the Indians' labor power continues to be the basic force driving the cultural imposition of the imaginary Mexico over the *México profundo*. The pincers of domination press inward in two different ways. They not only exploit and impoverish the communities, pushing them into misery, but they simultaneously deny and constrain their ability to develop in terms of their own Mesoamerican civilizational project.

On the ideological plane, each and every day one's own culture confronts a different way of understanding and caring about the world. The community is divided, thanks to the actions of Protestant missionaries, "progressive" teachers, and political factions representing external interests. Some causes are taken up by youth and provoke friction between the generations. Sometimes parents themselves encourage abandonment of the local culture. They do not want their children to speak "the dialect," or their daughters to wear traditional clothing, or their children to appear to be Indian. The symbols of stigma must be eliminated.

The fact is that stigma is one of the basic tools of cultural imposition. Stigma fulfills its discouraging functions in additional areas of daily life, as the social experience of many sectors of the Indian population has diversified, and as Indians have been obligated to sustain intense and multiple relationships with the dominant society. Work, migration, commerce, schooling, the media, and the multifaceted presence of the imposed culture within their own communities create new relationships. The imaginary Mexico's conviction that everything Indian is inferior manifests itself in all its actions, in all the projects that constitute cultural imposition. Harassment and the constant demand that Indians renounce who they are represent the most basic explanations for the presence of the imposed culture.

Let us look at a personal testimony. This is the way that Javier

Castellanos describes what happened in his community, Yojovi, in the district of Villa Alta, Oaxaca:

> The old men say that before, things did not change, that every-thing was always the same, but today things are very different. We had a bandstand where the musicians played, and we had good musicians. We had public baths and washbasins for clothes. We had benches where the young people sat to talk. But we ourselves tore them down. A schoolteacher convinced us that it was better to build a monument to the flag and tear down the bandstand in order to build it. We tore down the public baths to build the school. The washbasins we tore down because that was the place where the teachers' houses were to be built. Suddenly it seemed as if we wanted to destroy our village. After these things had happened, it seemed of little importance, but six or seven years later the people began to leave the community. Some said it was out of poverty, others that they wanted to see other places. But we had known worse poverty and no one abandoned the village. They say that in 1915 a plague of locusts came and ate everything that was green. There was not even grass to eat, and we might have wanted to leave, but we stayed in our village. We have seen illness among our animals. We have seen our brothers, children, and parents die without being able to cure them, but nevertheless, we never abandoned our village. And we cannot say that we left in order to see other places, because to do that you must have money, and that is something we do not have. What happened to us is what hap-pened to the bird we call *yase*. When someone touches its nest, even without hurting the eggs, the female destroys the nest and goes away. What we do not know is who came near and touched our nest. Practically speaking, that has been our history. We have spent our lives destroying ourselves. [Castellanos 1982]

In the material universe, in the forms of social relations, in thought and knowledge, and even in emotions, Indian peoples experience daily the schizophrenia of Mexican society. They live in a world that is split in two, opposed and incompatible in each and every aspect. When the resources of traditional medicine do not cure illness, one goes to the clinic. When that does not help either, one goes back to the *curandero*. If the piece of land for raising corn does not produce the bare essentials, the only thing left is to migrate like swallows, in whatever direction, through different skies. The flute and the drum of the ancestral dances can hardly be heard through the rock music of the loudspeakers, in the still-solemn maelstrom of the village fiesta. One does the ritual cleaning in the sweatbath [*temascal*] and afterward one has to offer one's hand to one's neighbor after mass. The stories of the *aluxes* are learned at the same time as the cartoons of Donald Duck.

There is the dream of the city, with its famous personalities and its mythic acts, along with the certainty of discrimination and unemployment, as opposed to the precarious but secure shelter of the extended family, of the godparents and *compadres*, of one's own language and well-trodden paths. Time spent in school interrupts participation in work, and instruction is deficient and third class, making the educational message doubly incomprehensible and foreign. The imaginary Mexico is inextricably intertwined with the *México profundo*. There is imposition and stubborn resistance: I fall and I rise again, I stop being but I return to existence because I still am, I yield and I protest, I accept and I reject. Above all, I endure.

Everything seems a permanent battleground. At moments, when the imaginary Mexico goes through illusory stages of expansion, the pressures increase. Indian lands are contended for with greater rancor, Indian labor is needed in greater quantity and with more urgency, cultural imposition increases and diversifies. The community seems to dissolve in the triumphal whirlwind of the imaginary Mexico. Youth emigrate to the degree that attachment to their own culture decreases. But the contradictory dynamic of dependent, savage, peripheral capitalist development is incapable of sustaining the storm's pressure. The expansion that seemed uncontainable reaches its limits and begins to recede. Resources become scarce and unemployment increases, public works and projects are abandoned, supply and demand increase. Then, as Eric Wolf pointed out years ago [1959: 214–232], the communities tend to close in upon themselves and customs that had been on the verge of being forgotten are revived. People participate and the vitality of Mesoamerican civilization emerges once more. There is memory and apprenticeship in all of this.

In summary, the daily life of Indian peoples, from the moment in which each one of them came under colonial domination, became a complex in which both one's own culture and the imposed culture were present. The relative proportions varied in different areas, depending on each case and each historical period. Even in situations in which one's own culture has been attacked to the point of existing only in minimal areas of domestic and communal life, the group, as a differentiated social unit, persists and has its own distinctive identity. It persists because of that minimal cultural nucleus of its own. That sphere, restricted as it may be, is structured by a cultural matrix that gives meaning and coherence to the actions of the group. It allows the group to confront domination through the processes of resistance, appropriation, and innovation. The daily presence of the imposed culture, on the other hand, is not perceived as an articulated and coherent whole, even though that is what it may be as seen from the dominant society. Rather, it is experienced within communal life as a range of actions and pressures that require particular responses, adequate to each situation. The only quality that all these influences share, from the daily perspective of Indian communities, is that they all come from outside, from the threatening, non-Indian world, and are therefore dangerous in principle and should be received with the deepest mistrust. This individualized handling of the imposed culture helps explain why certain cultural items are introduced in the communities with relative ease while others provoke resistance and are tolerated only when the sum total of forces present does not allow them to be eliminated.

## The New Battlefronts

As we have seen, the persistence of Indian communities, the basis of the *México profundo*, has been possible thanks to their ability to keep their own cultures. This necessarily implies a historical process that "actualized" Mesoamerican civilization, or brought it into the present. It is there, in those cultures forced to emphasize their mechanisms of resistance, that the profound vitality of Mexico glows. There the principles of a different civilizational project are safeguarded.

The dynamic relationship between the forces of domination and those of liberation constantly generates new forms of struggle and new spaces in dispute. This has given rise in recent decades to Indian strategies of asserting their rights that did not exist or were not manifested with the same clarity in earlier periods. One of the most notable phenomena has been the emergence of forms of political organization that produce other types of leaders, whose discourse and arsenal of tactics are not present in the daily struggles within the communities.

Many of the Indian political organizations that emerged at the beginning of the 1970s were adopted by the state in an effort to create defined and institutionalized groups that would speak for the Indian world. The nonexistence of Indian peoples as political units in the organization of the Mexican state, and the systematic denial and invisibility of real Indians in official ideology, blocked the recognition of an Indian spokesperson. At the same time, there was an intensification of conflicts with the communities, principally over land, and there was also a need to reinforce the legitimacy of a government that had been severely questioned in 1968. These factors made it advisable to try to create an Indian organization that would accept dialogue under the terms required by the government. As a result, then, of the First Congress of Indian Peoples [Primer Congreso Nacional de Pueblos Indígenas], held in Pátzcuaro in 1975, the National Council of Indian Peoples [Consejo Nacional de Pueblos Indígenas—CNPI] was created. It was composed of several dozen executive councils, which were to represent the different ethnic groups.

The creation of the CNPI obeyed a governmental decision. This sort of origin brought it into immediate disrepute with a sector of public opinion in the opposition. This meant that the CNPI was not accorded the attention it should have gotten in terms of the reaction of different Indian peoples to this new alternative for organization and a national presence. In practice, many executive councils remained simply as one more acronym, without the least real existence in the communities they supposedly represented. Nevertheless, in other cases, the leaders had or developed roots, and the executive councils became a conduit for expressing wrongs suffered and for presenting demands. On a national level, the meetings of the CNPI called attention to the most evident problems of Indian peoples. They sporadically alerted public opinion to them—a public opinion that was drowsy and shortsighted about that aspect of the national reality. Indirectly, the CNPI also brought about the rise of parallel organizations, independent of the government, tied in some cases to opposition political parties or, in other cases, completely autonomous.

Along with government efforts to create an Indian spokesperson, the consequences of other processes that had been maturing for years emerged, giving birth to new actors in Indian affairs. It will be remembered that one of the *indigenista* strategies of revolutionary governments since the 1930s had been to train youth from the Indian communities, to convert them into agents of de-Indianization. Little by little the number of Indian teachers and cultural promoters had grown, along with smaller numbers of nurses, agricultural extension agents, and other technicians and professionals. After the traumatic experience of brainwashing, through which they learned to renounce their own background and to disparage their relatives' culture, they joined the ranks of the "agents of change" who were to finally redeem the Indian by making him disappear.

During the 1950s, this process seemed to be going well and accelerating. But it happens that history is complicated, and apparent tendencies frequently change their symbols and their direction. The trajectory of the Indian teacher seemed certain and secure. After leaving the boarding school he would spend a few years in some community and could later aspire to make the leap for which his own training had prepared him. That is, he would cease to be an Indian teacher and would go to the city and build a career as a nonstigmatized teacher. This happened for some time, but there were many aspirants and the road was narrow. Some were frustrated at not being able to abandon the education of Indians as easily as they had expected. Others became aware that Indian reality did not correspond to the schematic and disparaging vision with which they had been indoctrinated. The fact is that many teachers and cultural promoters began to picture an alternative project of Indian education. In that effort, with its highs and lows and contradictions, its successes and failures, the Indian teachers have begun outlining a sort of school education that they regard as their own. They want education to be more inclusive and they have undertaken the task of giving it a content of their own, in which Indian languages and cultures occupy a place next to Spanish and "universal culture." In the field of education, then, a new battlefront has been created, in which the institutional spaces and decisions about the method and content of the education imposed by the state can be disputed.

The expansion of higher education has permitted Indian students to filter upward in different career fields. It has not been easy, of course. Living conditions in Indian communities do not favor going on to a university education. Neither does the deficient schooling of the aspiring Indian students, brutally accentuated by the necessity of managing in another language, another society, and another culture. These factors do not place Indian students in the best position to overcome the obstacles the educational system has put in place and finally earn a university degree. Nevertheless, a good number of them have managed to do so. Many desert and accommodate themselves as best they can in the ranks of those who believe in the imaginary Mexico. There they must contemplate alone the bitterness of an omnipresent racism. Others maintain or recover their Indianness and in some way contribute to the struggles of the Indian peoples. There are associations of students and Indian professionals that work, each in its own way, for the welfare of their home communities.

In recent years, sheltered by institutional situations within the governmental apparatus, special programs have been carried out. These seek to train Indian students in ways that do not imply their de-Indianization but that favor a process of reflection and a real appropriation of tools of understanding and action that can be put to the service of Indian projects. Thus, ethnolinguists of professional caliber have been trained, as have mid-level cultural promoters who work at studying, retrieving, and promoting their own languages, histories, and cultures. Other programs have also been directed toward Indian students, although without the clearly defined goal of reinforcing Indian cultures. These programs have trained anthropologists, social science teachers, and, notably, specialists in Indian education.

In the last few years, then, a new Indian sector has been created. In spite of its internal differences, it has in common a long urban experience and a secondary or university education. These factors allow it to deal with the dominant culture much more easily than can people whose only experience is living in their communities, and whose only external contacts have been through migratory labor. This new group is necessarily composed of individuals who say they are Indians, but who in general participate only sporadically in communal affairs. They are a new, urban presence on the national scene. They are necessarily a political presence, since by affirming their Indian identity they are claiming the right to participate as Indians in the public life of the country. Their actions reach beyond the local borders of their communities, without their having to renounce their origin or the cultures from which they come. In different ways they have opened a new battlefront. This is a momentous achievement since, for the first time, it places Indian demands in the arena of national debate in a different way than did *indigenismo*, which was of concern only to non-Indians. Now it is Indian speakers themselves who promote the debate, Indians who are capable of establishing the dialogue in terms of and using the kinds of arguments that are considered legitimate in the dominant society. The momentousness of this new presence is not invalidated by the fact that in some cases, the members of this new group have betrayed the trust put in them and exploited their situations for personal benefit, to the detriment of their local communities. Such situations exist and bring disrepute to the movement. They should be understood, although never justified, in the context of a national society in which corruption permeates all levels of political transaction and represents a temptation that is difficult to conquer. The urban Indians, it must be remembered, came to that atmosphere from a communal life that functions on other bases and principles.

Another argument that has been employed to label the urban Indian movement as spurious is the assertion that its representatives "are no longer Indians." In this case one must suppose that the only true Indian is one who is illiterate and miserably poor, and who does not speak Spanish or employ Western rationality. Anyone who does these things ceases to be Indian. Can there be a clearer example of the persistence of colonial ideology?

The new forms of struggle are also encountered on other levels. In some communities commerce, which had been in the hands of "ladinos," has been slowly recovered by local people. In its extreme form the process leads to the expulsion of the inhabitants who are not Indian and the re-Indianization of the geographic area. There are important instances of organizations that produce and commercialize handicrafts.

This process nearly always includes the recovery of techniques, raw materials, and traditional motifs that had fallen into disuse through the pressures of a voracious and degrading commerce. In the same way, the number of self-generated, local-level projects grows constantly. They promote techniques and products that had been abandoned, such as the use of precolonial terraces for cultivation, or they introduce new lines of production that generate little or no technological dependence. Some of these experiments have governmental support, but many others are based on local resources and initiative. In some cases there is complementary financing from private sources, national or international. Another of the new facets of the struggle is the growing capacity of many communities to secure external funds and administer them directly.

Another order of activities that should be mentioned is the appearance of an Indian press. It is still very incipient and unstable, but it points toward the appropriation of the printed word, something that has remained foreign to Indian cultures. The possibility of publishing texts in indigenous languages has stimulated the creation of the necessary alphabets, as well as the recovery of oral tradition and the beginning of a new Indian literature. An example is the magazine *Guchachi' reza*, published by the Folk Council [Ayuntamiento Popular] of Juchitán. The artistic movements in theater, music, and dance that have been initiated in various Indian regions are always based on the recovery of their own traditions. However, they frequently make use of new elements and resources that have been appropriated and that aim to create new and different forms of expression to extend the cultural space of community culture.

In the area of religious confrontation, the requirement of respecting tradition has been the point of rupture with those converted to different sorts of Protestantism. Protestant penetration has increased at a giddy pace in recent decades and raises questions that, for lack of adequate information, are difficult to answer . For example, some communities in Chiapas have been so deeply divided that the Protestant families have left their homes to form new communities in other places, especially in the jungle. What happens to them? What happens to their culture and their previous identity? Do they stop being Tzotziles? Do they stop being Indians? The imposition of a new religion in itself does not necessarily imply a change in ethnic identity or a rupture in cultural and historical continuity, as irrefutably demonstrated by the "spiritual conquest" of Mesoamerica. Contrary to the obvious wishes of the pastors and missionaries, the Protestant communities could become a new framework for the continuity of Mesoamerican civilization. This would be the case if their members were to appropriate the new religion and insert it, with modifications, into the matrix of their own culture, as happened centuries ago with Catholicism. At this point what predominates seems to be an attitude of total rejection of the past. But one cannot make a tabula rasa of the past, nor replace one's own culture from one day to the next. This process, with its current characteristics, is too new to be able to draw conclusions about final effects. It is worth remembering that in the first half of the sixteenth century there were groups of fanatical Indian youth who had been indoctrinated by the friars. They dedicated themselves to destroying the sacred images venerated by their elders and denouncing the "heresies" of their own parents [Moreno Toscano 1976: 45–46]. Those living through those times, particularly the friars, certainly believed that it was the beginning of the end for Mesoamerican civilization. Time very quickly proved them wrong.

In conclusion, it should be pointed out that the recent transformations of Mexican society have affected Indian peoples in different ways and have provoked new responses in various aspects of life. Along with traditional resistance, which has not been abandoned and whose existence cannot be denied, new initiatives have arisen to recover and modernize Indian cultures. New Indian actors are involved in them, within their own communities and in the broader spheres of national urban life. Many of these movements are not related among themselves and at times they are explicitly and implicitly contradictory. But put in a broader perspective, they constitute a proof of the vitality and viability of Mesoamerican civilization in modern Mexico.

# PART III.

## The National Program and the Civilizational Project

# 9.

# The Nation We Have Today

### The Shattering of the Illusion

It all happened very rapidly. It took only a few years, at the end of the 1970s, for the illusions and the euphoria of the oil mirage to pass. Next came the certainty that the model of development imposed on the country had now reached its end and that it had no more to offer. This was evident by December of 1982. It was necessary to stop believing in miracles, in immense treasures that appeared suddenly, assuring us the definitive solution to all our problems. An undeserved miracle it would have been, too, since it was not the result of a series of rational or steady efforts to generate the wealth the country needs, or to solve the problems that overwhelm it. Suddenly it seemed that all the mistakes, the interminable chain of absurdities, incompetence, and examples of short-sightedness, were not really so bad. In the end, they were justified by the final result: a country whose only challenge was to learn how to manage abundance. Shortly thereafter the false illusions and triumphal behavior of the imaginary Mexico came noisily crashing down. The country that remains is another one, very different from the Mexico imagined during the brief years of the most recent euphoria.

Today we must accept that Mexico is a poor country. We must acknowledge that there are large extensions of land that are not appropriate for "modern" agriculture and others that are eroded and produce less than before because they were exploited in an irrational manner. We must accept that things have reached the extreme in which our own agriculture does not produce enough basic products to feed the Mexican population even at the minimum required level. Our dependence grows because of hunger. The country that invented corn now has to import it.

Agriculture for export and for producing products for industry is unstable. In the first case, international prices and the restrictions on imports into the United States, the principal buyer, always place a question mark on the future of the market and frequently provoke acute crises for different products. These crises have to be resolved with scarce national financial reserves, and the cost is almost always paid by Mexican consumers. Neither do crops for industrial use seem to offer a promising future, at a time when industrial growth is stagnant and many firms are closing. And it is these kinds of agriculture, it must be remembered, along with cattle raising, that have taken over the best agricultural lands, displacing the Mesoamerican products that form the subsistence base for the immense majority of the population.

We cannot be confident about our raw materials as the basis for a secure and balanced international commerce. Prices and demand forces move in ways beyond our control and always to the benefit of the buyer, in a market principally controlled by the United States. The export of manufactured products is limited because Mexican industry, with isolated exceptions, is not competitive on the international level. One attempt at a solution has been to accept *maquiladoras* [foreign-owned assembly plants along the northern border]. The country has become a *maquilador* at an alarming rate, which means that we sell only the strength of Mexican arms so that others may become rich. And we sell it very cheaply. The dollars earned by the workers (how many million a year?) alleviate the misery of their families and add to the foreign exchange reserves. But *bracerismo* [selling our labor to foreigners] cannot be the solution for the Mexican economy. If we accept it as such, we must accept the inevitable political consequence, which is to declare the country dissolved and integrate ourselves into the North American economy and society.

Our industry is not sufficiently organized to satisfy the basic demands of the national market. Many superfluous things are produced, and, on the other hand, many things that are necessary are not produced. How much is spent in Mexico to produce, promote, and consume canned food, bottled soft drinks, alcoholic beverages, and throwaway containers? What does it cost, in this poor country, to create industrial employment aimed at producing garbage? In discussing this point we cannot pass over the role played by advertising—a force that promotes models of consumption that, put simply, impoverish and hurt the consumer. Much more than necessary is spent on "food" whose nutritional components have been obtained traditionally for a much lower price. For example, compare plastic bags containing industrially produced corn products with tamales, tortillas, and *atole*. In addition, these purchases divert a significant part of the precarious family budget, which would be better applied to real family needs.

In addition, because of the twisted nature of industrial development, the quality and the prices of many national products do not compete with the contraband foreign products sold openly on every side. This means a restricted market for selling national products and a continuous loss of foreign exchange. This happens in a country with 1,860 miles [3,000 kilometers] of border with the United States, across which millions of people pass annually. The "informal economy" in this process acquires an overwhelming importance not reflected in statistics. It is a way for a few to get rich and for the poverty of many others to be disguised.

Within the generalized poverty, there is economic inequality, which should be intolerably scandalous. A gross and insulting sort of squandering and waste exists, along with an inability to attend to the most elemental necessities of millions of countrymen. (Is it accurate to say "countrymen"? Can those Mexicans who put their money safely in the United States really belong to the same country?) The crisis has made the rich richer and everyone else poorer. The end of the "miracle" has made evident, for anyone who ever doubted it, the profound tendency toward inequality that has been implicit in the plan for national development.

The crisis obviously produces poverty, but not an evenhanded poverty, since even within the *México profundo* the effects are not equal. In the long run, of course, it is that majority population that pays the consequences, while a minority benefits and enriches itself to disgusting excess. Those sectors of the *México profundo* that have detached themselves from Indian and traditional campesino communities, that have enrolled themselves as subordinates in the imaginary Mexico, may well be those in the worst conditions and with the fewest resources to deal with the crisis. Here unemployment is at its highest, and exclusive dependence on the money economy intensifies the effects of inflation. There is also dependence on social services, which are not increasing and are actually being reduced for the contingents of marginalized urban poor. They, who found themselves obliged to choose a life and a job within the development plans of the imaginary Mexico, are the first and the most deeply excluded and the ones who must support the requirements of the economic contraction. Those upon whose work and poverty have depended the illusions of growth are those who must now pay the costs of the collapse.

The foregoing does not mean at all that Indians and traditional campesinos are at the margin of the crisis. In everything that relates them to the imaginary Mexico, they also pay debts they never contracted. The only difference, but a very important one, is the margin of self-sufficiency provided by the orientation of their culture. It is a precarious margin, certainly, but it is a margin that does not exist, or barely survives, in the urban sectors of the *México profundo*. In spite of the common misery, here, surrounded by asphalt, there are fewer ways to confront the crisis. At least, this is true for the moment.

Every Mexican is born owing a debt. The foreign debt today is unmanageable. If it were to be paid, the country would be poorer than it was before it went into debt. The loans served to fill in potholes, not to build a new and serviceable highway. The debt makes the economic development plan, as it has been developed, unfeasible. It also places the country in a feeble position for maintaining the degree of political autonomy that had been achieved. The pressures of the International Monetary Fund threaten to channel the political economy toward the sole objective of paying the debt. Bilateral negotiations with the U.S. government, on the other hand, carry the risk that Mexico's foreign policy may be included as something to be negotiated, through the inevitable pressures of *realpolitik*. The margins of autonomy constrict as the dependence that has accumulated reveals itself, implacable in all its dimensions and facets.

Some problems that were sidestepped during the crisis appear more dramatic today. The air pollution in Mexico City and other urban industrial zones is no longer a distant and improbable danger to be avoided. It is now a daily reality whose gravity cannot be exaggerated or hidden. We must reverse many urban policies, which have happily accumulated during administration after administration, that have made Mexico City one of the worst megalopolises in the world. We must repair the damages produced by a savage capitalism, which has made uninhabitable its own lair, where so many inhabitants of the *México profundo* are obligated to remain. We must rethink and rebuild our cities, without forgetting that they are the creation and the bastion of the imaginary Mexico. Their problems are not simply deviations, anomalies that can be repaired without rejecting the project of which they are the inevitable result. The city expresses, in its own way and with its own cancer, the unresolved contradictions of Mexican society and history. Its problems cannot be truly resolved if it maintains in all areas, even ideologically, its dominant position before the rural world and its role as the center for denying the *México profundo*.

Aggression against the natural world is not limited to the urban sphere. Mountains and forests are clear-cut, rivers and shorelines are polluted, the resources of the earth and the sea are destroyed, species become extinct, and in a thousand ways the ecological niches patiently created by nature and by man over thousands of years are altered. It is a suicidal effort whose only rationality is to earn the largest possible immediate profit, at all costs and perish whatever is in the way. Under the direction of the imaginary Mexico we have become splendid creators of deserts and efficient agents for destroying life on earth, in the water, and in the air.

And how do the Mexicans, our people, feel when faced with such encouraging prospects? There is a generalized frustration resulting from the shattering of illusions, however false these may have been. Employment opportunities close each year as eight hundred thousand Mexicans reach the age of eighteen, the symbolic dividing line between adolescence and adulthood. They have no reliable prospects, no security whatsoever that anything they may do will lead to something better in life. Open discontent is more easily seen in the middle classes and in broad sectors of the bourgeoisie. There insecurity reigns, rage against a country they wanted for their own as an inexhaustible supplier of satisfactions that would allow them a steady, eternal ascent. Now they look for someone to blame, not counting themselves among the candidates. Since the 1940s they have wanted to be more cosmopolitan than Mexican, and their uprooting is more profound when they see themselves as part of an impoverished country. It is not these people or their interests that are the best guides to find the path down which all may march.

The people of the *México profundo* are silent; they do not participate because they are denied the opportunity to do so on their own terms. They are an invisible and mute people as far as the imaginary Mexico is concerned. They are a people who endure with a patience that seems beyond limit. Here or there, sporadically, there is a cry of protest, an isolated outburst. The national political debate unravels—not in terms of its discourse, of course, but in terms of authentic participation—for lack of a constituency. The proposals of the Right reflect a nostalgia for the path already taken and a stubborn and crazy will to pursue it. The Left cannot manage to define a program that is halfway convincing. It overspecialized in criticism and now shows itself incapable of proposing a future that starts from our current reality, apart from the words that have become dull from so much overhandling. The real game of political decisions remains open for only a few, and its norms and procedures are paralyzed. It has become a parlor game, routine and predictable, more and more incapable of responding to what is really happening. Corruption continues, browsing through fields of privilege earned by a long history and by generalized acceptance as an admissible and acceptable form of conduct.

The picture is not complete, but these lines sketch the profile of the imaginary Mexico, today and in the immediate future. There do not seem to be any new miracles in sight.

What is going on here? It is certainly not a simple, fortuitous piling up of isolated problems, each independent of the other. It is not the accumulation of difficulties that overwhelms us. What immobilizes us is something much more profound: the fading away of one plan for the future and the incapacity to formulate another one that will not have the same pitfalls. In the same way, a new plan for nationhood cannot be made up of shreds and patches. It cannot be the sum total of particular measures that, under pressure from the crisis, attempt to attenuate each of the multiple and different manifestations of the previous model's breakdown. The only option, without doubt a difficult and arduous one, but nevertheless the only possibility, is to draw from the *México profundo* the historical will to formulate and undertake our own civilizational project.

When all is said and done, what we are speaking about is civilization. It is at the level of civilization that one measures the transcendence of the problems and recognizes the capacities and potentials of a people. It is there, in the civilizational project, that the fundamental information is to be found for designing the nation we want and are able to build in each historical period. From this perspective, what broke down was the civilizational model of the imaginary Mexico, a model that had been accepted as the only one possible.

**Founding a New Hope**

We were not able to construct an imaginary country and it would be insane to insist on doing so. Mexico is what it is, with this population and this history. We cannot persist in the attempt to replace it with something it is not. The task is simpler: to make it better from within, not from without. We must stop denying what it is and, to the contrary, take it for something that can be transformed and developed starting from its own potentialities. We must recognize the *México profundo*, once and for all, because without it there is no worthwhile solution.

What do we have as a basis for going forward?

We have varied natural resources, not so many nor as rich as we were led to believe by the image of the horn of plenty, but enough to permit a better quality of life for the Mexicans of today and the foreseeable future. If ours were a homogeneous society one might think that all those resources should be exploited according to a single production scheme, with a single set of goals, conceptions, and ways of working. But it is not homogeneous and, therefore, the resources mean different things and are exploited in different ways. Natural phenomena are converted into resources through culture, and here multiple cultures coexist. Each culture defines the natural resources it will exploit, the form in which it will obtain and transform them, and their final use and meaning. In addition, as we have seen, the Indian communities claim a part of those resources as exclusively their own, and they consider them inseparable from their history, culture, and patrimony. This link surely allows them to defend those resources better than if they were seen as "national" resources, the view taken by some sectors of the imaginary Mexico. Ultimately, the function of "national resources" seems to be to ensure personal enrichment for the few.

The diverse ways in which nature, work, and material production are understood are due to the presence of two different civilizations, Mesoamerican and Western. This diversity is not in itself an obstacle. It becomes an obstacle only when there is an attempt to impose a single economic rationality, and especially when that rationality radically denies any other. When this is not the situation, diversity in production is a resource of enormous potential, because it gives the whole society a vast arsenal of alternatives and new experiences for the management of natural resources. The different ways of understanding and working the earth, for example, become a problem and an obstacle only when all are measured with a device that is appropriate for only one of them. One such device is the market value of the crop produced per unit of area. Or, to take another example, work by artisans is judged "backward" if it is isolated from its social and cultural context and measured in terms of "productivity," defined as the largest quantity of products finished in a given period of time. Judgments of this sort result from applying a unique and exclusionary model of economics and civilization. Everything outside that model, everything that belongs to another civilizational project, is converted into an obstacle, a hindrance, and a cause of backwardness. All its potential is ignored and denied.

The same thing happens with knowledge. Mexican society has at its disposal a vast store of knowledge, the result of thousands of years of refinement and experimentation in the heart of the diverse societies of the *México profundo*. That knowledge has proven its validity to the degree that, first, it resulted in the development of Mesoamerican civilization, and, second, it has ensured the persistence of the peoples who preserved it and brought it into the present. This is knowledge about all areas of life and is necessarily tied to particular ways of understanding the world. It forms part of specific visions of the cosmos. Some of this knowledge, for example, that which allows the management of the surrounding natural world, cannot be mechanically transferred to other surroundings. It is not formulated in terms of explicit general rules. The inductive and deductive processes that generated it have made use of data from a limited universe, and those data rest upon local experiences, because of the isolation and social fragmentation imposed by colonial domination.

But their restricted validity in modern times does not imply any inherent inability of that knowledge to be developed, broadened, and deepened through systematic formulation. The problem is to reestablish the social conditions that would permit that development, conditions that have been systematically denied since the imposition of colonial domination. Meanwhile, and in spite of the foregoing, traditional knowledge constitutes an invaluable capital for all the peoples of the *México profundo*. It could be transformed into a resource for the country as a whole if its potential validity were recognized.

Here again the deeper problem is accepting the validity of another civilization and abandoning the arrogant assumption that one's own, Western way of understanding is the only certain and true one. It is enough to imagine an average family from the Narvarte suburb of Mexico City who had to survive, with the knowledge they possess, in the desert lands of Punta Chueca, on the Nayar Mesa, or in the jungle surrounding Nahá. There live the Seri, the Huichol, and the Lacandón, each group with a store of their own knowledge, which has allowed them to survive and prosper, in spite of everything.

Above all else, to move forward the country counts on its people, on those who, in the end, constitute the totality of Mexico. But the perspective of the imaginary Mexico allows Mexicans to be seen only as individuals, not as members of communities and societies forged through history. In the plans of the imaginary Mexico, real people are transformed into "human resources," interchangeable, isolated numbers that can be subtracted here or added there. The obvious social condition of being human is ignored. We forget that individuality exists only in the context of a given society, which in turn possesses a specific culture. Since in Mexico there exist various cultures, affiliated to two distinct civilizations, real Mexicans are individuals in different factual contexts, not in a single one common to all. What we can count on to move forward is not eighty plus million undifferentiated individuals in a common social and cultural system. Rather, it is something much more important and more promising: a variegated mixture of societies, each one of which possesses its own culture. That is to say, each individual, besides being an individual, belongs to a social unit within which he or she is the bearer of particular ways of living and making history. Taken together, we have a great number of different ways of organizing work, family, and community. We have a broad range of forms of expression. We can count on multiple knowledge and skills to face similar problems. We have different senses of ultimate importance. This will be the contribution of the *México profundo* and its rejected civilization, if and when we decide to build a common future with the *México profundo* and not against it.

There is another point we should consider in these times of frustration and disillusionment. Indian peoples have resisted five centuries of colonial oppression and domination. What is the basis for their decision to survive and endure? What are the sources of their will to continue making history for themselves? On what interior strength have they drawn to persist for centuries in their own vision of life, under conditions incomparably more difficult than those that in a few years destroyed the development plans of the imaginary Mexico? The spiritual force behind the will to endure is indispensable for formulating a new, viable, and authentic national program. The believers in the imaginary Mexico no longer have that will. They have little conviction to continue, although some try to disguise this fact, stubbornly recovering the ruins of the shipwreck and trying to rebuild the same, useless vessel. But, on the other hand, that same will gives life to millions of Mexicans, who exercise it in the specific acts of their daily lives, confident in their beliefs and in their attachment to what is their own. The argument may sound overly abstract, but there, in the *México profundo*, we also have the indispensable reserve of confidence on which to found a new hope.

From all that has been produced within the framework of the imaginary Mexico there is also much to retrieve and to put at the service of a new national program. What is imaginary is Western. It is imaginary not because it does not exist, but because, based on it, there has been an effort to build a Mexico different from Mexican reality. Western civilization exists and is present throughout the world. My effort is not to deny it, as it has denied Mesoamerican civilization. Neither would I deny that many elements of Western civilization can and should be employed to build a better Mexico for everyone. The country already counts on social groups that know how to employ and develop aspects of Western culture that they have made their own. There exist a store of important resources needed to carry out a new national program. We have scientists and technicians, artists and intellectuals, and they control knowledge and Western skills, which are useful today, and will be in the future. The problem is whether Mexican society does or does not have the ability to appropriate those resources and use them to promote its real interests. That is, are we capable of employing the knowledge and techniques of Western civilization without at the same time adopting the civilizational project that denies our underlying reality?

The matter can be summarized as follows. Diverse ways of manipulating reality, through knowledge, techniques, material instruments, and forms of social organization, acquire meaning only in the framework of a civilizational project. Such a project defines the reality to which we aspire. Only in terms of this project can we judge the relative merits of the cultural elements with which we try to manipulate reality, with which we find them to be better or worse, adequate or useless. The West has generated cultural elements as a function of its own project, but that does not mean that these elements are useful only there. Other civilizational projects, like the one we need, can also make use of them without changing their nature. It is also an act of reclamation, since the achievements of Western civilization were only possible thanks to the exploitation of peoples with different cultures. In the West that belongs to us, but not in that which is imposed upon us, there are also potential resources for moving forward.

Putting the situation in this perspective, Mexico counts on a vast arsenal of peoples and cultural elements and resources. They could be used to create a better and more just society, capable of offering its different members a full and higher quality of life. These are the bricks for building the new home of the Mexicans. They are the only ones that are really ours, but they are sufficient. Only the plans to attend to our immediate needs and to our infinite aspirations are lacking.

# 10.

# Civilization and Alternatives

## Substitution, Fusion, or Pluralism

In some way, we have to define and put into practice a new national program for the future. The risk of not doing so would be to accelerate internal breakdown and accentuate existing contradictions. It would encourage centrifugal forces, which detract from the very concept of an independent nation. It would tear down the national borders, which, even though seriously debilitated, still permit us to hope that dependence will not be translated into the dissolution of the country. Mexico as a country continues to be viable, because of its expanse, the size of its population, its productive potential, and, above all, the cultural resources that its people have been wise enough to conserve. It is viable, but it may not be in the future. Its viability will be threatened if the new national program is built along the margins of our national reality, ignoring the historical and civilizational processes that are still operating and that have a deep history. The national program must be defined in terms of civilization.

A first possible option would be to insist on the substitution project, which throughout this book I have called the imaginary Mexico. It is worth repeating that this project rests on the conviction that a substantial part of the reality of the country, that part which derives from Mesoamerican civilization and which forms the *México profundo*, should be replaced with a distinct reality. The other reality has presented itself in different garb in different historical periods, but it always turns out to be a version of Western civilization wearing somewhat different makeup. The model of the country we aspire to be is copied in every case from some other country recognized as advanced, according to the standards of Western civilization. In the current period, the model to imitate is of an industrialized country that assures its inhabitants higher and higher levels of consumption, especially consumption of material goods. The alternative forms of political and economic organization for achieving this goal are presented as opposed and irreconcilable, for instance, as either capitalism or socialism. But the ultimate objectives are the same; the only argument is over which road is better or shorter. It is a single civilizational project defined on the basis of the same suppositions. History is an infinite process of rectilinear advance. Advancement consists of greater and greater control over and capacity for exploitation of the natural world, for human benefit. The benefits generated by this advance are realized and expressed in terms of more and more consumption. And through this process, the ultimate human goals are achieved. On these assumptions of Western civilization rest its scales of evaluation and its definitions. Work is a necessary evil, which should be reduced as historical advancement proceeds. Nature is an enemy to be overcome, since humans fulfill themselves to the degree they become independent of nature. Greater production and greater consumption of goods are absolute, immanent values that require no justification whatsoever.

According to this civilizational project, there is no alternative but to accept Mexico as a backward and underdeveloped country. Even worse, it will become more so each day if the distance that separates us from the developed countries of the West continues to increase, which is and has been the tendency. Every day it becomes more difficult to imagine how in the hell we will manage to become a country on the cutting edge. Naturally, it is the *México profundo*, the Indians, the campesinos, the marginalized urban masses, who embody in a self-evident manner the backwardness and underdevelopment of the country.

The reasons can be debated. For some the exploitation to which those groups have been subjected is reason enough to explain their lack of participation in "Mexico as a developing country." For others the cause is laziness, ignorance, and the lack of initiative of the people composing those sectors. The first explanation points to a fact that is certain: the systematic, brutal, and multifaceted exploitation of the *México profundo*. But a hasty conclusion is drawn, and it leaves aside a fundamental fact, the existence of a different civilization. Given the other civilization, one can question the supposition that if exploitation were diminished or eradicated, the members of these groups would immediately adopt the imaginary Mexico's Western project. This way of analyzing the situation is also Western and leads to a substitution project; it does not admit any future other than that which derives from the civilizational project of the West. The second way of understanding the problem does the same thing, but in an ingenuous and hypocritical way. It eliminates the problem of exploitation from the analysis and not only denies any future to Mesoamerican civilization, but also attributes to it the causes of the "backwardness" of those who participate in it.

On one or the other road, or on the paths between them, one reaches the same conclusion. The plans of the imaginary Mexico must be extended, which implies the replacement of the cultures affiliated with Mesoamerican civilization.

Today, after the breakdown of the dream, reformulating the replacement project would involve many limitations and shameful adjustments. Up to now, government actions have led in one direction. Meanwhile, other promoters and beneficiaries of the imaginary Mexico are in doubt about whether to join the enterprise or to search for alternatives and personal security in some other place. The predictable worsening of the crisis in its political and economic aspects will force those who see only the project of Western replacement to define their positions.

There will be those who, within the general guidelines and objectives of the replacement project, insist that it can be converted into a national, mestizo project. This position appears to reject replacement, admitting that there are positive values in Mesoamerican civilization, which should be incorporated into the national plans. The fusion of civilizations is postulated as the way to create an authentic national culture, and thus a legitimate and viable national future. Earlier I tried to show the fallacy in what has been called Mexican "mestizo" culture, and I will not insist on the point. But it is well to remember that although the integration of two or more distinct cultures to form a new one is possible, it takes a very long time. The factors that lead to the crystallization of a new culture are not subject to the will of individuals. Rather, they result from broad social processes in which successive generations take part. The fusion of cultures and civilizations in Mexico may happen, but it certainly will not be in the foreseeable future, and it will not be the result of a decree or of the actions of one or two generations.

Ultimately, many of the initiatives and activities set in motion to reinforce the plans for a national mestizo culture are really intended to lubricate the machinery of imposition and expansion of the imaginary Mexico. The effort is to remove obstacles that are too obvious. Certain superficial concessions are made to the cultural practices of the *México profundo*, using a little local color as a cosmetic touch for the evident Western nature of the imaginary national plans. The central problem remains the inability to recognize and accept the other, which in this case is the other civilization, the Mesoamerican one. Without the prior steps of recognition and acceptance, there is no way of speaking seriously about a process of cultural fusion or *mestizaje*.

There is another alternative, derived precisely from the recognition and acceptance of Mesoamerican civilization, with all its implications. This would be a national development plan organized on the basis of cultural pluralism. Pluralism would not be understood as an obstacle to be overcome but, rather, as the content itself of the project, that which makes it legitimate and viable. Cultural diversity would not be simply a reality recognized as the point of departure, but, instead, a central goal of the project. The attempt would be to promote development of a multicultural nation without its ceasing to be exactly that.

Of course, the challenge is not easy. I hope I have been able to show that the differences between cultures, especially those that belong to different civilizations, are profound. They are differences of orientation in values, of the sense of what is ultimately important, of the conception of the world. The specific cultural matrix is what gives meaning and significance to such explicit traits as clothing, local *costumbres*, modes of production and consumption, and aspirations. As we have seen, there are not only differences but also contradictions and oppositions between the cultures of the *México profundo* and urban Western culture. The expectations are not the same nor is there a correspondence in many important aspects of daily life. Reconciling those oppositions is the major challenge of a national plan that takes pluralism as fundamental.

An ethnically plural nation requires that all power structures that imply the domination of some groups over the others be annulled and suppressed. In the case of Mexico, this means the suppression of the colonial order, which began five hundred years ago and has not yet ended. It means liberating oppressed peoples and cultures and bringing them into the present, through democratic participation in national life. This process must take place within a democracy that not only recognizes individual rights, but also emphatically asserts the rights of historical collectivities. National unity ceases to be a mechanical unity based on uniformity and instead becomes an organic unity integrating different sectors. These sectors should not be unequal or in a hierarchical relationship. Each one of them has the real right to manage its own affairs within the state, which unifies them and in relation to which they share certain interests and goals. It is a firmer national reality because it is more promising and more real than one conceived in terms of uniformity, one that denies the existence and the rights of groups that deviate from the accepted model.

What sort of country would Mexico be if it claimed its multiethnic nature? It would be one in which all the existing cultural potential would have the opportunity to develop and test its validity, a country with a larger number of alternatives. It would be a national society that did not reject any segment of the resources created throughout its history. It would be, in short, a nation that lives as a real democracy, in accord with its richly diversified cultural makeup. It would be a nation capable, therefore, of acting on the international scene from an authentic position of its own. It is one thing for a country to presume itself inferior and underdeveloped, as determined by an imposed scale. It is another for a country to understand itself as different by sustaining and affirming goals derived from its own history. One could then speak of an authentic decolonialization. It would not consist of fighting to follow smoothly the path that has been imposed on us, but, rather, defining and following our own path.

## Civilization, Democracy, Decolonialization

Western civilization developed in successive centers, gaining power and influence. After a certain point in its historical development, its dynamic of expansion was always accompanied by an inability to coexist with other civilizations. The West sees itself as the bearer of *the* universal civilization. As something unique and superior, it entails the negation and exclusion of any other, different civilizational project. The ruling classes in Mexico until the present have been dependent, not only economically, but in all areas. This dependence results from affiliation with a civilization whose sources and centers of decision making and legitimacy are far distant and not under local control. This situation has produced a creole variety of the dynamic of Western expansion, always badly copied and backward in relation to the advanced countries that served as models. It has always been crude, with a tendency to understand being modern simply as being stylish. For that reason it has promoted a subsidiary and spurious modernity.

The Arabs were in Spain for seven centuries but Spain is a Western country and not an Islamic one, however many Islamic traits may be present in the cultures of the peninsula. The West burst upon Mexico five hundred years ago, and in addition, we border Western civilization's most powerful country for 1,860 miles [3,000 kilometers]. To deny the West in some global way or pretend to isolate ourselves from its presence not only would be impossible, it would be idiotic. The task is how to assimilate the inevitable and necessary Western elements in an autonomous national development plan, without incorporating others that by their nature and dynamics would deny the possibility of pluralism. How can we build and use the machines without glorifying the machinery? How can we produce the goods we need without falling prey to consumerism?

Extreme positions may argue that this is impossible. These are cultural elements that have arisen through a complex historical process, goes this argument, and they are indissolubly linked to other principles and values of the Western civilization from which they arise. This argument is valid for explaining the origin and development of those elements, but it does not lead to the inevitable conclusion that other peoples cannot fabricate machines with a different civilizational meaning. It is not a problem of all or nothing. The question should perhaps be posed in these terms: we should learn to see the West from Mexico, instead of continuing to see Mexico from the West.

The foregoing would mean a substantial modification in the way the West is implanted in the society and culture of Mexico. Its historical condition of being a civilization of conquest contradicts any possibility of carrying forward a project based on plurality. Western civilization has been presented in this country in such a way that it is not compatible with a decision to respect and favor the development of other cultures. As a consequence, it is necessary to reassimilate the West or, more accurately, to assimilate it for the first time. It will be essential to divest from Western culture the necessary elements, separating them from the arrogant garb of their imperial past. It will be necessary to domesticate these elements and make them coexist with others of a different origin, which do not pretend to follow the basic orientation of Western civilization. The Western elements should exist among others and not be the only ones or the preponderant ones. In the final instance, they must place themselves at the service of a project that is not Western but plural, and in which Mesoamerican civilization must play the lead role.

The foregoing implies an essential renovation of democracy in its meaning and in its implementation, here and now. The Western notion of democracy, based on formal, individualistic criteria, is insufficient to guarantee the participation of an ethnically plural population. In fact, as we saw earlier, it becomes an obstacle, a mechanism that prevents the participation of groups that do not share that way of understanding democracy. Western-style democracy has functioned in Mexico to justify a structure of cultural control, limiting the development of Mesoamerican cultures. This makes necessary a critical, in-depth review of the mechanisms of representation, delegation, and exercise of power, in order to ensure that decision making respects the plural nature of Mexican society.

In a society that recognizes itself as plural and wants to be so, thinking about a national culture means abandoning the idea that it be uniform. The common elements will not be the specific cultural contents of the diverse groups that compose Mexico. The common characteristic will be, first of all, the will to respect each other and to live together in diversity. The national culture will be a larger sphere of fruitful coexistence, free to develop according to its own plans. The necessary convergences will be few, as we have seen: the decision to build and maintain an independent state, and the acceptance of the minimum norms and mechanisms required for the functioning of a multicultural state.

Since independence, the Mexican State has taken on the heavy burden of creating a nation that it considered nonexistent because it was not expressed in one uniform society. Perhaps the excessive growth of the state apparatus is due, in part, to the effort required by this task. A State that respected the cultural autonomy of its component societies and only regulated their coexistence, that handled general matters that went beyond the internal affairs of each, would certainly be a smaller State with fewer functions, and one that was more solid and efficient.

Here again the test of truth is democracy, and what it should mean for Mexicans. A highly centralized and omnipresent power is congruent with the idea that the State's job is to create the nation. It accomplishes this by imposing a cultural model, created from above, on the rest of society. The recognition of pluralism, the acceptance of a plural model, carries with it a real decentralization of power. It means a social decentralization of decision-making power, not just administrative decentralization by territory.

### The Paths toward Pluralism

It might seem that in speaking of civilizations and civilizational projects we are handling excessively abstract concepts. They may seem to have little or nothing to do with real, concrete problems and urgently needed decisions. Needless to say, this is not the case. Rather, we are dealing with different, inseparable levels of the same reality. My insistence on the civilizational dimension of Mexico's problems is due to my belief that this aspect is precisely the one that has been absent in the debate. Its absence prevents us from putting the immediate problems and the solutions that have been proposed in a broader perspective, one in which they can acquire their true and deeper meaning. For that reason the adoption of a new civilizational project has implications for the immediate tasks facing us. Consciously or unconsciously, each day we choose options in favor of or opposed to such a project.

It is thus proper to explore briefly some of the concrete actions that would contribute to putting into effect a program of national pluralism. We should not lose sight of the fact that the program itself, with all its relevant details, by its nature must be constructed with the contributions of the societies that have developed historically in Mexico, with their different cultures. The priority is how to create the conditions for liberating these oppressed cultures. Their liberation is necessary for them to participate on equal terms, without renouncing their differences, in the design and construction of the new society.

As we have seen throughout this work, local societies on a relatively small scale—hamlets, communities, villages, and neighborhoods—are the social systems that have made possible the continuity of the *México profundo*. It is in the heart of such groups that Mesoamerican civilization is lived daily and its cultural matrices preserved. This being the case, one can derive two complementary plans of action within a national pluralism project. On the one hand, it is necessary to recognize and reinforce the local societies as the fundamental, constituent units in State organization. On the other hand, it is necessary to generate the conditions for building or rebuilding broader levels of social organization that allow the development of local culture, starting within those same communities.

The first proposal is oriented toward reinforcing local communities and broadening their own cultural spheres. To begin with, it implies a revision of the current administrative divisions, to adjust them to the real territoriality of the communities. It was mentioned earlier that in many cases this correspondence does not exist, because administrative divisions have usually been defined and imposed by interests that have nothing to do with the historical trajectory and makeup of the communities. Municipal and *ejido* boundaries frequently carve up an original community. The barrios of the cities are ignored as the social and spatial base of city government. Their integrity is attacked by urban policies that respond to current fashion, to corruption, or to a technocratic vision derived from foreign models. The restitution of a local territoriality determined by the needs and the histories of real social systems should be one of the first steps of a national pluralism project.

Reorganizing a territorial division in accordance with the reality of the existing social systems is not the final goal. The recognition of territoriality is necessary, in the first place, to assure the local communities the physical space they require as the sphere under their direct control for carrying out communal projects. Of equal or greater importance is recognizing the territorial base of the fundamental sociopolitical units that constitute the Mexican state. A new organization of the national territory would thus express the first level of a new division of power. The local societies that have developed historically would be recognized as legitimate political units, with decision-making powers in an ever-broader spectrum of matters that concern them.

To achieve the foregoing as part of a pluralism program, it will be necessary to respect internal forms of social organization. The current scheme must be abandoned, since it admits or, rather, imposes only a single structure of local government with the same norms and procedures for all. Is there any definitive reason why communities that have elaborated and maintained other ways of assigning and legitimating local authority, using their own procedures, should be obligated to use a different system? Is it necessary, for example, that local authorities be elected every three years instead of being replaced annually, as happens traditionally in many communities? Is the universal, secret, direct vote (which in fact is neither practiced nor respected in most of the country) an intrinsically superior way of achieving authority, as opposed to a hierarchy of *cargos* representing service to the community?

Many of the reasons why indigenous governments have become weaker or suffered crises have to do with the external decision not to recognize them. If local and municipal budgets, for example, and the corresponding decisions about public works, education, civil justice, and other communal matters could be handled through the traditional authority systems, many of the reasons for avoiding election to an annual *cargo* would disappear. Reinforcement of the system, contrary to what might be supposed, would not mean rigidity and stagnation in the handling of community affairs. Quite to the contrary, the effective recovery of functions that colonial domination has taken away would lead to their becoming more dynamic and up to date. They have been blocked by external pressures, which allow no response except resistance and "conservatism." There are documented cases, for example, of youths assuming legitimate positions of authority when circumstances allow it, thereby modifying the *cargo* systems' tendency toward gerontocracy. This may occur without implying a break with the old system. Rather, it indicates a renovation of the capacity for self-government, according to local plans. There are also experiences, still isolated, of political struggle for recognition of local forms of government, a fact that indicates a rising consciousness about these problems.

The process will not be free from difficulties. It is easy to foresee that in many cases there will be an initial stage in which noncommunity interests will come forward. *Caciques* of different flavors and colors will try to take advantage of the new margins of local autonomy to increase their power and to augment their benefits and privileges. But the decision to return to the communities a broader and more effective control over their own affairs will at the same time unleash internal forces capable of confronting that risk. To the extent that the communities recover control over their cultures, they will have better and more powerful resources to eliminate the outside interests that have been imposed on them historically, and that are contrary to their own goals.

All the cultural processes that for five hundred years have been dedicated to the resistance and survival of the *México profundo* may now be reoriented toward the renovation and development of local cultures. This process will originate internally and not be imposed from outside. Nevertheless, the communities, at their own discretion, will be able to make use of many of the cultural elements that today belong only to the dominant society. The communities have been prevented access to those elements by the system of domination and exclusion. Or it may be that the elements have been rejected because there was an attempt to impose them as part of the same system. The recovery of cultural control will diametrically change this situation.

The range of actions that might be undertaken on a local scale, as the communities broaden the cultural spaces under their control, is very extensive. Actions would result first of all from local initiatives. But without a doubt the process would be accelerated if a general policy of support and encouragement were put into effect. There are already meaningful experiences with such policies. Educational policy must be revised in depth with the goal of leaving in the hands of the community an ever-larger number of decisions about the content, methods, general organization, and functioning of the school system. It will be necessary to direct sufficient credit and funding to finance self-directed productive projects, without trying to subject them to the rigid econometric policies of the imaginary Mexico.

All this requires more than simply "taking into account" the opinion of the communities. It requires accepting and respecting their decisions. In this process, it must not be forgotten that the communities of the *México profundo* have been subject for centuries to colonial oppression, with all the internal consequences that oppression produces and that have been discussed throughout this book. If in fact one wants to promote a national pluralism project, the process requires resolutely intensifying actions to recover local cultures and bring them into the present. One of the key points will be broad and intensive training of new community figures capable of making use of the opportunities created by the recovery of cultural control. However, this training must not uproot them or lead them to reject their culture. The new figures, cultural promoters in the broadest sense of the term, should be trained to value their culture and from that perspective to promote the critical appropriation of foreign cultural elements. This is a process similar and complementary to that which I have suggested at a national level. Here the effort would be to see the West from the viewpoint of the community and stop seeing the community from the perspective of the West.

To this point I have placed the emphasis on the local community, the fundamental nucleus of the *México profundo* and the indispensable unit of support for a national pluralism project. But cultural revitalization of the communities is not enough to foment a civilizational process, because this involves other levels of state organization. I have mentioned several times that one of the most destructive effects of colonial domination was the reduction of the social sphere of Mesoamerican civilization to the narrow limits of the local community. The goal is not just to recover a village level civilization, but to reconstruct the necessary cultural space to develop a modern civilization, valid today and into the future.

In reconstituting the state, in defining the recognized sociopolitical units that are a legitimate part of it, it is not enough to reorder the territory so as to make it congruent with the borders of historically defined local societies. It is necessary to go deeper, since the attempt is to repair the problems caused by colonial history. Social structures broader than the local ones must be created in order to provide the framework needed by the civilizational impulse, which lives on confined within the communities. Memory does not have to go back very far to remember that the creation and current borders of the states that constitute the federation, in the great majority of cases, have been the result of recent historical decisions and accommodations. And with some exceptions, those divisions are not based on deep historical continuity or on the real distribution of the population. There is not a Huastec state, nor a Maya one, nor an Otomí one, although all would have ancient reasons for existing. All would constitute necessary levels of social and political organization for those peoples to modernize their own particular civilizational projects.

This is not simply a problem to be resolved by redrawing state lines. It goes much beyond that. In recognizing the fundamental ethnic basis of those political units, whether states, districts, or municipal units, we would be affirming their right to organize their internal life and their participation in national affairs in their own way. They would be organized as a function of the ideas implicit in the locally dominant cultural tradition, the tradition that in turn defines and sustains that historical group. It is not, then, a simple change of names or a matter of boundaries between states. We are speaking of a decision giving the people of the *México profundo* the right to command levels of political organization broader and more complex than the local community. Such organization would allow them to qualitatively increase their capacity for reconstruction and for cultural development.

It is essential to restructure broader levels of social organization to assure the flourishing of Mesoamerican cultures. Respect for the right of local self-determination is different from respect for the right to organize at higher levels in the political structure. Many projects cannot be carried out within the limited framework of the local community, because they require participation and cultural resources that go beyond those limits. The destruction of some of Mexico's Indian peoples has reduced them to a single community. However, there are many others that include a large number of local communities, even though today they may be relatively isolated from each other. The goal is to pick up the thread of history that was temporarily broken by colonial domination. Insofar as the situation and conditions imposed by the twenty-first century permit, the goal is to favor the reconstitution of viable sociopolitical groups.

This again has to do with the problem of our democracy, since we must guarantee these peoples effective representation in all the areas of national government decision making. There is a deep irrationality in the fact that there are two senators for each one of the many recent states, which were often created in an authoritarian way in the heat of momentary circumstances. At the same time there are millions of inhabitants of Indian communities who have no assured representation in the legislative bodies. Their representation should be as differentiated peoples with their own historical legitimacy, and not based on the fictitious "universal" individual vote.

In the current situation, the possibility of legislative and structural changes recognizing pluralism and supporting the development of local cultures and Mesoamerican civilization is very remote, since there is no authentic representation of those peoples. Their affairs and interests, when they are recognized at all, are seen only from the perspective of the West and the dominant national project. It is imperative that we break the colonial mediation. It is imperative that we let the *México profundo* speak, and that we listen to its words.

### The Inevitable Dilemma

I have tried to show that the *México profundo*, bearer of a denied civilization, embodies the distilled product of a continuous process thousands of years old, the Mesoamerican civilizational process. During the last five centuries, barely a moment in their long trajectory, Mesoamerican peoples have lived subject to a system of brutal oppression that affects all aspects of their life and their cultures. The resources used by colonial domination have been many and have varied over time. However, stigma, violence, and rejection have been constant. In spite of this, Mesoamerican civilization is present and alive, and not only in the peoples who maintain their own identity and affirm the fact of being different. It is also present in broad majority sectors of Mexican society that do not recognize themselves as being Indian, but that organize their collective life on the basis of a cultural matrix of Mesoamerican origin. All these peoples form the *México profundo*. They have been systematically ignored and denied by the imaginary Mexico, which controls power and which assumes itself to be the bearer of the only valid plan for the country's future.

I have tried to trace, more through revealing examples than in rigorous sequence, the chronicle of disaster and the memorial of ignominy. It is a chronicle of disaster insofar as the current breakdown of the illusions cherished by the imaginary Mexico is not simply momentary stumbling, attributable to external circumstances. Rather, it is the inevitable result of a long history of obstinacy in trying to replace the reality of Mexico with another reality, which is itself a poor imitation of Western models. It is a memorial of ignominy, as seen and understood from the other side, from the viewpoint of the peoples who have lived with daily violence, exploitation, contempt, and exclusion. The effort has been to subject these peoples to a civilizational project that is not their own and that does not accept them. The memorial of this history, barely sketched here, is the necessary counterpart to our vision of Mexico. It is the other leg, without which we cannot begin to walk on any path whatsoever.

I have tried to show that today's crisis is not only the crisis of Mexico, but the breakdown of a development model that ignores the *México profundo*. We have sufficient although not inexhaustible resources, and we have at our disposal a great diversity of cultural systems. These systems provide different ways in which resources can be converted into useful elements for making human life more plentiful, according to the aspirations for fulfillment implicit in each culture.

At the same time I have tried to show how the efforts to impose a single model lead to a failure to make use of what we already have. They provoke a schizophrenic situation in which reality marches along its own path while the national plans for the future march separately, along an imaginary path.

In summary, I have tried to show that faced with the collapse of the illusion it is necessary to look inward and determine our real strengths. We must recognize our resources and abilities in order to formulate a new national vision, an authentic and therefore viable one. We must use the available plans and materials to construct our new, common home.

The conclusion, in my opinion, cannot be other than to try to construct a pluralistic nation in which Mesoamerican civilization, embodied in a great variety of cultures, has the place it deserves, a place that allows it to view the West from Mexico. That is to say, we should understand and take advantage of the West's achievements, from the viewpoint of a civilization that is our own because it was forged here in this land, step by step, since remotest antiquity. That civilization is not dead, because it breathes in the heart of the *México profundo*. The adoption of a pluralist project, which recognizes the validity of the Mesoamerican civilizational process, will make us want to be what we really are and what we can be. We will be a country that pursues its own objectives, that has its own goals derived from its own underlying history. In affirming our differences, to ourselves and to outsiders, we will be radically denying the would-be hegemony of the West, which rests on the supposition that difference implies inequality and that what is different is by nature inferior.

Finally, the intention of these pages has been to suggest that the problem of civilization cannot be seen as an insignificant one, as one that can be postponed given the current circumstances. I have insisted that it *is* the problem, because within it is defined the model of the society we want to create. The decisions we must inevitably make about reorienting the country constitute a choice of civilizational project beyond the immediate political debate that takes place within the boundaries of the Western vision—that of the imaginary Mexico. If in some way these pages have stimulated the reader to reflect on these problems, whether or not he or she agrees with what I have set forth, they will have fulfilled the purpose for which they were written.

# References Cited

Aguirre Beltrán, Gonzalo
    1967    *Regiones de refugio.* Mexico City: Instituto
            Indigenista Interamericano.

Anderson, Arthur J. O., and Charles E. Dibble
    1975    *Florentine Codex. General History of the Things of*
            *New Spain,* by Fray Bernardino de Sahagún. Book 12—
            *The Conquest of Mexico.* Santa Fe, N.M.: School of
            American Research; Salt Lake City: University of
            Utah.

las Casas, Fray Bartolomé de
    1953    *Brevísima relación de la destrucción de las Indias.*
            Buenos Aires: Ediciones Mar Océano. First published
            in 1552.

Castellanos, Javier
    1982    El cultivo del maíz en Yojovi, Villa Alta, Oaxaca. In
            *Nuestro maíz,* vol. I. Mexico City: Museo Nacional de
            Culturas Populares.

Chávez, Adrián I.
    1979    *Pop Wuj (Libro de Acontecimientos). Traducción*
            *directa del manuscrito del padre Jiménez.* Mexico
            City: Ediciones de La Casa Chata, Centro de
            Investigaciones Superiores del INAH.

Cook, Sherburne F., and Woodrow Borah
    1977    *Ensayos sobre historia de la población: México y el*
            *Caribe,* vol. I, Prefacio. Mexico City: Siglo XXI.

Florescano, Enrique, and Isabel Gómez Gil
    1976    La época de las reformas borbónicas y el crecimiento
            económico, 1750–1808. In *Historia general de México,*
            vol. II, pp. 183–301. Mexico City: El Colegio de
            México.

Gamio, Manuel
 1960    *Forjando patria*. Mexico City: Editorial Porrúa. First
         published in 1916.

Gibson, Charles
 1964    *The Aztecs under Spanish Rule: A History of the
         Indians of the Valley of Mexico, 1519–1810*. Stanford,
         Calif.: Stanford University Press.

González, Luis
 1976    El liberalismo triunfante. In *Historia general de
         México*, vol. III, pp. 163–281. Mexico City: El Colegio
         de México.

González Navarro, Moisés
 1954    Instituciones indígenas en México independiente. In
         *Métodos y resultados de la política indigenista en
         México*. Mexico City: Memorias del Instituto
         Nacional Indigenista, vol. VI.

Guzmán Bockler, Carlos
 1970    El ladino: un ser ficticio. In *Guatemala: una
         interpretación histórico-social*, by Carlos Guzmán
         Bockler and Jean-Loup Herbert, pp. 101–121. Mexico
         City: Siglo XXI.

Herrera y Tordesillas, Antonio de
 1944–   *Historia general de los hechos de los castellanos en
 1947    las islas y tierra firme del mar océano*. Asunción del
         Paraguay: Editoria Guaranía.

Katz, Friedrich
 1972    *The Ancient American Civilizations*. New York:
         Praeger. First published in 1969.

Kirchhoff, Paul
 1967    *Mesoamérica. Sus límites geográficas, composición
         étnica y caracteres culturales*. Suplemento de la
         Revista Tlatoani. Escuela Nacional de Antropología e
         Historia. Originally published in 1943.

Lafaye, Jacques
 1977    *Quetzalcóatl y Guadalupe. La formación de la
         conciencia nacional en México*. Mexico City: Fondo
         de Cultura Económica. First published in 1974.

Martínez, José Luis
 1976    México en busca de su expresión. In *Historia general
         de México*, vol. III, pp. 283–331. Mexico City: El
         Colegio de México.

Mendizábal, Miguel Othón de
 1929    *Influencia de la sal en la distribución geográfica de*

*los grupos indígenas de México.* Mexico City: Imprenta del Museo Nacional de Arqueología, Historia y Etnografía.

Molina Enríquez, Andrés
1909     *Los grandes problemas nacionales.* Mexico City: Imprenta de A. Carranza e Hijos.

Monsiváis, Carlos
1976     Notas sobre la cultura mexicana en el siglo XX. In *Historia general de México,* vol. IV, pp. 303–476. Mexico City: El Colegio de México.

Moreno Toscano, Alejandra
1976     El siglo de la conquista. In *Historia general de México,* vol. II, pp. 1–81. Mexico City: El Colegio de México.

Muñoz Camargo, Diego
1947     *Historia de Tlaxcala.* Mexico City: Publicaciones del Ateneo Nacional de Ciencias y Artes de México. First published in 1892.

Museo Nacional de Culturas Populares
1982     *Nuestro maíz.* Mexico City: Museo Nacional de Culturas Populares.

Paz, Octavio
1977     Prefacio: entre orfandad y legitimidad. Preface to *Quetzalcóatl y Guadalupe,* by Jacques Lafaye, pp. 11–25. Mexico City: Fondo de Cultura Económica.

Ricard, Robert
1947     *La conquista espiritual de México.* Trans. Ángel María Garibay K. Mexico City: Editorial Jus/Polis. First published in 1933.

Ruz, Alberto
1981     *El pueblo maya.* Mexico City: Salvat Mexicana de Ediciones, Fundación Cultural San Jerónimo Lídice.

Wolf, Eric
1959     *Sons of the Shaking Earth.* Chicago and London: University of Chicago Press.

Womack, John, Jr.
1969     *Zapata and the Mexican Revolution.* New York: Knopf.

Zavala, Silvio, and José Miranda
1954     Instituciones indígenas en la colonia. In *Métodos y resultados de la política indigenista en México.* Mexico City: Memorias del Instituto Nacional Indigenista, vol. VI.

# Bibliographic Appendix

As I indicated in the Introduction, the purpose of this Appendix is to give general readers an initial orientation to works that will allow them to delve more deeply into some of the major points dealt with in these pages. For this reason it does not pretend to be an exhaustive bibliography and does not even list all the works that were helpful in the writing of this book. I have marked with an asterisk (*) the texts from which direct quotations have been taken, so that the interested reader can corroborate them and go beyond the quotes in the text itself.

### General Works

The collection of works about Mexican history that was most useful is the *Historia general de México*, published in four volumes by El Colegio de México in 1976. I made particular use of the chapters by Alejandra Moreno, Enrique Florescano and Isabel Gómez Gil, Luis González, Carlos Monsiváis, and José Luis Martínez. Two works deal specifically with the history of *indigenista* policy in Mexico: *Métodos y resultados de la política indigenista en México*, published in 1954 by the Instituto Nacional Indigenista, with selections by Alfonso Caso, Silvio Zavala and José Miranda, Moisés González Navarro, Gonzalo Aguirre Beltrán, and Ricardo Pozas; and *La política del lenguaje en México: de la colonia a la nación*, by Shirley Brice Heath, published by the INI in 1972. A pioneering book to which I owe inspiration and orientation on various subjects is by Eric Wolf: *Pueblos y culturas de Mesoamérica* (Editorial ERA, 1967). A more recent work is by Gonzalo Aguirre Beltrán: *Lenguas vernáculas, su uso y desuso en la enseñanza: la experiencia de México* (Ediciones de la Casa Chata, CIESAS, 1983).

### Precolonial Mesoamerican Civilization

Of the interpretations of the Mesoamerican civilizational process, the ones that seem most complete to me are the book by Eric Wolf already

cited and the section about Mexico in *The Ancient American Civilizations*, by Friedrich Katz, published in London in 1972 by Weidenfeld and
Nicholson and unfortunately not yet translated into Spanish. A classic
paper by Paul Kirchhoff is *Mesoamérica: sus límites geográficos,
composición étnica y caracteres culturales*, published by the SAENAH
in 1960. Other general works are *Agricultura y sociedad en Mesoamérica*,
by Ángel Palerm (SEPSETENTAS, 1972); *Una visión del México
prehispánico*, by Román Piña Chan (UNAM, 1967); and the volumes
published by the INAH under the collective title *México: panorama
histórico y cultural*, written by various specialists.

The Aztec world is the best documented. Among the more compre-
hensive general works can be cited *El Pueblo del Sol*, by Alfonso Caso
(Lecturas Mexicanas, FEC-SEP, 1983); *Los antiguos mexicanos a través
de sus crónicas y cantares*, by Miguel León Portilla (Lecturas Mexicanas,
FCE-SEP, 1983); *Pensamiento y religión en el México antiguo*, by
Laurette Séjourné (Lecturas Mexicanas, FCE-SEP, 1983); *Tenochtitlan
en una isla*, by Ignacio Bernal (INAH, 1959); and *La vida cotidiana de los
aztecas en vísperas de la Conquista*, by Jacques Soustelle (FCE, 1956).

Regarding Maya culture I highly recommend the last work by Alberto
Ruz, *El pueblo maya* (Salvat y Fundación Cultural San Jerónimo Lídice,
1981). It is also essential to consult the *Pop Wuj* in the direct translation
by Adrián I. Chávez (Ediciones de La Casa Chata, CISINAH, 1979).
About the Otomí there is the book by Pedro Carrasco, *Los otomíes:
Cultura e historia prehispánicas de los pueblos mesoaméricanos de
habla otomiana*, published by the UNAM in 1950.

Some recent works that may provide more information about particular aspects of Mesoamerican civilization are *Historia de la agricultura:
época prehispánica*, edited by Teresa Rojas Rabiela and William T.
Sanders, published in two volumes by the INAH in 1985; and *Formación
del estado en el México prehispánico*, by Brigitte Boehm de Lameiras (El
Colegio de Michoacán, 1986).

Of course, the work of the chroniclers and conquistadors is essential
to consult, but one should not forget that their vision of precolonial
Mexico is necessarily and fundamentally distorted by the colonializing
roles their authors played.

### The Colonial Regime

Apart from the appropriate sections included in the general works
mentioned at the beginning of the Appendix, the reader will find the
following titles of interest: *Los aztecas bajo el dominio español (1519–
1810)*, by Charles Gibson (Siglo XXI, 1967); *Quetzalcóatl y Guadalupe:*

*la formación de la conciencia nacional en México,* by Jacques Lafaye (FCE, 1977); *La conquista espiritual de México,* by Robert Ricard (Jus/Polis, 1947) (however, the translator decided to omit paragraphs from the original text in French, thinking them unsuitable); *Rebeliones indígenas de la época colonial,* María Teresa Huerta and Patricia Palacios, eds. (SEP-INAH, 1976).

## The Nineteenth Century

For the central theme of this book, especially for government policy toward the peoples of Mesoamerican civilization, the work of Moisés González Navarro cited in the section on general works is essential. Another work by the same author that should be read is *Raza y tierra: la guerra de castas y el henequén* (El Colegio de México, 1970), and an inseparable companion work, *La guerra de castas en Yucatán,* by Nelson Reed (ERA, 1976). A general view from the middle of the century is found in *La estructura económica y social de México en la época de la reforma,* by Francisco López Cámara (Siglo XXI, 1967). The Indian presence in the city is studied by Andrés Lira in *Comunidades indígenas frente a la ciudad de México* (El Colegio de México, 1983). For the Indian rebellions, see *Movimientos campesinos en México durante el siglo XIX,* by Leticia Reyna.

## Contemporary Indian Cultures

On this subject the bibliography is very large. Unfortunately, there is no ethnographic compendium in Spanish that presents a satisfactory panorama of contemporary Indian cultures. The best summaries are in the works by Eric Wolf and Gonzalo Aguirre Beltrán and Ricardo Pozas, previously cited. Also by Aguirre Beltrán are *Formas de gobierno indígena* (UNAM, 1953), and *Medicina y magia* (INI, 1963), which give general views of these topics. The best source of information is found in numerous monographs that describe the cultures of particular communities. The Instituto Nacional Indigenista (INI) has published more than seventy titles by Mexican and foreign authors that cover a broad spectrum of the country's ethnographic panorama. In their character as classics of Mexican ethnography, the following should be mentioned: *Yalálag: una villa zapoteca serrana,* by Julio de la Fuente; *Los peligros del alma: visión del mundo de un tzotzil,* by Calixta Guiteras Holmes (FCE, 1965); *Chamula, un pueblo indio de los Altos de Chiapas* (INI, 1959); and *Los elegidos de Dios: etnografía de los mayas de Quintana Roo* (INI, 1978), by Alfonso Villa Rojas. For understanding the importance of corn in indigenous communities, see the testimonials brought together in *Nuestro maíz*, in two volumes (Museo Nacional de Culturas Populares, Mexico City, 1982).

## *Indigenismo* and Indian Problems

The pioneer work is *Forjando patria*, by Manuel Gamio (Porrúa, 1960). The best historical analysis is by Luis Villoro, *Los grandes momentos del indigenismo en México*. The theoretical foundations of *indigenismo* are formulated by Gonzalo Aguirre Beltrán in two works: *El proceso de aculturación* (UNAM, 1957) and *Regiones de refugio* (Instituto Indigenista Interamericano, 1967). Among early works critical of *indigenismo* are *Las clases sociales en las sociedades agrarias*, by Rodolfo Stavenhagen (Siglo XXI, 1969); *Los indios en las clases sociales de México*, by Ricardo Pozas and Isabel H. de Pozas (Siglo XXI, 1971); and *De eso que llaman antropología mexicana*, by Arturo Warman et al. (Nuestro Tiempo, 1970). Regarding the new Indian political movements, there is my book, *Utopía y revolución: el pensamiento político contemporáneo de los indios en América Latina* (Nueva Imagen, 1981), and the *Cuadernos de CADAL* (Centro Antropológico de Documentación para América Latina). The theoretical framework that served as a basis for the structure of this book was developed in my essay "La teoría del control cultural en el estudio de procesos étnicos," *Papeles de La Casa Chata* 3 (CIESAS, 1987).

# Index

*Acción integral indigenista,* 118–120
Acosta, Father José de, 12
Advertising, 154
Agave plant, 11–12, 49
Agriculture: agrarian reform, 64, 108, 111, 112, 121; appropriation in, 137; and capitalism, 46; collective agriculture, 122; and concept of time, 38; development of, 4–6; diversified cultivation, 121, 125; for export, 153–154; Indian agriculture, 25–26, 94, 125; mechanization of, 125; of Mesoamerican civilization, 4, 11–12, 46, 47, 127, 154; and missionaries, 84; modern methods of, 115, 153; and natural resources, 11; as principal economic base, 7, 32, 44; production for industry, 153–154; and self-sufficiency, 28; tools used in, 26; and tributary system, 93. *See also* Corn
Aguirre Beltrán, Gonzalo, 24, 92, 118, 119
Alamán, Lucas, 106
*Alcaldes mayores,* 90, 93, 95
Alcoholism, 82
*Alegría,* 12
Altamirano, Ignacio M., 105, 107
Anáhuac, 80, 97
Apaches, 99
Appropriation, and cultural resistance, 135–138, 139, 143
Archaeology, 3, 54, 55, 113
Architecture, 113

Art: depiction of Indian in, 53–55; of Indians of Mexico, 148; murals, 54, 55, 113, 114; nationalistic character of, 53, 112–113. *See also* Handicraft production
Augustine, Saint, 84
Augustinians, 83, 84
Autonomous Department of Indian Affairs, 117
*Ayuntamiento,* 44
*Azada,* 26
Azcapotzalco, 71
Aztecs: and colonial domination, 78; ethnic identity of, 76; glorification of, 113; and Mesoamerican religion, 9; museum exhibits, 54; and Náhutalization, 87; and precolonial domination, 71–74

Banderas, Juan, 99
Barrios, 30, 45, 48–49
Beans, 11, 25
*Benemérito,* 101
Blacks, 42–43, 79, 85
Boas, Franz, 115
Bockler, Guzmán, 51
Bolaños Cacho, Manuel, 104
Bone setters, 45
"The Book of Events," 4–5
Borah, Woodrow, 81
Bourbon Reforms, 95
Bourbons, 100
*Bracerismo,* 154
Buddha, 114

*Caciques*, 78, 82, 89–90, 92, 171
Calles, Plutarco Elias, 108
*Calpixque*, 73
*Calpulli*, 71
*Campadrazgo*, 52
Campesinos: and government participation, 109; and Indian culture, 58; replacement of, 46; and Revolution of 1910, 112, 115; self-sufficiency of, 155; and technological modernization, 121; and underdeveloped nation status, 164
Canals, 6, 10, 26
Canary Island immigrants, 102
Capitalism: and agriculture, 46; and imposed culture, 143; and Indian self-sufficiency, 28; and Indian social organization, 36, 37; in Mexico, 121; and Mexico City, 156; and substitution project, 164. *See also* Economics
Cárdenas, Lázaro, 64, 108, 117, 122
*Cargos*: and capitalism, 37; organization of, 35, 136, 140, 171; priests' system of, 85; in rural communities, 45, 52; social authority of, 36
Caso, Alfonso, 119
*Castas*, 79, 91, 97, 103
Caste distinctions, 16
Castellanos, Javier, 141–142
Castellanos, Manuel, 101
Catholic Church: and anticlerical legislation, 65; and appropriation, 135–136; and colonial system, 75, 83–88; economic control of, 94; popular Catholicism, 136, 149. *See also* Priests; Protestantism; Religion
Cattle ranching: and haciendas, 92; and Indian land, 42, 52, 124, 154; stimulation of, 121
Central America, 98
Central Mexico, 6–7
Centralists, 99–100
Certificates of inaffectability, 121
Chac, 74
Chapultepec Park, 54
Chávez, Adrián I., 5, 7
Chiapas, 7, 130, 148

Chichén, 7, 70
*Chichimeca*, 24, 76. *See also* Nomadic northern Indians
Chihuahua, 99
Children, 30, 134, 135
Chiles, 11, 25
*Chinampas*, 6, 10, 26, 93
Chinese immigrants, 102
Cholula, 7, 80
Chontales, 7
Christ, 114
Christianity: and colonial domination, 75; and evangelization, 85–87, 89; and Indian nobility, 83; and popular religion, 136; and racial issues, 18; and Western civilization, 57. *See also* Catholic Church; Protestantism; Religion
Cihuacóatl, 54, 71
Cities: and colonial power, 47, 52; and education, 105; growth of, 51, 122, 124; housing of, 49–50; and imaginary Mexico, 122, 156; Indian culture in, xviii, 47–53, 55–57; and *indigenismo*, 118; industry in, 121; mestizo migration to, 51–52; rebellions in, 130–131; in refuge regions, 50; segregation in, 48; and television, 123. *See also* Mexico City; Urban life
Civilization: confrontations between, xv, 57, 59, 61–62; and democracy, 167–169; differing paths of, 103; national program for, 163–167; new vision for, xvii; and pluralism, 169–174; in precolonial Mexico, 9–10, 70–75. *See also* Mesoamerican civilization; Western civilization
Civilizational project, 161–162, 176
Classic period, 6, 70
Clavijero, Francisco Javier, 96
Clothing, 45, 106, 141
CNPI (Consejo Nacional de Pueblos Indígenas), 145
Coahuila, 105
Codices, 54
*Cofradías*, 85, 138. *See also* Saints
Collective agriculture, 122

Colonial domination: and cities, 47, 52; as common experience, 24; compared with precolonial domination, 71–76; continuing effects of, 58; and cultural control, 67–68, 70–76; and cultural diversity, 65; and democracy, 166; and destruction of Mesoamerican civilization, 62, 172; effects on Indians of Mexico, 22–23, 76–79, 88–93; and European settlements, 48; and imaginary Mexico, xix; and Indian culture, 129; and Indian relations, 42, 79; Indian resistance to, 22, 129–135, 139, 160–161; and Indian social organization, 23; and Indian territorial distribution, 25; justification of, 62; and knowledge base, 159; and ladino cultural identity, 51; and *México profundo*, 132, 134–135, 159–160, 174; and national culture, 67; rejection of innovations from, 134–135; and religion, 75, 80–81, 83–88; and segregation, 63; and urban colonial power, 47; violence of, 79–83; and Western civilization, 64. *See also* Dominant society

Colonial society: duality of, 78–79; and Indian languages, 20; of New Spain, 94; and racial subjugation, 16, 24; and segregation, 16–17; social hierarchy of, 18, 61; structure of, xvi; view of Indian culture, 8–9, 133

Comanches, 99

Commercial interchanges: and ecological niches, 6; and European settlements, 48; free trade, 101; and Indian exploitation, 93; of Indians of Mexico, 32, 70; international, 154; local control of, 147–148; markets, 32, 49, 72, 94; under Aztec domination, 72–73. *See also* Economics

Communal land. *See* Indian land

Communal life. *See* Social organization

*Compadres*, 52, 137, 138, 143

*Concheros*, 49

*Congregaciones*, 82

Consejo Nacional de Pueblos Indígenas (CNPI), 145

Conservatives, 63, 106

Constitution of Apatzingán, 96

Constitution of Cádiz, 97

Constitution of 1917, 64, 108

*El Consulado de comerciantes*, 95

Consumption, 121, 154, 163–164, 167

Cook, Sherburne F., 81

COPLAMAR, 120

Corn: cultivation of, 4, 8, 44; haciendas' exploitation of, 92; importation of, 153; indigenous classification of, 14; invention of, 11; and *milpas*, 25; scarcity of, 131

Corporal punishment, 82–83, 101

*Corregidores*, 90, 91

Cortés, Hernán, 80, 82, 89

Cosío Villegas, Daniel, 114

Council of 1555, 85

Counter Reformation, 87

Crayfish, 49

Creel, Enrique C., 103

Creoles: and colonial administration, 94; and Counter-Reformation, 87; and ideology of mestizo Mexico, 106, 110; mestizos mistaken for, 79; and Mexican independence, xix, 94–98; nationalism of, 95, 113; as power group, xv; rejection of, 111; view of Indian, 102

*Cuatequitl*, 91

Cuauhtémoc, 113

Cuba, 99

Cuban immigrants, 102

*Cues*, 86

Cult of the talking crosses, 131

Cultural control: and colonial domination, 67–68, 70–76; of cultural elements, 135; and democracy, 168; and imposed culture, 139–144; and Indians of Mexico, 112, 119, 135; and mass media, 123–124; and Revolution of 1910, 108; rewards of, 109–110; theory of, xx

Cultural diversity: of Indian culture,

22–23, 41; and land, 41–42; of Mexican society, 41–44, 57–58, 61, 116, 158–162; and national culture, 65; as obstacle to progress, 62; and pluralism project, 166–167, 168; in rural communities, 44–47

Cultural elements: and appropriation, 137–138, 139; control of, 135; of imposed culture, 132; preservation of, 119; and Western civilization, 167

Cultural homogeneity, 110, 116

Cultural matrix, 143–144, 174

Cultural *mestizaje*, 17, 24, 110, 128, 165

Cultural missions, 117, 120

Cultural patrimony: as cultural capital, xvii, 67; differences in, 119; of imaginary Mexico, 103; of Indians of Mexico, 40, 45, 139; of *México profundo*, 67, 132; of oppressed groups, 136; and Revolution of 1910, 110; separation from, 18

Cultural relativism, 115

Cultural schizophrenia, 56–58, 65–67, 69

Cultural traits: and civilization, 10; and cultural regions, 42; and de-Indianization, 17; of Mesoamerican civilization, 8, 41

Cultural unity: and colonial domination, 61–63, 65, 67; and cultural control, 68–69; and elimination of Mesoamerican culture, 62, 66; and Western civilization, 63–66

*Curandero*, 142

Customary law, 127, 140

Dams, 6, 26

Day of the Dead, 49

De-Indianization: as civilizing, 105; and cultural continuity, 24, 42; and education, 105; and haciendas, 44; and Indians in cities, 53; as integration, 115, 116, 119; and mestizos, 17–18; of rural communities, 45–46; special programs preventing, 146; and youth, 145

Dead-letter laws, 65

Democracy: and civilization, 167–169; and colonial domination, 166; and imaginary Mexico, 127–128; in Mexica society, 71; and Mexico, 169; and pluralism project, 168; and representation, 174; and Western civilization, 66. *See also* Government; Politics

Departamento Autónomo de Asuntos Indígenas, 117

Díaz, Porfirio: attitude toward Indian, 99, 105; and immigration, 102; and indentured servants systems, 65; overthrow of, 64, 108–111; and peace, 97

Díaz Zulueta, José, 103

Diego, Juan, 95

Diet. *See* Foods

Domestic animals, 12, 26, 28

Dominant society: and appropriation, 137; and cultural control, 124; dependence on, 121; and imposed culture, 144; Indian use of cultural elements, 131; and political life, 127–128; and precolonial domination, 70–75; pressures on ethnic groups, 46, 143; and traditional rites, 133–134. *See also* Colonial domination

Dominicans, 83

Echeverría period, 123

Ecological niches: alteration of, 124; and commercial interchanges, 6; conservation of, 156; and cultural development, 8, 42, 45; diversity of, 42, 72

Economics: and agriculture, 7, 32, 44; and Catholic Church, 94; development of, 115; economic regions of Mexico, 42; foreign debt, 156; and foreign interests, 108; of Indians of Mexico, 26, 28–32, 36, 127; and indigenous problem, 117; informal economy, 155; and land, 33; and middle class, 123; mixed economy, 121; monetary economy, 89, 93,

155; post–World War II, 121; and substitution project, 163. *See also* Capitalism; Commercial interchanges; Self-sufficiency

Education: as achievement of revolution, 126; higher education, 126, 146, 147; and imaginary Mexico, 105, 126, 146; and imposed culture, 141, 143; and Indian culture, 146; and Indian languages, 114, 146; of Indians, 52, 105, 115, 117–118, 120, 145–146; and indigenous problem, 117; and *México profundo*, 126; of middle class, 122; rural school system, 117; of Vasconcelos, 114

*Ejido* lands, 44, 124. *See also* Indian land

El Nacimiento, 24

Elites: discontent of, 157; and Indian culture, 55–56; and Indians in cities, 53; and racial issues, 18

*Encomienda* system: conflicts with priests, 81, 83; development of, 89; and forced labor, 82, 90; rebellions against, 130; view of Indian, 101; and Yucatan, 99. *See also* Tributary systems

Endogamy, 30–31

English immigrants, 102

Environmental protection zones, 124

Epidemics, 81–82

*Espeque*, 26

Ethnic groups: Aztecs as, 76; extinction of, 23, 46; Gamio's views on, 116; Indians of Mexico as, 21–22, 45; of Mexico, 41–44, 61–69; pressures from dominant society, 46, 143. *See also* Indians of Mexico; Mestizos

Ethnic pluralism, 120

European aristocratic refugees, 122

European immigrants, 103, 105

European invasion, 3, 8–9, 12, 61, 79

Exports, 121, 153–154

Fairs, 32

*Fajina*, 31

Family, 29–30, 37, 49–50

*Fatiga*, 31

Fauna, 12

Federalists, 99–100

Fernando VII, 96

Fiestas, 49, 52, 133, 136

First Congress of Indian Peoples, 144–145

*Fiscal*, 136

Fishing, 26, 28

Florescano, Enrique, 94

Flour mills, 91

Foods, 5, 26, 46, 49, 51

Forced labor: and *encomienda* system, 81, 82, 89, 90; and Indian communities, 91–92; and Indian population, 24, 82, 90; rebellions against, 130; and *repartimiento*, 78, 82, 90–91. *See also* Labor

Foreign debt, 156

Formative period, 5

France, 96, 97, 127

Franciscans, 83, 84, 85

Free enterprise, 101

Free trade, 101

French settlers, 42–43, 102

Fuente, Julio, 119

Fusion project, 165

*Gachupines*, 102

Gamio, Manuel, 114, 115–117

Gante, Pedro de, 85

*Gente de razón*, 20, 50, 98, 140

Geographical names, 13–15

German immigrants, 102

Gibson, Charles, 82, 84, 90, 100

Gilberti, Maturino, 84

Godparenthood, 137, 138, 143, 152

Gómez Gil, Isabel, 94

Gómez Morín, Manuel, 113

González, Luis, 101

González Navarro, Moisés, 94, 99, 101, 102, 104, 105

Government: bureaucratic power of, 109; and Indian political organizations, 144–145; of Indians of Mexico, 35–37; rebellions against, 130; and Revolution of 1910, 109; in rural communities, 44–45. *See*

*also* Democracy; Politics; Social organization
Grapes, 92
Great Chichimeca, 24
Guadalupana, 95
*Guadalupanismo*, 95
Guadalupe, Treaty of, 99
Guatemala, 51
Guilds, 91
Gulf of Nicoya, 7

Haciendas: and corporal punishment, 82; and de-Indianization process, 44; indentured servant systems of, 65; and Indian land, 92; and Indians of Mexico, 100; labor force for, 91; in New Spain, 94; and priests, 93; rebellions against, 130; in Yucatan, 99
Handicraft production: appropriation in, 137; and commercial interchange, 32–33; commercialization of, 55, 147–148; of mestizos, 44; and nationalism of Revolution, 113; and self-sufficiency, 28, 44
Henequen exports, 99
Herbalists, 34, 45, 49. *See also* Medicine
Herrera y Tordesillas, Antonio de, 130
Higher education, 126, 146, 147
Holy Office, 85
Honduras, 7
Huastec Indians, 25
*Huauzontles*, 49
Huey Tlatoani, 71
Huichols, 140
*Huipiles*, 44
Huitzilopochtli, 9, 73
Human beings, interrelationship with nature, 10–13, 15
Human sacrifice, 74
Hunting, 26, 28
Hunting and gathering societies, 4, 8

Imaginary Mexico: aspirations of, 103; and cities, 122, 156; and colonial domination, xix; and democracy, 127–128; development model of, 67, 120, 153–158, 175; and education, 105, 126, 146; failure of, xvii, xviii; and fusion project, 165; Gamio as spokesperson for, 117; and imposed culture, 140; Indian participation in, 155; and individualism, 160; Liberal policies of, 100; and marginalization of majority, 65–66, 122; new face of, 120–128; participation in Revolution of 1910, 111; and racial subjugation, 146; relations with *México profundo*, xvi, 67, 69, 106, 125, 128, 141, 174; views on Indians, 104; and Western civilization, xvi, 107. *See also* Dominant society; Mexico
Immigrants, 102–103, 105
Import substitution, 121
Imposed culture, 132, 139–144
Indentured servant systems, 65
Independence. *See* Mexican independence
Indian communities, 53, 64, 91–92
Indian culture: and acculturation, 45; and affirmation of group, 133; and agriculture, 25–26; and appropriation, 137; and art, 53–55; autonomy of, 39–40, 135; and *cargo* system, 36–37; changing nature of, 139; in cities, xviii, 47–53, 55–57; and colonial domination, 129; and commercial interchange, 32–33; and concept of time, 38–39; cultural patrimony of, 18, 40; and cultural schism, 57–58; definition of, 19–23; diversity of, 22–23, 41; and education, 146; and elites, 55–56; and family, 30–31, 37; folkloric vision of, 128; and imposed culture, 139–144; ladino adoption of, 51; and land, 33–34; and medicine, 34–35; and middle class, 56–57; modernization of, 149; and nature, 27, 37–38; preservation of, 119; profile of, 23–40; and rebellions, 131; rejection of, 18; and religion, 38–39; and

resistance, 132–138; and ruling groups, 64; in rural communities, 44–47; and self–sufficiency, 28–29, 31–33, 37, 39; and settlement patterns, 31; and territorial distribution, 24–25; uniformity of, 78; value of, 116; and work organization, 29–30, 31, 38. *See also* Social organization

Indian land: break up of, 100–101; and cattle ranching, 42, 52, 124, 154; as communal property, 33, 37, 103; defense of, 158–159; loss of, 92, 143; and Mexican expansion, 124; and population distribution, 24; and rebellions, 130; renting of, 90; and sacred sites, 33–34; and self–sufficiency, 34

Indian languages: census data on, 20; in cities, 49; diversity of, 105; and education, 114, 146; and evangelization, 86–87; geographical names in, 13–15; and geographical place names, 13–15; ladino adoption of, 51; and Mesoamerican civilization, 8; and mestizo Spanish, 17; in Mexico City, 52; number of, 22; publishing in, 148; and resistance, 138–139; in rural communities, 45; women as transmitters of, 139; and women's role, 29–30

Indian population: census data on, 20, 22; decline in, 81–82, 90; and *encomienda* system, 82, 90; precolonial, 15–16; recuperation of, 92, 106, 120; territorial distribution of, 24

Indian resistance: and appropriation, 135–138, 139, 143; armed, 130–132, 139; to colonial domination, 22, 129–132, 139, 160–161; culture of resistance, 132–135, 143; daily strategies of, xvii, 132–139; and *indigenismo*, 120; and innovations, 134–135, 138, 139, 143; linguistic, 138–139; and Mesoamerican civilization, 58; and political organiza-

tions, 144–148; rebellions, 102, 130; and Revolution of 1910, 64; and self–sufficiency, 135

Indians of Mexico: agriculture of, 25–26, 94, 125; in art, 53–54; census data on, 20; and children, 30; in cities, 47–53; classification of natural world, 38; and colonial domination, 22–24, 25, 42, 76–79, 88–93; colonization of northern Mexico, 98; commercial interchanges of, 32, 70; conditions of, 101; conflicts between, 82; contemporary reality of, 39–40; decision-making abilities of, 67–68, 132, 135, 139; and democracy, 174; discrimination against, 18; economics of, 26, 28–32, 36–37; education of, 52, 105, 115, 117–118, 120, 145–146; as enemy to Mexico, 103–107; genetic traits of, 15–18; government of, 35–37; and haciendas, 100; ideological exaltation of, 53–54, 95, 96, 113; and imposed culture, 139–144; as inferior, 77, 84, 96, 101, 104, 105, 115, 141; kinship relations, 30, 37; as labor force, 24, 47, 62; local community organization of, 23, 78, 129, 169–170, 172; marginalization of, 65–66; and medicine, 34–35; and Mesoamerican civilization, 3; and mestizos, 17, 111; and Mexican independence, 96, 98; in Mexico City, 48; migration to cities, 51–52; military recruitment of, 104–105; and monetary economy, 89–90; new sector of, 147; and politics, 52, 144–149; prejudice against, 19, 53; press of, 148; as priests, 85; religious domination of, 83–88; and revolutionary Mexico, 111, 112, 114–120; segregation of, 62; self-determination of, 119; as slaves, 82; social organization of, 20–21, 30, 47, 119; somatic traits of, 15; and Spaniards, 77; and underdeveloped nation status, 164; values of, 21; and Western

civilization, 62–63. *See also* Forced labor; Nomadic northern Indians; Self–sufficiency; *headings beginning with* Indian; *and names of specific tribes*
Indigenismo, 53, 115–120, 145, 147
Indigenous Coordinating Centers, 118
Indigenous languages. *See* Indian languages
Indigo, 92
Individualism: and imaginary Mexico, 103, 160; and Indian values, 36–37; and liberals, 65, 100; of Protestantism, 125; in urban life, 50
Industrial development, 121, 124, 153–155, 163
Informal economy, 155
Infrastructure, 121
INI (Instituto Nacional Indigenista), 117, 119, 120
Innovations, and cultural resistance, 134–135, 138, 139, 144
Inquisition, 85
Instituto Nacional Indigenista, 117, 119, 120
Integral indigenous action, 118–120
Integration: and de-Indianization, 115, 116, 119, 120; of Mestizos, 110–111; of *México profundo*, 114
International Monetary Fund, 156
International School of American Archaeology and Ethnography, 115
Irrigation water, 92
Italian immigrants, 43, 102
Itzás, 7
Itzcóatl, 71

Jalisco, 106
Jesuits, 87–88, 93, 106
Juárez, Benito, 105

Katz, Friedrich, 71, 73
Kickapoo, 105
Kinship relations, 30, 37. *See also* Family
Kirchhoff, Paul, 7–8
Kukulkán, 74

La Mesilla, Treaty of, 99
Labor: *bracerismo*, 154; and dominant society, 46; forced, 24, 78, 81, 82, 89, 90–92; free, 91; indentured servant systems, 65; Indians of Mexico as, 24, 47, 62, 78, 81, 88; migratory, 147; wage labor, 44 91, 46, 140
Labor unions, 109, 121
Ladinos, 50, 51, 119, 147
Lafaye, Jacques, 86, 95, 96
Lake Nicaragua, 7
Land: and cultural diversity, 41–42; erosion of, 92; and independence, 97; landowning oligarchy, 108; in rural communities, 44; and tributes to Spain, 89; and violence, 125. *See also* Indian land
Languages: distribution of, 8; of elites, 56; as ethnic identifier, 45; indigenous origins of, 14; in precolonial Mexico, 74; of rural communities, 45. *See also* Indian languages; Náhuatl; Spanish language
Las Casas, Bartolomé de, 81
Law: anticlerical legislation, 65; customary, 127, 140; dead-letter laws, 65; Laws of Cádiz, 100; Laws of the Reform, 100
Left, proposals of, 157
Legal equality, 100
Lerma River, 7
Liberals: and colonizing northern Mexico, 98; and cultural homogeneity, 110; and Indians of Mexico, 101, 105; and individualism, 65; and legal equality, 100; and mestizos, 110–111; and private property, 100; and Western civilization, 63
Literature, 114
Local community organization, 23, 78, 129, 169–170, 172. *See also* Social organization
Luther, Martin, 75

*Macehuales*, 71, 78
Madrid, Miguel de la, 120
Magazines, 123

Maguey, 11–12, 92

Manifesto of the Union of Technical Workers, Painters, and Sculptors, 113

*Maquiladoras*, 154

Marginalization, 65–66, 127

Markets, 32, 49, 72, 94. *See also* Commercial interchange

Marroquín, Alejandro, 119

Martínez, José Luis, 105, 107

Mass media, 123–124

*Matlazáhuatl*, 81

Maximilian, 101

Maya Indians: glorification of, 113; and lack of military domination, 70; population of, 23; religion of, 74; and Toltecs, 7; under Aztec domination, 72; and War of the Castes, 131; in Yucatan, 6, 99

Mayo, 99

*Mayordomías*, 35–36, 49, 136

Media, 123–124

Medicine: appropriation in, 137; bone setters, 45; herbalists, 34, 45, 49; and imposed culture, 141, 142; of Indians of Mexico, 34–35, 115, 120; and indigenous problem, 117; and medicinal plants, 127; in rural communities, 45, 46; vaccinations, 134, 135

Merchants, 94, 95

Mesoamerican civilization: agricultural tradition of, 4, 11–12, 46, 47, 127, 154; attacks on language, 138; categorized as Indian, 76–79; and Catholicism, 136; in cities, 49; co-existence with Western civilization, xv, 159; and colonial domination, 62, 172; confrontation with Western civilization, xv–xvi, 57–58, 59, 61, 70, 166; and cultural control, 70; cultural heritage of, 3, 24, 39, 41; development of, 4–10; effects of colonial domination, 23; and fusion project, 165; Gamio's views of, 116; and higher education, 126; and imposed culture, 141;

and Indian languages, 13–15; invalidation of, xvi; and media, 124; and medicine, 115; and Mexican cultural diversity, 41; and *México profundo*, 1, 174; and monoculture, 125; and nature, 10–13, 27; and nomadic northern groups, 9, 24; as obstacle to progress, 62; and pluralism project, 168, 170, 175–176; political domination in, 72–73, 74–75; population distribution of, 24–25; and Protestantism, 148; racial composition of, 15–18; religious systems of, 9, 73–74; and *repartimientos*, 90–91; in rural communities, 47; and social hierarchy, 43; and Spanish evangelism, 85; and substitution project, 163, 165; viability of, 149. *See also* Civilization; Indians of Mexico; *México profundo*

*Mestizaje*, 17, 24, 110, 128, 165

Mestizos: in colonial society, 79; and de-Indianization, 17–18; and fusion project, 165; ideology of, 106; and independence, 96; integration of, 110–111; Mexicans as, 15; Mexico as mestizo country, 64, 112, 165; and *México profundo*, 112; migration to cities, 51–52; as power group, xv; as priests, 85; and rural communities, 46; social differences from Indians, 17, 43; social inferiority of, 16

*Metate*, 11

Mexica, 54, 71, 73–74, 76, 130

Mexican Constitution, 127

Mexican independence: and creoles, xix, 94–98; and Indians of Mexico, 96, 98, 103–107; and territorial definition, 98–103

Mexico: border defense, 98; and capitalism, 121; colonial origins of, xvi; colonial roots of, 97; constitutional history of, 65; cultural continuity of, 4; cultural diversity of, 41–44, 57–58, 61, 116, 158–162; cultural groups of, 41–44, 61–69; and democracy, 169; federalists/centralists struggles, 99–100; geographical names of, 13–15; geography of, 9; human occupation of, 10–13; image of, xviii–xix; independence of, 63, 97, 169; influence of corn, 11; knowledge base of, 159–160; and media, 123–124; as mestizo country, 15, 64; modernization efforts, 103–107; national program development, 158–162; as poor country, 153; precolonial, 9–10, 70–75, 113, 129; reconstitution of, 173; regions of, 42; revolutionary policies of, 111–112; rural culture of, 44–47; and substitution project, 164; territorial definition of, 98–103, 173; and Virgin of Guadalupe, 95; and Western civilization, xvi, 167. *See also* Imaginary Mexico; Mexican independence; *México profundo*; New Spain; Revolution of 1910

Mexico City: air pollution of, 156; and communal lands, 100; education in, 106; and Indian languages, 52; Indians of, 48; labor force of, 91

*México profundo*: and appropriation, 137; and colonial domination, 132, 134–135, 159–160, 174; and communal land, 100; composition of, 1; cultural patrimony of, 67; defensive responses of, 124; and education, 126; exploitation of, 164; and federalists/centralists struggles, 99; and fusion project, 165; integration into society, 114, 120; knowledge base of, 159; and media, 124; and Mesoamerican civilization, 174; and mestizo ideology, 112; and Mexican expansion, 124; in Mexico City, 156; and middle class, 123; participation in Revolution of 1910, 111, 112; and pluralism project, 171–172; and political activists, 125–126; and postrevolutionary Mexican development, 120–121; and priests, 125; production and

consumption of, xvii; and Protestantism, 125; recognition of, 158; relations with imaginary Mexico, xvi, 67, 69, 104, 106, 125, 128, 141, 174; and religion, 136; resistance of, xvii, xix; and revolutionary Mexico, 113–115; social organization of, 127–128, 129; and substitution project, 163; and underdeveloped nation status, 164; urban poor of, 155. *See also* Campesinos; Indians of Mexico

Michoacán, 84, 100

Middle class: of cities, 56–57, 122–123, 124; discontent in, 157; and *México profundo*, 123; and Revolution of 1910, 111, 122

Midwives, 45

Mier, Servando Teresa de, 96

Militarism: and Indian recruitment, 104–105; in precolonial Mexico, 70–71, 73, 74; of Revolution of 1910, 109; of Spaniards, 80

*Milpas*: and Mesoamerican agriculture, 11; products of, 25, 44; replaced by wheat, 92; and self-sufficiency, 28; and settlement patterns, 31

Mining, 42, 48, 91, 94

Missionaries, 81, 83–88

*Mitotes*, 86

Mixed economy, 131

Mixtecs, 23

Modernization programs: of agriculture, 115, 153; and campesinos, 121; and dominant society, 46; and Indian culture, 149; in Mexico, 103–107

Molina Enríquez, Andrés, 110

Monetary economy, 89, 93, 155

Monoculture, 46, 121, 125

Monsiváis, Carlos, 113, 114

Moors, 75

Mora, José María Luis, 102, 105, 106

Morelos y Pavón, José María, 96–97

Moreno Toscano, Alejandra, 82, 83, 149

Mormon immigrants, 102

Motagua River, 7
Motolinía (Toribio de Benavente), 85
Municipal elections, 127
Muñoz Camargo, Diego, 80, 82
Murals, 54, 55, 113, 114
Music, 113

*Naboríos*, 91
*Nacos*, 53
Nahua, 14, 23
Náhuatl, 56, 74, 86–87
Náhuatlization, 87
National Council of Indian Peoples, 145
National culture, problems of, 61–69
National Indian Institute, 117, 119, 120
National Museum of Anthropology, 54, 55
National patrimony, 97
National program: for civilization, 163–167; development of, 158–162; substitution project, 163–165
Nationalism: and art, 53, 112–113; of creoles, 95, 113; Indian as symbol of, 53; of Revolution, 13
Natural order, 77
Natural resources: and adaptations for human life, 11; and agriculture, 11; in Classic period, 6; conservation of, 156; and cultural diversity, 158; and imaginary Mexico, 103; and Indians, 119; state control of, 110; use of, xvii
Nature: as enemy, 164; human interrelationship with, 10–13, 15; Indian interrelationship with, 27, 37–38, 47
Nervo, Amado, 107
Netzahualcóyotl, Lord of Texcoco, 71
New Spain: caste distinctions in, 16; Catholic Church as landholder, 87; colonial society of, 94; as creole homeland, 96; exploitation of Indians in, 88; founding of new settlements in, 48; and independence, 97; Inquisition in, 85; missionary activity in, 83, 85, 87; as two repub-

lics, 77. *See also* Mexico
Newspapers, 123
Nomadic northern Indians: appropriations of, 135; as *chichimecas*, 76; and Mesoamerican civilization, 9, 24; and mining, 48; resistance of, 130; as slaves, 82; as threat to imaginary Mexico, 104
*Nopales*, 12, 49

Oaxaca, 6
Oil industry, 56, 108, 123, 124, 153
Olives, 92
Olmecs, 5, 6
Othón de Mendizábal, Miguel, 12

*Paisanos*, 51
*Palenques*, 79
Pánuco River, 7
*Parajes*, 30, 45
Patron saints, 87. *See also* Saints; *and names of specific saints*
Paz, Octavio, 106–107
*Pelota mexteca*, 51
*Peninsulares. See* Spaniards
People of the Sun, 9, 54, 71
Pimentel, Francisco, 105
Plantations, 91
Pluralism project: and cultural diversity, 166–167, 168; and democracy, 168; and ethnic pluralism, 120, 168; and local societies, 169–170, 172; and Mesoamerican civilization, 168, 170, 175–176; and national pluralism, 169–174; and social organization, 170–171; and territorial division, 170, 172; and Western civilization, 168
Politics: conservatives, 63, 106; corruption in, 157; and European invasion, 61; and Indians of Mexico, 52, 144–149; left's proposals, 157; liberals, 63, 65, 68, 100, 101, 105, 110–111; national, 157; political activists, 125–126; and political life, 127–128, 144–149; and Revolution of 1910, 108; right's proposals, 157; and substitution project, 163. *See*

*also* Government
*Pop Wuj*, 4–5, 7
Popular Catholicism, 136, 149
Population. *See* Indian population
Posada, 113
Pozas, Ricardo, 119
Preclassic period, 5, 6
Precolonial Mexico, 9–10, 70–76, 113, 129
Press, 123, 148
Prickly pear cactus, 12, 49
Priests: attitude toward Indians, 84, 88; and evangelization, 86; and haciendas, 93; and independence, 96; and Indian languages, 87; Indians as, 85, 106; and internal life of Indians, 85; and land, 125; role of, 137; and tributes, 89. *See also* Catholic Church; Religion
Prieto, Guillermo, 94
Primer Congreso Nacional de Pueblos Indígenas, 145
*Principales*, 36, 78, 137
Private enterprise sector, 109
Private property, 100, 103
Proletarianization, 45
Protestantism, 37, 125, 141, 148
Public works, 120
*Pulque*, 49, 92
*Pulquerías*, 106
Purépecha, 23

Quetzalcóatl, 74, 77, 114
Quiché Maya, 4–5
Quiroga, Vasco de, 84

Racial issues, 15–18
Racial subjugation. *See* Subjugation
Radio, 123
Ramírez, Ignacio, 105
Ranching. *See* Cattle ranching
Rebellions, 130–132, 139
Reciprocity, 30, 36, 44, 138, 140
*Reducciones*, 82
Refuge regions, 24, 50, 92–93, 118
Religion: and appropriation, 136; and *cargo* system, 45; and colonial domination, 75, 80–81, 83–88; colonial

opposition to, 77; community control of, 136–137; confrontations of, 148; and creoles, 94; and medicine, 34–35; of Mesoamerica, 9, 86; and *México profundo*, 136; and precolonial political domination, 73–74; and rebellions, 130–131; in rural culture, 44. *See also* Catholic Church; Christianity; Protestantism
Remojadas, 6
*Repartimientos*, 78, 82, 90–91
Resistance. *See* Indian resistance
Revolution of 1910: and art, 112–113; and communal land, 100; and ideological exaltation of Indian, 53; and *indigenismo*, 115–120; as mestizo project, 111; motives for participating in, 111; tribulations of, 108–115; and Western civilization, 62, 63; and Zapata, 64
Ricard, Robert, 83, 85, 87
Right, proposals of, 157
Rivera, Diego, 54
Rodríguez Puebla, Juan, 106
Ruling groups: and Indian culture, 64; of Indians of Mexico, 78; as minority, 66; and Western civilization, 63. *See also* Government; Politics
Rural communities, 43, 44–47, 52, 105, 122
Rural school system, 117
Ruz, Alberto, 70

Sáenz, Moisés, 117
Sahagún, Bernardino de, 85–86, 118
Saints: *cofradías* for, 85, 138; fiestas for, 49, 52; and geographical names, 13; and *mayordomías*, 35–36, 49, 136; patron saints, 87. *See also* names of specific saints
Salary. *See* Wage labor
San Gregorio School, 106
San Juan, 100
Sánchez, Bachiller Miguel, 95
Santa Anna, Antonio López de, 99
Santiago, 100
School of Santa Cruz de Tlatelolco, 85

Segregation, 16–17, 48, 62, 63

Self-sufficiency: and commercial interchanges, 32–33; and economics, 28–29, 37, 39, 140, 155; and Indian land, 34; and Indian resistance, 135; and monoculture, 125; in rural communities, 44; and wage labor, 31

Settlement patterns, of Indians of Mexico, 31

Sierra, Justo, 101

Sinaloa River, 7

Slaves: and African culture, 43; Blacks as, 43, 79; for domestic service, 91; Indians as, 82; Maya Indians as, 99; and *palenques*, 79

Social hierarchy: of colonial society, 18, 43, 61; of Indians of Mexico, 78; of Mexico, 97–98; and Spanish colonizers, 43

Social organization: appropriation in, 137; and *cargos*, 35–37; in cities, 50; communal work projects, 31, 90–91; continuity of, 87, 90; effects of colonial domination, 23; of Indians of Mexico, 20–21, 30, 47, 119; and indigenous problem, 117; innovation in, 138; local community organization, 23, 78, 129, 169–170, 172; of Mesoamerican civilization, 6–7, 78; of *México profundo*, 127–128, 129; and pluralism project, 170–171; and rebellions, 131; and reciprocity, 30, 36, 44, 138, 140; restructuring of, 173–174; in rural communities, 44–45, 47

Socialism, 164

Sociedad Indianista Mexicana, 102

Spain: agricultural techniques of, 84; French triumph over, 96; Mexican distancing from, 106; nobility of, 95; as Western country, 75, 167

Spaniards: arrival of, 6; and colonial society, 79; domination of, 95, 96; and fall of Tenochtitlán, 71; and Indians of Mexico, 77; militarism of, 80; royal appointments of, 94; separation from Indians, 48

Spanish Constitution of 1812, 97

Spanish language, 14, 17, 45, 117

Squash, 11, 25

Student movement, 123

Subjugation: and caste distinctions, 16; and colonial domination, 75, 76–77; and colonial society, 16, 24; and decision-making abilities, 132; and imaginary Mexico, 146; and Indian culture, 24, 131; of Mesoamerican civilization, xvi, 58; and precolonial domination, 70–75, 76; of rural communities, 47; and Western civilization, 58

Substitution project, 163–165

Suffrage, 127

Sugarcane, 92

Syncretism, 136

Tabasco, 7

Talking crosses, 131

Technology, 33, 101, 103, 121

Tehuacán, 5, 8

Tehuacán, 106

Television, 123

Templo Mayor, 80

Tenochtitlán: and Aztecs, 9, 71; and commerce, 72; Cortés' assault of, 82; fall of, 130; and precolonial domination, 73

Teotihuacán, 6, 7, 8, 70

Tepic, 106

*Tequio*, 31

Texcoco, 71

Textile mills, 91, 94

Tezcutzingo, 10

Theocratic chiefdoms, 6

Thomas, Saint, 77

Time, in Indian culture, 38–39

Tlacaélel, 54, 71, 73

*Tlacoyos*, 49

Tlaloc, 74

Tlatelolco, 81

Tlaxcaltecans, 80, 82

Toltec culture, 7

Tonantzin, 95

*Topiles*, 35, 136

Totonacs, 6

Tourism, 55, 124

*Town and Country* magazine, 56, 122

Trades, 91
Tributary systems: abolition of, 97; and agriculture, 93; after colonial domination, 78, 85, 88–90, 92; in precolonial Mexico, 71–73; rebellions against, 130. *See also En-comienda* system
Triple Alliance, 71, 73
Tula, 7
Turkeys, 12

Unemployment, 155
United States: agricultural exports to, 153–14; and agricultural workers, 46; constitutional model of, 97, 127; as example of Western civilization, 63; and Indian domestic workers, 52; informal economy with, 155; and Mexican foreign debt, 156; and Mexican middle class, 56; and Mexican territory, 98; and Treaty of Guadalupe, 99
Urban life: and colonial power, 47; and imposed culture, 140; Indian heritage in, 47–53, 58; individualism in, 50; markets of, 49; and *México profundo*, 1; middle classes of, 56–57; and new Indian sector, 147, 149; poor of, 155, 164; and rural life, 43; and unemployment, 155. *See also* Cities; Mexico City; Rural communities

Valley of Mexico, 6, 26, 71, 81
Vasconcelos, José, 114
*Vecindades*, 49–50
Velasco, Luis de, 77
Veracruz, 6, 100
Vigil, José María, 101
Violence: of colonial domination, 79–83; of Indians, 105, 139; and land, 125; of priests, 84
Virgin of Guadalupe, 95
Virgin of Tepeyac, 95

Wage labor. *See* Labor

War of the Castes, 131
War of flowers, 74
Wealth, 103, 122
Western civilization: and civilizing Indian, 105; coexistence with Mesoamerican civilization, xv, 159; and colonial domination, 64; confrontation with Mesoamerican civilization, xv–xvi, 57–58, 59, 61, 70, 166; cultural elements of, 167, 175–176; and democracy, 66; development of, 167; elements of, 167; as imaginary, 161; and imaginary Mexico, xvi, 107; and Indians of Mexico, 62–63, 118; and individualism, 50; and Mexican independence, 63; and pluralism project, 168; and Spanish evangelism, 85; and subjugation of non-European cultures, 75; and substitution project, 163–164; superiority of, 116. *See also* Civilization; Imaginary Mexico; Mesoamerican civilization
Wheat, 92
Wild plant foods, 26, 28
Wolf, Eric, 143
Womack, John, 112
Women: as domestic workers, 52, 56; as language transmitters, 139; role of in Indian society, 29–30; and *tequios*, 31
Work. *See* Labor
World War II, 121, 122

Yaqui, 99
Yojovi, 142
Yopes, 130
Youth, 35, 143, 145, 171
Yucatan, 6, 7, 23, 74, 99

Zamacona, Manuel María de, 103
Zapata, Emiliano, 64, 112
Zapatistas, 111
Zapotec Indians, 6, 23
Zumárraga, Juan de, 86, 95

## DATE DUE

UPI 261-2505 G